The Hunting Imperative

The Hunting Imperative

BIOGRAPHY OF A BOY IN AFRICA

By
Richard Harland

Rowland Ward Publications
Johannesburg

ISBN 0-9584188-7-X

The Hunting Imperative Copyright © Richard Harland 2001

First Edition October 2001

Rowland Ward Publications
P O Box 2079, Houghton 2041
South Africa
Tel:(27 11) 728 2542
www. rowlandward.com

Edited by Brian Marsh

Photographs by kind permission of Paul Grobler & Maryanne Birch

Cover design by Lionel McMurray, Collage Graphics
Printed & bound by Waylite Press, Johannesburg

For Brita

Place Names

Names are used as they were at the time of the narrative.

Southern Rhodesia	≈	Zimbabwe
Salisbury	≈	Harare
Umtali	≈	Mutare
Marandellas	≈	Marondera
Sipolilo	≈	Guruve
Sabi River	≈	Save
Lundi River	≈	Runde
Nuanetsi River	≈	Mwenezi
Portuguese East Africa	≈	Mozambique
Wankie National Park	≈	Hwange
Que Que	≈	Kwekwe
Northern Rhodesia	≈	Zambia
Ruanda	≈	Rwanda
Bechuanaland	≈	Botswana
Tanganyika	≈	Tanzania

Contents

	Acknowledgements	ix
	Parochial Terms	x
	Foreword	xi
	Introduction	xiii
1	Born To Hunt	1
2	Little Boy, Big Game	9
3	Elephants & Eagles	17
4	Last Days Of The Belgian Congo	25
5	Pluto's Episode	29
6	Solving Problems Schoolboy Style	33
7	On Official Business	45
8	Bandazi & The Straw Hat	51
9	Slightly Extra-Territorial	59
10	College Life	63
11	Big Ivory, Bad Buffalo	67
12	Killer Elephant	73
13	Rainy Nights	79
14	Moving On	85

15	Game Ranger	95
16	Death In The Corridor	107
17	The Buffalo Man	115
18	Elephants Here, There, Everywhere	121
19	Wanderlust	127
20	Msimbiti Experiences	133
21	A Patchwork Of People	143
22	Touched By The Sun	151
23	New Territory	159
24	The Good, The Sad And The Scary	167
25	In The Mud; In The Rain; In The Drink; In The Corridor	173
26	The Vet Gets His Virus	185
27	King Of Tuskers	191
28	Dark Deeds	199
29	Defying Death In Darkest Europe	207
30	Brass On The Anthills	213
31	The Snake-Snatcher	221
32	Back To The Bush	229
33	A Meander Through Safari Land	233
	Epilogue	249

Acknowledgements

Jennifer Swift for sowing the seed - "Write it down".

Mellonie Tucker for deciphering the pencilled scrawl, then typing it.

Ed Matunas for kindly allowing quotes from *Modern African Adventures*.

Paul Grobler who taught the boy elephant hunting.

Tsuro Fifteen Sibanda: he was always there.

Brita, for patience and constructive criticism.

Brian Marsh, whose prodigious advice and encouragement made this book.

Parochial Terms

Veld: Afrikaans for open countryside, wilderness.

Kopje: Afrikaans for a low hill.

Vlei: Afrikaans for a hollow in which water collects during the rainy season; a wetland.

Veldschoen: Afrikaans for a strong leather shoe or boot.

Biltong: Shade-dried meat similar to 'jerky'.

Bwana or Baas: Boss, master.

Lowveld/Highveld: Areas roughly below/above 2 500ft elevation.

Pan: Depression, sometimes acres in extent, holding rain water for several months of the year; occasionally permanent.

Kraal: A group of traditional African huts; a corral for holding cattle.

Jesse: Derived from the Makorekore word 'muchesa' meaning a dense thicket. Composed of multi-stemmed shrubs 10 to 20 feet high and covering areas from small patches to hundreds of acres in extent, particularly in the Zambezi Valley.

Foreword

I n the mid-1900s most Southern Rhodesian farmers' sons grew up with rifles and shotguns in their hands, hunting the baboons, bush pigs, plains game and game birds that abounded on farms at that time. Richard Harland was one of them, but few – if any – had the big game experience that he had accrued when still in his early teens. At 14, accompanied by only an African tracker, he was hunting buffalo on the vast Devuli ranch in the south-eastern lowveld. That same year, already determined that his future lay in elephant hunting, he met Paul Grobler, the country's doyen in that particular field, who took him under his wing. Paul was an honorary officer of the game department who had an open permit to shoot problem animals on privately owned farms and in the tribal lands.

A few weeks after meeting him, Richard shot his first elephant under Paul's direction, a crop-raider in the tribal lands, and the following year, by which time he had notched up a respectable score of crop-raiders, Paul was sending him solo on elephant control. Paul recommended to the game department that Richard be made an honorary officer and, at 17 while still a schoolboy, he became the youngest member ever to be appointed to that prestigious position. He too could now buy licences for crop-raiding elephant he shot which allowed him to sell the ivory, and by now all his spare time was spent hunting elephant. The sub-title of this most interesting book, *Biography of a boy in Africa*, could well have read *Biography of the most unusual schoolboy in Africa*. "Unusual" Richard most certainly was!

After two years at Gwebi Agricultural College at his father's insistence, he had come to realise that the days of making a living by hunting elephant for their ivory had come to an end, and he applied to join the game department. Because he and his reputation were well known he was immediately accepted and sent to *Gonarezhou* in the south-eastern lowveld, where he was employed on half-pay (not yet being 21; the required age for the job) and put onto shooting out the elephant and buffalo in the tsetse fly corridors. These chapters are filled with thrilling hunting incidents, a wide range of bush-lore and interesting observations, the history of the country's misguided tsetse fly eradication policy, and numerous hairbreadth escapes.

By now the period of extensive elephant control had come to an end and Richard became a partner in a snake-venom venture, catching and keeping Africa's most dangerous and venomous snakes. He only got bitten once (remarking simply that he had been drinking and the snake hadn't). During this time he married Brita, a young girl from a farming family in the Midlands, who finally persuaded him to opt for a less dangerous and more settled life.

I had once met Richard, almost 40 years ago, when he was a student at the agricultural college. His class was brought down to visit pioneer game rancher George Style's Buffalo Range Game Ranch, where I was manager. The brand new concept of 'sustainable utilisation of wildlife resources' (now better known as 'game ranching' and previously banned – "no profit from wildlife" then being the rule) was still in its infancy, and I was called upon to deliver the lecture. I am sure my talk was extremely boring, public speaking being the least of my talents, but I noticed one lad's eyes never left my face, and the young Richard collared me afterwards to ask for more details about this little known but fascinating industry.

I had the game management rights of the half-million acre Nuanetsi ranch, situated on the Nuanetsi river only a few miles up-river from where Richard resided during his game ranger days. Inevitably my wife, Jillie, and I heard tales about the young ranger's exploits, his boss Warden Tim Braybrooke being a regular visitor to our home, but we never met. Today Richard and Brita are two of our closest friends, but we only really came together at the commencement of his book, which I was privileged to be asked by the publisher to edit.

Today Richard is a highly successful farmer and businessman and in no way resembles the harum-scarum youngster he once must have been. Having swapped his rifles for fly-rods, he and Brita travel to different waters in distant countries, and with a deep passion for opera that Brita shares, they make regular trips to Vienna and many other venues to hear their favourite performers. Jillie and I regret the lost years, but we have caught up with the Richard of those days from the contents of his book, which I recommend to all interested in reading a highly unusual hunting story.

Brian Marsh
Zimbabwe

Introduction

Predation by certain species upon others always existed on Planet Earth and will continue for the duration. Humans are predators but unlike lions, eagles or sharks, not every individual is required, or has the ability, to kill. Throughout history, communities had a social structure containing some hunters or fishermen who did the job of providing animal protein for their groups, and archaeological evidence of prehistoric predatory hominids suggests the instinct, the genetic formula, to hunt has been with us for a long time. The existence of butcher's shops and supermarkets does not cause the hunter's inherited characteristics to change.

The early hunter needed to ensure that he could acquire animal protein more or less regularly, and to this end he conserved the source as a matter of common sense. Leaving enough breeding stock to maintain sustained yield, selecting old or non-productive individuals when practical and conserving the habitat of prey species, are all factors governing the activities of hunters, past and present. In a sometimes bizarre world, over-populated and combative to excess, one of the abiding constants is the effort of the hunting fraternity, by and large, to help conserve the environment and wildlife for the future. Admirable, considering how uncertain 'the future' so often appears to some of us in the second millennium.

ONE

Born To Hunt

Born with a full complement of 'hunters genes' in rural Africa, I make no apologies for allowing the predatory instinct to influence my life from an early age. I served the hunter's apprenticeship appropriate to the time and place in which I found myself and relentlessly pursued all opportunities which could further hone the skills and increase the experiences. My goal was to eventually specialise as an elephant hunter which I achieved at the age of fifteen. There were ups and downs along the way; fortunately, mostly ups!

The catapult period was short-lived as the first .177 calibre air rifle, a Diana, arrived on my sixth birthday. Doves and other birds featured frequently for lunch, while dozens of rats shot in the farm chicken houses were fed to the cats.

Aged seven, I committed the cardinal sin of pointing a gun at something I did not intend to kill and, what is more, I pulled the trigger. The unfortunate target was the backside of our African cook, Ninepence by name, who happened to be walking some distance ahead of me up the hill from our vegetable garden, back to the house with arms full of produce. I was probably frustrated by the fruit-eating bulbuls, starlings and mousebirds managing to out-manoeuvre me all morning in the orchard, and simply took a pot-shot at Ninepence to speed his progress up the pathway. He was wearing heavy-duty khaki shorts and I knew the pellet would hardly be felt through them. Wrong! The uphill flight of the projectile resulted in it striking Ninepence's behind square on. Vegetables flew in all directions and an extremely vexed cook came back down to earth, ready to attack, only to find the enemy had retreated in haste. I owned up to the

crime and was soundly thrashed by my father but nothing like what happened to an acquaintance, Richard Palmer.

The Palmers, who were staunch supporters of the Agricultural Shows, were a well-known farming family from near Umtali, a large town on Rhodesia's eastern border. Mr. Palmer had a magnificent Hereford bull ready for exhibition but its enormous pair of testicles proved too great a temptation to young Richard who punctured them with just one tiny lead pellet. The unfortunate animal had to be destroyed just a few days before the show. Us kids elevated Richard to near-hero status but his father apparently felt differently!

My next step up in weaponry was my father's .22, an Australian-made Slazenger. My father had no interest in hunting, firearms or wildlife in general. He loved farming, growing crops, constructing dams and farm buildings, fixing things and playing tennis. Born in London in 1913, he came to join his elder brother, Dick, on a farm in the east of the country near the small village of Rusape.

Mother was born of English parents in Ceylon and the family settled in Rhodesia when she was seven. She married my father in 1938; sixty two years later she still lives on the family farm. A woman of extraordinary energy and zest for life, she is a passionate gardener, lover of nature and the 'outdoors'. She always understood and accepted the hunting imperative which dominated her eldest son's development. I have two older sisters and a younger brother who were all far more normal and better balanced children.

The use of the .22 rimfire greatly expanded my spectrum of hunting opportunities, providing the self-training in stalking of steenbok, duiker, dassies (or hyrax) in the rocky hills, guineafowl and francolin. In those days Dad and Uncle Dick employed a number of young white men to supervise the African farm workers and I would frequently accompany them on night shoots. Three or four of us would drive around the crops in an old Land Rover, one fellow holding a spotlight, another using a shotgun and I had the .22 or my mother's .410. Springhares, which dug up newly-germinated maize, offered really difficult targets as they bounced at speed across the fields, with the Land Rover hurtling over contour ridges and swerving all over the place to keep up with the erratic course of the animals. Scrub hares were also found in the lucerne fields at night. We favoured eating the springhares and gave the others to the farm workers. An occasional porcupine might be shot in the maize and this was a prized delicacy.

Going to boarding school at the age of seven was a rude shock to my system. I hated it. I disliked the authority and regimentation, and found

In Luangwa Valley with Rob Waller

With my first hero, Rob Waller

Luangwa Valley, 1953

Springhares are good to eat

With my brother Adrian and Tsuro - Devuli Ranch

Devuli Ranch - Author, Mbwana, Tsuro

10.75mm Mauser bullets from Devuli buffalo

difficulty in studying things which were of no interest to me. However, I did enjoy learning to read and write, and was quickly delving into the family library of hunting books which my mother had collected. One of my greatest pleasures was to spend hours absorbing the wondrous stories of John Hunter, John Taylor, Selous, Martin and Osa Johnson, Jim Corbett, J.H. Patterson and others.

Sunday morning at Ruzawi School was free time during which a couple of friends and I would roam the surrounding farming areas, exploring the granite outcrops, timber plantations and indigenous woodlands. Once a fellow explorer, Phil Deere, climbed with me to a group of boulders high up on a *kopje* where we discovered a large clay pot on a slab of rock containing a swarm of bees. The thought of all that honey was too much for us eight-year-olds, so we gathered a few rocks and pelted the pot till it was smashed, releasing thousands of extremely angry bees which attacked us in great style.

Phil took off in one direction and disappeared while I dashed, panic-stricken by the stings and wildly beating at the mad swarm around my head, straight over the side of the *kopje* down an almost vertical drop of at least fifteen feet. Hitting a clump of bushes and severely grazing my hands, arms and legs on the rough stone, I scrambled blindly away, stumbling over rocks and through nettle patches while still being given the odd bee sting, until I reached level ground. Seeing a watercourse some distance away in a grassy vlei I ran on, plunging into the first small pool where I sank into foul black mud a foot deep.

Cattle used this pond as it was well churned up and reeked of dung. I didn't care. Shaking, shivering, hurting and burning, I lay in the cool, soothing muck and screamed for Phil. He screamed back and soon came along looking like hell, shirt torn, bleeding from cuts and grazes and tears streaking his face. Discovering that we were both still alive boosted our shattered little spirits and the decision was made to get back to school in case we fell ill. We knew about bees stinging people and animals to death.

The matron on duty took one look at the pair of urchins and was about to throw a tantrum when Phil collapsed in a faint in the dormitory doorway. That shocked her and when I explained that a rogue swarm of bees had attacked us and we escaped by running through thorn bushes and hiding from them in a mudhole, she turned pale and rushed off to call the school's nursing sister, the formidable and much-feared Miss du Plessis. Phil was carried off to the sick bay while I sat on my bed, head swollen and throbbing, having the barbed stings pulled out by the matron with a pair of tweezers. She stopped counting after thirty, all taken out of my head, neck and shoulders. My hands and forearms each had plenty more.

Barely able to see and too painful to move much, I was gently showered and put to bed. Sister du Plessis came round and made me take some medicine, glaring down at me for a moment, then made the inevitable comment in her coarse, Afrikaans-accented best bedside English.

"Yoo shtoopit childe."

Both Phil and I recovered within a day or two, but I sometimes wonder if this dose of poison had a long-term effect on my system. I have since been stung often by bees, very often by hornets (on occasion by five simultaneously), four times by various species of scorpions and once bitten by a night adder. The minimal effects I feel, with very little swelling and only a brief period of pain, I believe indicates a high resistance to these toxins; a direct result of the bee episode?

A real live hero entered my life in the shape of a new farm manager, Rob Waller, one of three men who have profoundly influenced my life. A gentle, humorous, six-feet-four giant, Rob devoted countless hours to teaching me about firearms, hunting and bush-lore. Our endless discussions on guns and game, coupled with my ravenous appetite for reading about the adventurous lives of hunters and explorers, firmly implanted the ambition to be a big game hunter. Most importantly, he taught me to always keep both eyes open when shooting, a habit which I later valued highly when tackling dangerous game at close quarters.

Our family regularly visited areas of Rhodesia, Nyasaland and Portuguese East Africa during the school holidays, frequently camping in remote, wild places and meeting some weird and wild characters. I recall being entranced by a Mr. Stock who owned a little motel at Birchenough Bridge on the Sabi River, for Mr. Stock had been mauled by a lion - and lived!

While on these bush trips another exciting revelation came to me. It was the vegetation. Every time we travelled into the bushveld of the Zambezi Valley, the Sabi lowveld or the Kruger Park, I felt a surge of excitement when the first mopane trees and baobabs were sighted. The harshness of the dry, grey expanses of leafless mopane woodland, thickets of jesse or scrubby combretums filled me with a yearning to get in there and hunt the big game I knew lived in these exotic places.

The heat and dust, the parrots, hornbills and sparrow weavers were all essential, magical ingredients of this atmosphere in the land of elephant, buffalo and lion. Many decades later, I still experience both a tingling anticipation and a strange calming of the spirit when I travel down into game country from the highveld, that 'msasa' tree highland plateau of Zimbabwe. 'Mopane' people and 'msasa' people actually are different sub-species, I'm convinced!

Undoubtedly my most exciting pre-teens safari was to the Luangwa Valley with Rob Waller. Fifty years ago, this part of Northern Rhodesia must have ranked as some of southern Africa's finest game country, and we camped in two areas, Nsefu Reserve and Luambe Park. Accompanied by a game guard carrying a .404, I walked my legs off (I had to take three strides for one of Rob's) through beautiful flood plains and mopane forests, filming reel after reel of 16mm cine with Rob's camera.

Puku antelope abounded, elephant were everywhere and huge herds of buffalo came to drink at the river in front of camp. We saw a black-maned lion deftly kill a lone buffalo bull by simply pulling the muzzle sideways as the bull bucked, thereby throwing it off balance and causing it to fall heavily onto the bent neck which apparently broke or dislocated. Once, a black rhino charged us, probably annoyed by the sound of the camera, whereupon our guard fired a shot into the ground between us and the oncoming snorter. That did the trick and I was much relieved to see the rhino gallop off as there were no trees nearby to climb. Rob was most excited and congratulated me on standing my ground. I didn't think I had any choice!

Shortly after the Luangwa trip, Rob presented me with his Army & Navy .450 Nitro Express double rifle in it's canvas-covered wood case complete with silvered oil bottle and a dozen rounds of solid ammunition. The piece had been much used as was shown by the slight parting of the barrels next to the front sight ramp. The soldering had cracked for a couple of inches from the muzzles where the right barrel was attached to the rib. Rob cured the little problem by fitting a radiator hose clip just behind the sight ramp which closed the hairline crack when it was tightened. Rob had not done a great deal of big game hunting and was not planning to do any in the future, and had probably picked up the old double at some sale for a few pounds.

For a ten-year-old a double elephant rifle is just too much gun, and holding it in the fork of a tree was the only way I could fire it without being flattened by the weight and recoil. I would only shoot it once or twice each school holiday but I swooned over that cannon, laying it next to my bed at night, cleaning and fondling it daily, and sneaking glances at it standing in the corner of my bedroom in between reading my hunting books.

Before I had a chance to use my beloved .450 on a real hunt, the licensing of firearms was tightened up and Rob was concerned that trouble was brewing as he had never bothered to register it. Mistakenly, he was also convinced that the barrels could not be rejoined at the muzzles. He insisted on destroying the old rifle. I was devastated but respected his decision.

A couple of years on I had saved enough money from selling rabbits, hares and game birds to buy a 'sporterised' .303 SMLE. This was big league

stuff for me and my father agreed to my taking an occasional kudu bull and reedbuck. Bush pigs were no longer safe and the resident troops of baboons had a very nasty shock coming. I soon learnt that the 215gr soft nose round was a real killer, far more effective than the pointed 174gr military bullet.

At the age of twelve I moved on to the senior school, Peterhouse, again as a boarder. This fine institution, near the town of Marandellas and only three years old, was modelled on the English Public School concept, being privately funded, very expensive and largely staffed by the best of British teachers. My housemaster, Tony Mallett, had a thunderous voice, was a great sportsman and wielded a cane with the force of a baseball striker. His lovely wife, Vivienne, was the secret fantasy of us pubescent lads and I'm sure she knew it. Much was the jubilation when the Malletts produced a son, Nicholas, who later became well known as coach of the South African Springbok rugby team.

The Malletts occasionally visited my parents during the holidays and when Nick was a toddler, my mother gave them a couple of domestic rabbits for him to play with back home. At that stage a friend, Neville Buch, and I were well into the falconry game. We enjoyed hunting with black sparrow-hawks and I was also training a martial eagle. This huge raptor with a 7½-foot wing-span had a voracious appetite which was a problem for a schoolboy who could only breed white mice in sufficient numbers to feed the smaller hawks.

I had permission to keep dead doves and bits of guineafowl or hare in a freezer at the science laboratory but on occasion a crisis would arise when I had nothing to feed my eagle. One of Nick Mallett's pet rabbits would have to be sacrificed. After all, the hunter is at the apex of the food pyramid so prey species, like rabbits, must expect to fulfil the course of nature.

Midnight would find two shadowy teenagers, wearing socks over their tennis shoes for non-squeak progress through the dormitory, moving down the stairs and along the corridor leading to the back of the housemaster's dwelling, furtively creeping along the wall of the garage to the rabbits' pen. One of us had a grain bag, the other carried a hockey stick. Once over the wire netting, we would raise the box under which the prey slept and whack one, pop it into the sack and slip away, desperately stifling giggles so as not to rouse the Malletts' dog.

Twice, during visits to our home, the Malletts embarrassingly admitted that "another of little Nicky's pets had simply disappeared" and asked my mother if she could spare a replacement. I, of course, had to depart in haste when this subject arose.

The requirement for Nick's rabbits fell away when Rob Waller lent me his

.45 Webley revolver and taught me how to cut down .410 shot shells to fit it, with which I could poach birds and squirrels on the school farm and surrounding countryside. Neville also smuggled his Browning auto .22 into school, so game birds and even dassies appeared on the menu for our hawks and the martial. Neville and I received canings for smoking, drinking, bunking out, stealing food from the kitchen, missing classes and many other crimes, but our guns and shooting escapades were never discovered.

Map of Southern Rhodesia

TWO

Little Boy, Big Game

Farming friends, whose son was also at Peterhouse, invited me to join them hunting on Devuli ranch for two weeks in the school holidays. This was enormously exciting as it would be my first hunt in the lowveld I yearned to visit; real game country! Although George Cross, my thoughtful host, had bought only plains game licences for his son Robin and me, I knew buffalo, elephant and big cats were there, and that some buffalo permits were issued to hunters.

Aged thirteen and armed with my recently acquired .303, plus a farm shotgun for game birds, I was beside myself with impatience as George Cross carefully loaded the farm truck and Land Rover with the safari requirements. I was accompanied by a young African, Tsuro, some years older than myself, whom Rob Waller suggested I should take along as a helper. Tsuro ('rabbit' in local dialect) Sibanda originated from Portuguese East Africa and had been working on our farm for a couple of years, where Rob had noticed his cheerful character and enthusiasm for hard work. Thus began our friendship which lasts to this day; an extraordinary relationship forged by many years of hunting dangerous game together.

At last we left for the lowveld, crossing the magnificent Birchenough Bridge over the Sabi river and passing the motel of Mr. Stock (of lion-mauling fame). Journeying on south we passed herds of impala, kudu and zebra, with an occasional group of cattle seemingly in the middle of nowhere. Passing massive baobab trees, unusually huge Sabi Star plants covered in their pink and white flowers, expanses of almost bare mopane trees and water courses flanked by evergreen giants, we rolled on, reaching the camp site late that afternoon.

9

The original Devuli ranch, covering 650 000 acres, was owned by two Englishmen, Despard and Lucas Bridges. The brothers had large ranches in Chile, Argentina and South West Africa and were true colonisers in the British tradition, overcoming incredible obstacles in setting up this vast ranching operation in a highly inaccessible part of Africa. After finding and buying Devuli in 1919, they employed a young English lad, Donald Somerville, as an assistant in 1920. Don ran the business of developing and stocking the huge concern, married Despard's daughter Tinita, and fittingly became a partner and managing director. He died in 1966 after 46 years on Devuli.

I was fortunate enough to meet Don on this hunting expedition and discovered from him that the company offered a few buffalo to hunters each season at a cost of £5, provided one had a Wildlife Department licence which also cost £5 per head for either a bull or a cow. He advised me to write to him personally if I wished to secure a buffalo for the following season. Looking at me with a smile he said, "You're certainly a keen young hunter but little boys and big game can be a dangerous mix. Do you have a suitable rifle for buffalo? And how old are you, Richard?"

"Thirteen, sir. Yes, I will borrow my uncle's 10.75mm for buffalo, sir. He shot an elephant with it once," I bubbled.

"Have you shot anything on this hunt?" he asked.

"Yes, sir. I've taken my quota of impala and kudu and I got my bushbuck today, so I've finished."

"Remarkable. I believe you're the only hunter this season to fill his quota and you still have five more days. Good luck for next year."

I applied for, and Don Somerville granted, two buffalo permits the following season, along with the usual plains game. This time I invited my school pal, Neville Buch, to join the safari. My mother, a true bush lover, came along as did my young brother, Adrian. One of our Land Rovers was loaded onto the 5-tonner driven by the farm driver and we set up camp on a new site in the riverine forest flanking the Sabi river.

The ranch provided an employee as the local guide and tracker. A tall, powerful man by the name of Naison introduced himself, grinning widely when he discovered we were to hunt buffalo.

"I have never hunted *nyati* with *mafana* (little boys) before. But, I think we will find them." His self-assurance and encouraging words gave me great confidence and I could hardly contain my impatience to get out hunting the next morning.

At home, a number of the farm workers were of the Muslim faith necessitating hallal, the ritual of cutting the throat of all animals killed for

food, so that they could eat the flesh. We had brought one 'qualified' Muslim, an elderly, wizened character named Mbwana, to do the honours. Naison, Tsuro, Mbwana and I were off in the Land Rover at first light, leaving Neville to hunt for plains game with two of our staff. Naison duly told me to stop, whereupon we all leapt out of the vehicle to study the fresh tracks and dung of a herd of buffalo.

Naison was addicted to his home-made snuff. Whenever he needed to ponder over a situation the little round tin would appear from a pocket and a pinch of the deadly black powder was inhaled into each nostril. I tried it once, sneezed for ten minutes and thought I'd blown a few arteries. But Naison never, ever sneezed; his eyes didn't even water.

I watched him circling around in the grass; dark piercing eyes scanning like radar, pinches of snuff being sniffed apparently subconsciously. Shortly he announced the verdict: we would follow. Wait a minute, I thought, this man must explain just what the hell he is seeing and thinking. No longer a total beginner myself, I recognised the true hunter that Naison was and I wanted all that knowledge for myself. Besides, I was going to be a big game hunter and must learn about buffalo!

Naison patiently explained how he established the number of animals, around thirty, by knowing that they had crossed the road early in the pre-dawn hours. They were spread out feeding with the tracks thinly covering several pathways through the scrub. Later on, he said, when the sun was up a bit, they would bunch up closer to cover a good distance by mid-morning before slowing down to rest and chew the cud. These were hunted animals and could put many miles between the Sabi river, where they drank, and their resting place over the next few hours. He showed me spoor of some adult bulls, and where one of them had turned around to stand and watch the back trail for any predators possibly following. From droppings, urine and chewed grass, he said they had passed by two to three hours earlier.

Several miles of Naison's incredibly quick, unerring tracking brought us into scrub-covered country, when we heard the first grunt of a buffalo. The wind, little as it was, had been favourable all morning. Telling Mbwana to stay back, the three of us moved on slowly towards the herd. My heart was thumping but I felt all my senses were really sharp as I followed on Naison's heels. Uncle Dick's 10.75x68mm Mauser felt good and solid in my hands. It was accurate, as I knew from several shots at a target, but apart from John 'Pondoro' Taylor's condemnation of the effectiveness of the round on elephant, I had no other knowledge of this calibre.

We had been spotted because the herd suddenly crashed away through the bush, glimpses of great, black shapes showing through the clouds of

dust as Tsuro and I followed Naison at the run. Abruptly, Naison turned sharp right, still running, and shortly we broke into an open area and there were the buffalo. A big cow was nearest to us, standing side-on. As she swung her head away to take off, I fired at the shoulder. The herd panicked, smashing their way into surrounding bush, tails up and hooves pounding.

A short while later we heard a loud yell some way off in the direction in which the buffalo had gone. I suddenly remembered we had left old Mbwana behind us and that the herd had turned back after the first alarm. We decided to find him first before following up the wounded cow.

We soon located him by calling as we moved through the bush. I was relieved to see him and astonished to find a dead buffalo next to the small tree in which Mbwana was clinging precariously. Checking that the buffalo was truly dead, we convinced the old guy to come down and cut it's throat. His huge knife was seriously blunt and he took ten minutes to saw through the inch-thick hide while Tsuro and Naison teased him mercilessly.

We reconstructed the hunt as follows: only one buffalo had initially seen us, spooking the herd which did not really know the direction or source of the danger. After a short rush, some grey louries (go-away birds) had called out ahead causing the herd to turn back which Naison had detected, making him rush off to intercept the group. When Mbwana was faced with the stampeding buffalo he leapt into a spindly sapling which promptly bent over, with Mbwana's backside swinging barely a foot above the rushing mob. When they passed he dropped out of the tree only to find a lone buffalo coming for him, head up and ready to kill. He turned to run, saw another tree within yards and scrambled up just in time, as the attacker, my wounded cow, slid to a stop, staggered and fell over dead.

My first buffalo hunt was retold with much laughter around the campfires that evening, but Mbwana was firm on it being his last buffalo outing; he would henceforth only attend to impala and suchlike! Fine by me, I thought, staring into the flickering flames. My big game career had begun today and suddenly the idea of hunting plains game was no longer an attraction.

"This is the life," I mumbled to myself in a satisfied, sleepy trance.

Borrowing an old farm Land Rover, Tsuro and I were back on Devuli the following year. We stopped by the headquarters to pay our respects to Don Somerville. "There's a wounded buffalo around there," he warned. "If you can kill it, the company will take the meat and hide and not count it on your licences."

What a challenge! I had bought three buffalo licences with sole use of the area for two weeks. The previous party had shot and lost a buffalo and the idea of pursuing it really got my imagination and adrenalin going. Recalling

the many accounts in my hunting books about wounded buffalo being extremely dangerous, and almost unstoppable when charging, made the prospect highly exciting. Don confirmed that Naison would be available as our tracker and that he also knew the area in which the buffalo had been hunted. Naison was something of a hero, having taught Tsuro and I volumes of bush craft and hunting skills the previous year.

My uncle, Dick Harland, had again lent me his Mauser 10.75 for which I was grateful and had confidence in since shooting my first buffalo with it. I soon learnt that 'Pondoro' Taylor was right; the round is hopeless on big, tough animals. However, at this time, I had no option but to use it and be thankful!

Driving on south through the wonderful, wild expanses of mopane and baobab country, we arrived at a clearing on the Sabi river's west bank; a beautiful camping site in evergreen forest. Naison duly arrived during the afternoon and assisted Tsuro and I in setting up our simple facilities and cooking the evening meal. He was sure the wounded buffalo was living in the riverine thickets further downstream and we decided to investigate the next day.

The raucous screeching of the Natal francolin woke me early and we soon collected our gear and set off in the old open-top Land Rover, following a track running parallel to the river, the chill of the dawn air adding to the tense excitement I felt. Some miles passed before Naison called a halt, suggesting we walk on down the track to check for buffalo spoor crossing.

An hour later we located signs of a small herd that had travelled during the night to drink at the river and soon found their returning spoor heading west into the dry country. There was an outside chance the wounded bull might have joined this group, and anyway I reckoned it would be folly to pass up a chance of getting an animal on the first day. Naison stared at the tracks, thoughtfully sniffed a pinch of snuff, then nodded to himself.

"What do you see, Naison?" I asked, intrigued.

"I know this herd. They have a favourite area to stay in the day time. It is very far and the other hunters usually give up following them. And there are some big bulls, even though the herd is only about forty in number."

Five hours of Naison's incredibly fast tracking, some through easy country, some through thick, tall grass with a myriad of cattle paths, proved his point! The dung was now fresh and we moved more cautiously until Tsuro hissed and pointed. The buffalo were lying down amongst dry, grey thickets of combretum (rooibos) bushes. The wind was favourable and I signalled to the others to wait while I stalked the herd.

Closing on them, I spotted two bulls lying in a clearing to the left of the

main group but as I crept towards them, the breeze shifted and one bull stood up, facing and staring straight at me. I shot him in the centre of his chest at which he stumbled sideways for a few steps then came at me. Firing for the brain had no effect whatsoever and my third shot, also for the brain, similarly failed and he kept coming, when he suddenly slowed, shaking his head before falling over with a bellow. Quickly reloading the Mauser's magazine, I approached and finished him with a neck shot.

To my astonishment, the second bullet had simply chipped a small crater in the front of the bull's boss while the third had entered next to the left eye, no doubt passing under the brain and having zero stopping effect. The following day, while butchering the carcass at camp, we found the first shot had passed through the heart which, fortunately, had caused him to fade out before he reached me on his charge.

The disintegration of the bullet on his boss, with a few pieces of metal still stuck in the horn, really disturbed me. Bullets recovered from the body shots were almost unrecognisable. John Taylor was right! In later years, similar shots with the .458 Win. Mag. had no problem drilling through the bosses of the most determined buffalo bulls.

That evening we discussed the possibility of trying to locate the wounded one again. Naison had been doing his mental homework and came up with a novel suggestion. He suggested we go via his home in the morning and collect his dog, which he assured us would be a great partner in the riverine jungle if we came up with the buffalo. He would be our early warning system, so to speak, which sounded good to me. I knew Don Somerville would not disapprove. Any means of accounting for this animal would be acceptable.

Arriving at Naison's kraal early next morning, Tsuro and I were highly amused when our man yelled from the Land Rover, "Poison, here, Poison." Whereupon a long-legged mongrel shot out of a hut and bounded up to us. Naison lifted him into the vehicle which excited him with it's smell of buffalo meat.

We searched for spoor again along the track near the river and eventually found day-old signs of a single buffalo. We followed, hoping to establish whether it was the wounded one, and if it was still living in this area. Poison, accompanying us, at one stage put his nose into the breeze and moved off purposefully. We followed and soon found where the buffalo had been lying down, leaving a large clot of congealed blood on the leaves. Things looked interesting!

We decided the bull had slept here during the night, moving off in the pre-dawn hours. He obviously was sticking to the forest along the Sabi river

which was, in parts, as dense and leafy as any jungle. That he was still bleeding almost a week after being shot, showed us the wound must be deep and possibly in an area like a leg or the neck where movement would keep it open. I looked at Poison, thinking I really was pleased to have him along! I had never followed up a wounded buffalo and doing so in thick undergrowth was scary.

Naison, with Poison at his side behaving like a well-trained gun dog, picked his cautious way along the bull's track, pausing frequently to listen. I followed, nerves taut, with Tsuro just behind. Trumpeter hornbills flew over, yelling loudly. Francolins, Heuglin's robins and other birds made far too much noise and I wished they would shut up. They were oblivious to the serious business at hand!

A sudden crash of an animal smashing through the forest startled me and Poison growled ominously. The sounds faded out of earshot as whatever it was continued it's panic-struck escape. We grinned at each other and Naison, encouragingly, said "Nyati. Next time, maybe he will not run away!" We soon came to the place where the buffalo had again been lying down, leaving blood and pus. The tension was now extreme as we followed the flattened vegetation at a snail's pace, finding where the bull had stopped running and turned around to listen for us. Smears of blood were high up on the bushes. Even Poison looked poised for action as we stalked on through the undergrowth. All four of us knew what may happen at any moment!

Seconds before it happened, I had an urge to move some paces to Naison's left and as I stepped past some scrub into an open space the buffalo charged Naison from close range. Poison had already rushed at the bull, barking furiously, and as I fired I saw the horns sweep down at the dog. Poison disappeared into the greenery, still barking. I fired again for the buffalo's neck, at which he dropped with a crash into some bushes and I shot finally for the heart.

Reloading the magazine, I called for Naison who appeared grinning from behind a small tree trunk just to one side of the dead bull. Tsuro came from somewhere and Poison limped onto the scene, still barking. I examined the dog while Naison described how the buffalo had given Poison a glancing blow which had bowled him over, but this had distracted the attacker's attention from Naison, allowing him to dodge behind the tree. Poison had only suffered a bruising and was soon walking normally. We all sat down and relived the action with nervous humour and relief.

The bullet from the previous hunter had gone diagonally through the neck, missing the vertebrae, arteries and wind pipe, but damaging the

muscles. One of the ranch managers called at our camp during the afternoon and we handed over the buffalo to him, explaining the agreement with Don Somerville.

Sitting around the campfire that evening, we roasted piles of fresh liver and Poison feasted on a heap of steak. The day's events were recounted, Naison sniffing snuff and cracking jokes about hunting with the *mafana*. He then made a strange comment, saying my *midzimu* (ancestral spirits) spoke to me. Asking what he meant, he in turn asked me why I had moved to one side and ahead of him just before the buffalo attacked. Answering his own question, he continued by saying my 'spirits' made me do it so I would be able to shoot in time. So, my spirits were responsible for saving him from the bull, not me, my rifle and Poison!

I recalled that urge to change position seconds before the bull had charged unexpectedly, and was strongly impressed to discover my intuition had actually functioned. I resolved never to disregard it and consequently found the power developed over the years of big game hunting and also during Rhodesia's bush war.

We continued to look for more buffalo and duly filled the other two licences, both reasonable bulls, after lots of hard hunting. At the end of my two week period the biltong had dried and we managed to pile the sacks high on the Land Rover for the journey back to the farm at Rusape.

Tsuro and I returned for other buffalo hunts over the following two years, in between ivory hunting expeditions. We always took Naison a gift and dog biscuits for Poison. In spite of Poison and my *midzimu*, I was proud of the success of that hunt; it laid the foundation for my confidence in hunting dangerous game. But I never used a 10.75 rifle again.

THREE

Elephants & Eagles

School holidays were busy times. The Devuli buffalo hunts were the highlight and there was also plenty of good hunting to be had on our 11 000 acres at home. Although I had lost most of the desire to shoot duiker, steenbok and even kudu, the animals that offered a real challenge physically were baboons and bush pigs. I was blessed with great athletic ability, playing most sports and ultimately captaining both my house rugby team and the school's athletics. I also represented the school in tennis, squash, hockey and cricket. Pursuing baboons up and down great granite domes and broken *kopjes* undoubtedly kept me very fit for school sports. Or was it the other way round?

Bush pigs offered the most exciting action when hunted at night in ten-foot high maize for which I used a double 12-bore shotgun loaded with SG or SSG. Tsuro and I patrolled slowly and silently along the edge of a block of maize, extending anywhere from twenty to fifty acres, keeping on the leeward side of the wind. Tsuro carried a torch and his axe, and had strict instructions to stay in one place once I entered the maize.

At any time between eight o'clock and midnight, the pigs started feeding. The loud crack of breaking maize stalks was the signal for me to sneak through the dense stand of vegetation, stopping frequently to gauge the direction the pigs were taking. They also stopped often, waiting silently for any sound or scent of a predator, before continuing with their rowdy chomping of juicy maize cobs.

Eventually, with luck, I might get within a few yards of the guzzling sounds. Kneeling down with the shotgun held horizontally, the butt tucked against my hip bone, and judging in the pitch dark the direction to point the

muzzle, I fired both barrels one after the other, quickly stood up, stepped into the nearest row of maize stalks and reloaded. Meanwhile, the pigs smashed their way in any direction, sometimes passing down 'my' row within inches of my legs. Outside of big game animals, this was the most challenging, exciting style of hunting I could have.

After a silent wait of up to ten minutes, I called to Tsuro to meet me where I stood. If I had heard a shot pig giving out dying sounds, we used the torch to look directly for it. If not, we searched for blood and followed very slowly, shotgun off safe and ready. Should the torch run low on power or we reached the edge of the land, we went home to sleep and returned in the morning to follow up. I then carried the .303 and Tsuro the shotgun. We had no dogs, so did the tracking until we either found the wounded pig, or if only lightly hit, it might have escaped onto a neighbouring farm. We worked hard to retrieve our pigs; corn-fed hog is delicious to eat and I made a few quid selling the surplus.

We had good sport with game birds too, as guineafowl, Coqui francolin and red-necked francolin were common. The government doctor from Rusape Hospital, Ken Davey, middle-aged and an avid hunter, had a pointer dog and was my most frequent partner. Several years later, Ken joined me for some elephant control in the Tsetse Fly Corridors of Gonarezhou in his capacity as an honorary officer.

One evening at school I was invited by a teacher to watch a home movie of himself shooting an elephant. Also present was the person who had taken the teacher on the hunt and done the filming. His name was Paul Grobler and he quickly became my new hero. Paul and his wife Marie, farmed tobacco not far from Peterhouse and I soon became a frequent visitor to their home. Many Sundays I walked the five miles to the farm and spent hours listening to Paul's hunting stories.

A rugged, sun-tanned man with luxuriant black hair parted in the centre, Paul had the looks and easy going self-confidence to have starred in any Hollywood movie as the 'Bwana White Hunter', except of course, he *was* the big game hunter in reality. Frequent forays into the tsetse fly areas along the borders of the Zambezi Valley to reduce elephants, plus call-outs by D.C.s (District Commissioners) to deal with crop-raiders, gave Paul enormous experience. In later years, he gave up farming and developed a substantial business with his son Stephen, in safari hunting, crocodile farming and kapenta fishing, all on the great Lake Kariba, plus having the contract to process thousands of elephants culled by the culling teams to reduce populations in the national parks.

One day Paul asked whether I would like to come elephant hunting

School friend Terence Nicholls and Author (with SMLE .303) on poaching trip

Two of a kind - Martial eagle with Author

Paul Grobler

Target practice, pygmy style

Author with pygmies in Ituri Forest, Congo

during the school holidays. At last he had made the invitation I had been praying for! He offered to lend me his .458 Winchester Magnum, a rifle made by the British firm, Birmingham Small Arms; an ordinary field-grade piece with a muzzle-brake consisting of five slots on each side of the barrel. The rifle fitted me well and was fairly lightweight but the back-blast from the 'shark's gill' slots made it very noisy. Naturally, I fell in love with the BSA.

Our first elephant hunt was in the Pfungwe district, along the Mazoe river near the Mozambique border. The whole area we covered seemed to be rugged, hilly country and, although elephants had been through some days previously, we never came across fresh signs. I was astounded by the agility of the elephants after walking for three days among these deep valleys and steep slopes following their heavily worn paths. Even Paul joked that they were related to baboons. The only game we saw were kudu.

We had to return for Paul to attend to his farming but he assured me he would either receive a call from a District Commissioner, or we could check out a different area on speculation. I promised I would be near the telephone for the next couple of weeks.

Days later Paul called. Elephants were raiding crops in the Mtoko district, only a couple of hours drive from his farm. We met at the small village of Macheke and headed north, arriving at a stream in the middle of a wild, uninhabited part of the tribal area that afternoon. Paul had hunted this country before and knew elephant liked to come here as the nearest villages were far away, so we set up our simple camp right there.

Walking upstream for an hour before sunset, we found elephant signs a day or so old of a herd of cows and youngsters. Tsuro was with us and I told him to learn everything he could from Paul's trackers, Petro and Bennet. As Petro was also a good bush cook, Tsuro picked up a few ideas in that department as well.

Early in the morning we walked rapidly downstream hoping to come across fresh signs of elephant and were in luck by mid-morning. Probably the same herd, numbering ten to fifteen head, had drunk at the stream, wandered about feeding, then at about sun-up by our estimate, moved northwards. We followed, catching up with them within two hours.

Paul was a great coach. He described many times all the angles for shots on elephant. Now he took us in slowly, whispering a commentary on what he intended to do and what he anticipated the actions of the animals to be as we closed to shooting distance. He was disappointed to find no bulls present, nor any cows with reasonably sized tusks. I was too excited to care much about the size of ivory! Paul pointed, as a big cow walked to a tree in front of us, saying, "Brain shot when she stops."

The boom of the .458 and simultaneous collapse of the elephant surprised me; it was so sudden, so final. Immediately reloading, I saw a clear shot as the herd charged across our front, and a second elephant dropped. Paul had also fired and I was not sure if we had shot the same animal. Apparently not, as he loped off at a trot, calling, "I shot one, come!"

The herd had run down into a small valley, then reappeared on the ridge of the other side. One animal was slowing up, no longer running with the rest. I stopped and aimed at it's head, again broadside on but nearly a hundred yards distant. The big cow dropped at the report, clearly brain shot; an absolute fluke! Paul and the two trackers stopped dead in their tracks and turned to look at me, their jaws sagging in surprise. We hurried on to make sure the elephant was really down for good, and that it was the one to which Paul had given a heart shot. He shook my hand and congratulated me on the exceptional shot but I knew it was just luck.

This first elephant hunt was so interesting. I learnt a great deal from Paul, such as: how to control my excitement at close quarters to big game; how to approach and assess a herd; to identify the matriarch (herd leader); to take into account the odd animal wandering on it's own; and many other observations. Not least was the wind. Petro donated me his little ash bag afterwards as I had never used one before. This was made from a six-inch square of old handkerchief, loosely filled with a heap of dry, white wood ash and tied at the neck with a piece of string. When shaken, the bag gave out a puff of white powder which indicated the direction the wind was blowing. That was the last time I ever shot at an elephant at that distance!

Paul was keen to show me the position of the brain in an elephant's skull, so Petro, Bennet and Tsuro started straight into skinning the head of the first cow, then chopping into the skull bones under Paul's direction. The brain cavity was just where I had imagined it and I studied it closely, then went to the other animals to point out to Paul the angles from front and side for a bullet to find it's target. From that day, I specialised in brain shots on elephants, developing the skill to a high level of deadly efficiency. However, it was only years later that the real secret dawned on me. I had quickly, and unconsciously, developed an ability to mentally 'see', or envisage, the position of the brain from any angle without having to look at external reference points such as ear holes, eyes, wrinkles on trunk, temple bones and so forth. I could instantly aim at the brain itself, almost as if I had an X-ray vision of it. That I possessed this uncanny gift only became apparent to me after talking with other hunters later in my career.

The next morning we stopped at a farmhouse to telephone the D.C. who would send word to the villagers in the area to collect the meat and bring

the ivory in to his office. Journeying on to the Groblers' farm, I told Paul of my intention to go back to Devuli ranch for more buffalo hunting. He obviously recalled my problems with the 10.75 Mauser; I had shown him the bits of full-metal-jacket shrapnel recovered from previous buffalo.

"You must take the .458 with you," Paul casually offered, as if lending out a hat or pair of shoes. Before I could stammer a reply, he took my breath away by continuing, "I have just bought a .460 Weatherby so you can keep the BSA if you like and pay me when you can. Let's make it eighty pounds and that's with some boxes of ammo thrown in."

I could hardly believe it. I soon scraped and scrounged the money to pay Paul, and over the ensuing couple of years I also bought his Short-Wheel-Base Land Rover and Marie Grobler's little Vauxhall Victor. I had, at times, varying degrees of teenage passion for their two lovely daughters, May and Pauline, but totally failed to make any acquisitions in that direction.

At Tsuro's insistence, I taught him to shoot both the .303 and .458. He had already proved his ability with a double shotgun on pigs but using the sights of rifles was new to him, as were bolt-actions and magazines. Soon, Rob Waller promoted him to 'shootaboy', which entailed patrolling the lands of tobacco and maize armed with one of the farm's ancient single-barrel 12-bores. Baboons were a fairly serious threat to tobacco; a big troop could break down dozens of plants in just minutes. Once maize carried maturing cobs, baboons by day and bush pigs by night proved an ongoing battle to control. Right up Tsuro's street – while I slaved away at horrible school. And knocking off Nicky Mallett's rabbits with a hockey stick was not really in the same league as a pig hunt!

However, hawking with our black sparrowhawks provided fine opportunities for Neville Buch and I to get into the farmlands around school and enjoy ourselves over the weekends after Saturday sports. The hawks, which had been wild-caught some weeks after leaving their nest in a plantation of eucalyptus trees, knew how to hunt but had not yet left their parent's territory and were therefore young enough to be tamed and trained without excessive trauma. A farmer friend and experienced falconer, John Hough, taught us how to set up his 'do-gazza' nets in the plantation with a half-grown live chicken tethered to a peg placed in the centre of the trap as the bait. The movement of the chicken as it pecked and scratched in the leaves attracted the young raptors, one of which would fly down to attack its prey, only to get tangled up in the nets. A quick dash from our hide where we were watching with binoculars and the prize was ours.

Then followed the tedious period of days with the hawk in a dark room during which it slowly became accustomed to sitting on the gloved hand, to

feeding on it and then, by allowing a bit of light in, to seeing its master up close. All the labours and frustrations during weeks of confidence-building were hugely rewarded by the first 'free' flight of the trained bird, when it returned to the glove instead of disappearing over the horizon forever!

The natural prey of the black sparrowhawk, besides rats, mice and squirrels, ranges in size up to francolin for the male and guineafowl for the larger female, in spite of the fact that the hawk is considerably lighter than an adult guineafowl.

In falconry parlance, there are two distinct categories of the discipline, using one or the other class of raptor, namely 'Long-wing' (falcons) or 'Short-wing' (goshawks and sparrowhawks) which have completely different hunting styles, and thus rather dissimilar training methods and field techniques. Falcons, with their long, pointed wings, short tail feathers and short legs, hunt by cruising high above the countryside and diving down (stooping) onto prey either on the ground or flying across an open area. To have one's falcon 'waiting on' up in the sky while the falconer, either with a couple of beaters or better still, a pointer dog, searches for something to put up for the bird, requires plenty of open countryside. However, as they are 'protected birds', ownership of the falcon species is disallowed unless under special permit, which schoolboys are most unlikely to obtain.

Sparrowhawks, with short, broad wings and long tails are built for manoeuvrability while chasing prey through trees and brush. They 'still hunt', moving from one vantage point to another to sit and wait for something to show up. We could therefore carry our hawks into various terrains, including grassland and planted fields, which gave us greater flexibility in hunting opportunities. We were also fortunate in having the use of a pointer, borrowed from one of the housemasters, Norman Davis, brother of the internationally renowned music conductor, Sir Colin Davis. The dog was friendly (like its owner) but quite untrained, had much enthusiasm for its role and was certainly better than no dog at all.

The hawk soon learnt to watch the pointer working ahead of us. As soon as the leather hood was taken off its head the bird tensed up for action, bobbing its head as it followed the dog's progress. The specially-made brass bells on each leg tinkled as the hawk irritably shook its legs as it felt the restraining tug of its jess or leather straps. Should a covey of francolin be put up within range, one slipped the bird, even giving it a flying start with a thrust of the fist, and then followed as fast as possible.

Once I lost my hawk in an open, rolling expanse of tall thatching grass and search as we might we could not find where it had gone down following a Swainson's francolin it was chasing. Not even Mr. Davis' dog could locate

it. After a wide ranging search over many acres I heard the bells tinkling somewhere at ground level. Pushing my way through the six foot high grass, I came upon an antbear's burrow with my hawk standing at the entrance, covered in red mud and looking thoroughly annoyed. Obviously the francolin had dive-bombed down the tunnel to escape and the raptor followed suit but being much longer legged, could not actually pursue the prey to the tight end of the burrow! He must have been down there for ten minutes in the moist red subsoil, absolutely terrifying the wits out of poor Mister Swainson while going mad with frustration. He flew up to my glove for a small reward, eyeing me scornfully as I laughed at his grubby appearance.

I have shot elephant and buffalo using .505 rounds that I developed and reloaded myself, and caught trout, bonefish and tarpon on home-tied flies, but these very satisfying accomplishments are nothing compared to sitting down to a dinner of francolin or guineafowl taken by my own bird of prey, captured wild, then co-opted into working as a hunting partner.

The martial eagle, along with the black eagle and the crowned eagle, rates as one of the largest raptors of southern Africa, with females reaching a wing-span of over seven feet and capable of killing monkeys, young baboons, and small antelope such as steenbuck and young duiker. I obtained a female chick from the nest a friend found in a small national park near Salisbury and raised it at school with the intention of training it to hunt guineafowl, hares and monkeys on the farm. I also figured that it may be possible to interest the bird in springhares and scrub hares at night with a spotlight.

The rearing of the eaglet, giving it sufficient exercise to gain strength and then teaching it to recognise prey animals and birds, was a lengthy, time-consuming job. The nestling period alone is about one hundred days. Two main drawbacks of raptors reared from a young age are, firstly, they often become 'screamers', calling out monotonously for hours, and secondly, they have not learnt to hunt and kill, although once the young bird has fed on whole animals and birds it seems to remember what is edible. The main problem is for it to learn the techniques of attacking from the air, pursuing a moving creature and capturing it successfully.

The training of the bird 'to the glove' is the easy part unlike with wild-caught hawks, although coping with the phenomenal strength of the eagles' grip was a different matter. With a spread of eight inches from the tip of the rear talon to that of the centre front toe, when the bird was excited or feeding on the glove and exerted maximum pressure with its feet, the pain of the talons through thick leather was often too great to bear. Crushing a

hare's skull was no problem for those vice-like weapons.

The first night hunt with the martial was a great success, mainly due to the utter stupidity of a young scrub hare which obligingly sat still in the light of the Land Rover's headlamps. The eagle did not seem to recognise it initially, so I instructed Tsuro to throw something at it to get it moving. The jack handle was the nearest projectile to hand and Tsuro flung it towards the target. The two-feet length of steel rod bounced once, end-over-end and cracked the hare on the cranium, laying it out cold, feet kicking in the dust. The martial, realising here was an easy kill, took off leisurely to cover the ten yards to the prone hare and grabbed it.

I was determined to have a more professional performance than this, so I picked up the eagle with the hare onto my gloved hand, then offered a piece of dove, hoping the martial would seize it and let go of the hare. Still holding my arm plus the prey in its one foot, the other struck with lightning speed at my right hand holding the dove, the force of its grip stabbing a sharp talon right through the end of my first finger. The bones in my hand started creaking as if shaking hands with Arnold Schwarzenegger. Almost speechless with pain, I told Tsuro to disengage the hare from the eagle's grip and throw it down on the ground. This he accomplished with much difficulty, eventually parting the body from the head which the talons still held against the glove. As the decapitated corpse hit the ground the eagle went for it, but without the courtesy of releasing my mangled right hand, resulting in me landing flat on the ground with the martial doing its best to pull me towards the out-of-reach hare. Only then was I released in favour of a more succulent meal. Here endeth the lesson, I decided, unceremoniously dumping the eagle with its meal on the floor in the back of the Land Rover, and heading home feeling definitely the worse for wear.

Apart from one further night hunt, when my eagle took two springhares in great style, I never hunted with it again. My parents decided I had too many distractions at school and that my academic achievements were not what they should be. Absolutely nothing to do with the disappearances of Nick Mallett's pet rabbits, but I was told that my martial must stay at home and that Rob Waller would look after her. This was devastating news as I loved my eagle and had great plans for future hunting. A month after returning to school I received the news that one day, while Rob was exercising the bird, it had flown out of sight. Two days later it was found drowned in a water tank.

FOUR

Last Days Of
The Belgian Congo

Rich country, poor country; vast territory, ghastly governments. In fact a typically African situation but on a huge scale. Imagine a European king owning a private estate of nearly 1.5 million square miles containing incredible natural resources and wealth, plus abundant slave labour. King Leopold of Belgium was granted the Congo Free State in 1885, after he had sent Henry Stanley to explore the possibilities of road, rail and river communications from the Atlantic coast up the Congo river to the hinterland. Unfortunately, the King turned out to be a somewhat tyrannical landlord.

Eventually the atrocities committed by Leopold against the people and the environment came to the notice of the western world and he was forced to give up the country to the Belgian government in 1908. Belgium did very little for the Congo for the next fifty years and independence in 1960 came almost as a shock to the ill-prepared Africans. The political turmoil, coup and counter-coup, murder, genocide and U.N. interference resulted, after a few years, in Joseph Mobutu becoming president with the support of America and other western governments. For over thirty-five years this megalomanic tyrant wrecked the country before being ousted by yet another dictatorial despot. Poor Congo - Leopold, Mobutu, Kabila. Who next?

The year before Independence, when I was fourteen years old, my parents decided we should visit the Congo during school holidays. A wise decision it turned out to be as it became almost impossible later with the fighting. The family sedan, a Vauxhall Velox, heavily laden with five of us plus luggage for the six weeks of travelling, proved worthy of the task of completing the 4500 miles through some of Africa's remotest regions.

The journey took us north-east through Southern Rhodesia to cross the Zambezi into Northern Rhodesia at the Chirundu bridge, then due north via Lusaka and the Copperbelt to Elizabethville (now Lubumbashi), our first stop in the Congo. More days of travelling, via the tin mining town of Manono and Albertville on the shores of Lake Tanganyika, brought us to Bukavu on the south side of Lake Kivu.

Kivu, at an elevation of 4800 feet, is surrounded by mountains covered in tropical greenery, banana plantations and chinchona trees, from whose bark quinine is extracted. Lake Kivu must be one of Africa's loveliest lakes, with clear blue waters, no bilharzia or crocodiles, and two great volcanoes smoking away just to the north of the lake. Ten years earlier, in 1948, a huge lava flow came down and reached the waters of Lake Kivu. We crossed the rough, undulating black rock on the road to Goma on the lake's north shore, finding a species of fern already well established on the sterile surface. Goma, a pleasant little town on the Congo border, with its more attractive neighbour, Kisenyi, a mile inside Ruanda territory, were the centres forty years later of some of Africa's most horrendous human slaughter.

All our passports and travel documents were stolen from our rooms at the Kisenyi Hotel but the police recovered everything from a nearby vacant plot the following morning. Much relief all round! Palm trees, well-kept gardens, the beach with its umbrellas and bikini-clad blondes, the food and language all gave a distinct impression of the French Riviera, at least until we visited the market. Here one was struck by the brightly coloured clothing worn by the crowd, with an occasional Tutsi elegantly robed in white, striding along head and shoulders above the milling throngs of Batwa people.

Motoring on northwards through Uganda took us into the Queen Elizabeth National Park, past Lake Edward and up the Semliki river back into the Congo to a town named Beni. The last fifty miles crossed the Equator in the hills just west of the magnificent Ruwenzori mountains, popularly known as the 'Mountains of the Moon', and passed through spectacular montane forest, home to mountain gorillas and chimpanzees. In 1925 the Virunga National Park was established to preserve a part of this wonderland for the great primates but they are still subjected to poaching activities. Lake Edward and its surrounds were suffering from a huge over-population of hippo resulting in the total destruction of grasses for miles around the lake. We met a Rhodesian who was on contract to cull five thousand of them; the meat was to be used to feed the people from various mines and towns in the region. We saw buffalo facing starvation and dead hippos in small pans.

Passing Mt. Hoyo at the eastern end of the vast Ituri equatorial rain

forests, we found occasional groups of Mbuti pygmies on the roadside, coming and going to the villages of the Lese tribespeople with whom they had a sort of symbiotic relationship. The pygmies brought meat, ivory and forest foods to exchange for cooking utensils, knives, tobacco or beer but, as the Balese considered themselves masters of the BaMbuti, no doubt the little people got a poor deal.

Further north into the Haute (Upper) Congo region we stopped in a village called Bunia to buy fruit at the market. There were several woman wearing the most hideous adornment of the 'duck-bill', a wooden disc in the top lip which is gradually enlarged from childhood till it may reach several inches in diameter. It was said girls thus mutilated would not be taken by the slave traders. I tried unsuccessfully to have my sister go in for this tradition, but she sensibly decided lifelong virginity was not for her.

From Bunia we took a track due west into the Ituri jungle for a hundred miles to a tiny outpost, Epulu, where we stayed in lodgings composed of small timber chalets. Here we saw the remains of Pat Putnam's homestead, an American who had stayed there for many years studying pygmies until his death some years prior to our visit. The Efe pygmies lived in larger communities than the BaMbutis, with strong bonds throughout the 'extended' family, the whole lot living in little leaf-covered dome-shaped huts in a clearing. We watched them having target practice with their tiny bows and arrows, preparing poison for the arrows, cooking meals and dancing. Fascinating people, largely unspoilt by European ways, and born hunters by definition. How I yearned to hunt a forest elephant or buffalo with them, but alas, no .458!

One of the more interesting projects the Belgians had instigated in the early 1900s was the domestication of elephants, and the centre of this was Garamba Park in the north-east corner of the Congo. At Epulu a fine herd of a dozen elephants was kept, although it appeared they did very little physical work for their keep. We enjoyed watching their evening drink and bath in the Epulu river, followed by a stroll back to their paddock where each was chained by a back leg and heaps of greenery left for them to browse on overnight. Some of the bulls had lovely long slender tusks and I shudder to think what became of these animals with the anarchy of civil war. C'est l'Afrique!

A portion of forest near the camp was fenced in for a group of okapi which were completely tame and bred quite happily; not surprising considering their docile temperament in captivity, although in the wild they are extremely shy and elusive. The beautiful dark colouring of the body, with wraparound stripes on rump and forelegs and white stockings below, make this one of the forest's most exotic creatures. We also saw bongo and forest

buffalo at Epulu but regrettably our days there soon came to an end and the return journey began.

With my mother's encouragement, we had a small 'museum' at home filled with all sorts of natural history objects and, having been taught rudimentary taxidermy by Rob Waller, I had preserved a few birds and rodents. Rob lent me a .22 pistol to take on the Congo journey, which I simply hid away with no thought of a permit and I had some shot shells with me just in case an interesting small creature needed collecting for the museum.

The road through the forest traversed occasional patches of open grassland, and once a most colourful bird flew across the track some way ahead of the car, prompting the family to call on me to get it for the museum. The road was several feet below the surrounding ground and storm-water drains were cut into the banks like small canyons. The bird seemed to disappear into one of these. I noticed a couple of pygmies a bit further on when my father stopped the car. Jumping out with the pistol, and loading a rat-shot cartridge in the breech, I did not see where the pygmies went but stalked along looking down each drain channel for the bird.

Suddenly it flushed out ahead of me and I tried a quick shot at it but missed. To my surprise it landed further along, so on I went. Passing a couple more drains, I slowly peered around the corner of the next channel off the road, pistol ready. The moment the pygmies, who were ten yards along the trench, saw me, one drew his bow and shot. Thanks to quick reflexes, I ducked down and the arrow went over me. They obviously thought I was after them. Shocked, I sprinted back to the car, leapt in and wound up the window! Telling my father to drive on, we passed the drain to see my two would-be assassins with bows at the ready but they did not try to give the Vauxhall a dose of 'curare' poison. The chatter in the car was rather like a troop of excited monkeys, and I took exception to my little brother's comment that there would be less of a squeeze on the back seat if I had let the pygmies shoot me. So much for my family's gratitude, with me risking my life in Darkest Africa for their benefit!

Taking a number of different routes on the journey south, the varied countryside and people were of never-ending fascination, contributing to the relative harmony amongst the five of us in the car. Apart from a puncture or two, the only other mishap occurred when my sister ate too much fruit, resulting in the coining of the term 'granadilla whiffs', and adeptness at rapid winding down of the car windows to avoid asphyxiation.

Barely a year after our adventure, the Congo descended into disaster and we were thankful to have experienced the old colony before it changed forever.

FIVE

Pluto's Episode

Shortly after the Belgian Congo journey, I had an unexpected call from Paul Grobler asking me to join him on a hunt. The District Commissioner at Mtoko wanted elephants chased out of his area. Within an hour I had the .458, Tsuro, blankets and some food packed into my mother's car and she drove us to Paul's farm, sixty miles distant. He was ready with his men, Bennet and Petro, and we set off immediately on the three-hour drive to the northern part of Mtoko.

We camped near a perennial stream a couple of miles beyond some villages whose inhabitants told us of the dangers they had experienced with a herd of elephant over the past week. Twice at night the animals had come into the kraals, upsetting some grain storage huts and breaking down precious pawpaw and mango trees. Two men, who were out looking for honey and caterpillars, had been chased a couple of days previously. One had been up a tree, chopping a hole into the hollow trunk to reach a beehive while his friend had a small, smoky fire going at the base of the tree to keep the swarm at bay.

Hearing the elephants breaking trees some way off, they decided to hurry up with the honey extraction. The one with the axe cut more vigorously into the tree to enlarge the entrance to the hive, and possibly the chopping sounds annoyed the elephants. Unbeknown to him, his friend below, seeing a couple of cow elephants advancing at speed, dropped a handful of burning grass and took off for the horizon.

So engrossed was the honey collector with peering into the hole and reaching for the dripping combs, he belatedly noticed the heat and smoke reaching him up in the tree. The tall grass around his perch was ablaze. The

shrill blast of an angry elephant trumpeting promptly loosened his grip on the branches. The poor fellow dropped a dozen feet into the fire, but shot out of there and successfully escaped the hostile jumbos. I couldn't help envisaging the man's legs running in mid-air before hitting the ground, like Pluto the dog doing 'wheel-spins' in the cartoon movies!

In true African fashion, the two men gave us their account with great histrionics and hilarity and, due to his unpronounceable name, I labelled the one guy Pluto. We welcomed their offer of assistance in locating the herd, and set off along a path to visit a couple of small villages in the vicinity. Paul pointed out to me the semi-digested seeds of pumpkin, sorghum and maize in the elephant's droppings along the path. Teasing Pluto, he pretended to pick out a piece of chewed beeswax, shaking his head and grumbling about people who wasted good honey by feeding it to elephants.

An hour's walk from our camp, with the morning dew still on the grass, the deep bass, booming calls of ground hornbills resounded nearby and, almost in answer, the sound of a village drum reached us. Pluto and his friend spoke a few words to each other followed by the announcement that the elephants had been around the village. We took the next fork in the path and headed in the direction of the thumping drum.

Minutes later, Petro said he smelt marulas and suggested we find the tree to check if elephants had fed on the fruit. Around the massive trunk of the big tree the grass was flattened and scattered with fresh elephant dung. With all of us circling the area, we soon picked up the herd's spoor going off in a meandering fashion as they spread out and fed.

Rapid tracking brought us up to the elephants within the hour. They were still moving but less dispersed, and we tallied up about twenty animals in the main group. The wind blew directly into our faces, so Paul gave us a whispered plan of action. He and I would shoot one each, preferably juvenile bulls or cows without calves at foot, and particularly not to kill the lead cow, as without the matriarch the herd would have its social and command structure temporarily devastated.

"Are you ready for action?" Paul murmured. I nodded, my heart thumping as loud as the village drum. He signalled to the five Africans to stay put, and I soon realised why. With a last shake of the ash bag to check the light breeze, he rapidly moved from bush to bush and tree to tree, keeping low in the patches of tall grass, straight into the herd of elephant!

This technique of 'swooping' on a herd is one I used frequently in later years but it demands several basic requirements: the elephants cannot be in dense cover; the hunter must be absolutely confident of his own abilities,

particularly on quick brain shots at close quarters; and he should 'use enough gun' with total faith in the rifle's reliability. Essentially, he must become an 'elephant man' through much experience of hunting and observing these great animals. The born hunter who hones his talents with continuous practice can develop his skills to a stage where many details involving the approach to the quarry and the positioning for the shots are observed and quickly mentally processed, yielding an automatic, instinctive attack plan.

In the elephant hunting context, some of the elements will be: the number and disposition of the animals, particularly the identification of the probable matriarch and any bulls; the direction of the wind and the herd's movement; any possible vantage points like termite mounds or high ground; and the likely flight paths of the various individuals once the shooting starts. Then, there is the all-important 'feel' of the situation facing the hunter. Does he feel right about doing a swoop on these elephants? Has he developed that intuition which will tell him, "Don't do it?" The 'slowly, slowly' approach is the one to take if there are any doubts.

Why, then, even consider a swoop attack at all? The professional elephant hunter or experienced game ranger will be evaluating his options as the hunt progresses, and foremost will be the number of animals he might put down. Crop-raiders would require one or two be shot to frighten them seriously enough to keep them away for a long time. In a Tsetse fly corridor, the objective would most likely be to eliminate the herd, particularly if some had been shot previously and the remainder still did not leave the area. In either case, the hunter might find the herd close to entering dense cover, or perhaps the wind beginning to shift around, or one animal showing suspicion of danger, so the quick assault is chosen.

I knew nothing of these things as I stood next to Paul with half a dozen elephants seemingly towering over us, all within five or ten yards. At Paul's indication I shot one cow and this prompted two others to charge us which we each put down with frontal brain shots, just yards apart.

"Reload your magazine," ordered Paul.

We stood still as the trumpeting, growling crowd of now-terrified jumbos crashed away through a huge thicket of jesse. Our African comrades came along, grinning widely and chattering excitedly as they examined the dead beasts. Paul cut a length of straight stem from a shrub and tried pushing it into the bullet channels, which worked on the .458 holes, but not his .460's entrance hole which had closed up in the thick, hard hide. The .458 solids had travelled directly to the brains on both my shots.

We had time to return to camp, have a quick meal and reach Paul's farm

before nightfall, so we left instructions with Pluto to have the tusks sent to the D.C. We would advise the other villages of the whereabouts of the meat on our way out. As we left the scene, I saw Pluto and his friend cutting into the temple glands of the elephants to extract the bits of twig that are often found buried in the ducts and are used in concoctions for medicinal applications.

Still full of excitement, I plied Paul with questions on the drive back, learning much more of the art of being a successful big game hunter. Two days later back at school, I was the envy of my like-minded pals who could barely believe my incredible experience of facing up to charging elephants.

SIX

Solving Problems
Schoolboy Style

Persistence is as essential in hunting as it is in the pursuit of girls. It's probably a fairly common occurrence that the two activities should seriously clash in a 16-year-old's life. The Peterhouse School Dance was in a week's time and my proposed partner, a most desirable lass, had accepted the invitation. Then the elephants interfered!

Paul Grobler sent a message saying he needed to see me so I slipped out of school after dinner that night and walked to his farm. He had received word that elephants were being a nuisance in the tribal area near the Nyagadzi river, east of the small settlement of Mrewa. Paul had already advised the District Commissioner that he was unable to attend, but that I would be available!

It was nearly midnight when I sneaked back into the dormitory, but found it hard to sleep with the excitement I felt. Then there was the other problem – my girl. To wait for the day after school broke up, go dancing, then only the following day get home, load up and drive to the hunting area was just too much of a delay. I phoned her in Salisbury the next morning and got what I deserved!

"If you go off hunting elephants, I shall never speak to you again," my sweetheart avowed. Sadly, she kept her word and remained inconsolable. Really, she could have blamed Paul!

I also phoned my friend, Tony Schreiber, at the game department, requesting a couple of elephant licences be posted to me, and called my father asking him to send a cheque to Tony for them. The last few days of school term took weeks to drag past.

The little Austin A40 was not heavily laden. I had recently acquired the

well-used vehicle with my post office savings and all we needed were blankets, some pots, clothes, tinned food and maize meal, and the .458 rifle.

"Wish I was coming with you. Good luck," my mother called encouragingly as we drove off. She has always had a boundless love for nature in its widest sense. My father had grunted noncommittally when told I would be away hunting elephants for some days, maybe a week, possibly longer. Thankfully, he did not care and therefore had no objection!

Late afternoon found us hot and dusty at the end of the road. We had passed the last occupied homestead where the farmer's pretty wife had glanced at my hunting licence, smiled approval for us to camp by a stream on the farm boundary, and advised me that there were no roads from there into the tribal area.

Our camp on the stream bank was positively spartan. Just a fire for cooking and the Austin in which our goods and chattels remained until required. We slept on a canvas sheet on the ground near the fire. The nights were not cold so a couple of blankets each sufficed.

We walked for four days. Leaving camp at sunrise and returning eight or ten hours later, we covered maybe fifteen to twenty miles daily, carrying a packet of biscuits, a tin of baked beans or Vienna sausages for sustenance, and a water bag. We found signs of elephants a week or more old. This was harsh, arid country, much of it burnt out from bush fires. It was a no-mans-land literally, lying between the sparsely inhabited farmlands through which we had travelled and the tribespeople way to the north.

The elephants, when resident in this wilderness, would travel far at night to raid the people's sorghum and pumpkin plots, then usually drink from their shallow wells and streams, causing cave-ins and mudholes, and maybe once a year, kill someone who had the temerity to venture out of his hut at night. If the D.C., a game department ranger or honorary officer was available to hunt a troublesome herd, the elephants would normally vacate the region, heading far north or east, into the low country of the Mazoe and Ruenya rivers which flow to the Zambezi.

Using my rifle ramrod tipped with a sharpened brass jag, Tsuro and I speared small barbel in the pools at night with the help of a torch. Freshly fried fish was a tasty change to the tinned food which accompanied our *sadza* (corn meal) for supper. Tsuro was definitely more advanced than I was at bush cooking and enjoyed preparing our simple meals, particularly since my mother had given him a few spells in the kitchen learning from her new cook, Kainos (Ninepence had retired after many years service; Kainos stayed for more than forty years). While cleaning my rifle I watched Tsuro squatting in front of the fire, holding a little frying pan over it containing baby catfish

'Duck-billed' woman, Bunia market

Okapi

Evening bath in Epulu river, Ituri Forest

Paul Grobler and crop-raider

My first ivory with Paul

fillets looking and smelling like something from a city restaurant. Next to his feet were two small black pots, one full of *sadza*, the other containing gravy simply concocted from a packet of soup powder. With his head inclined to one side to avoid the smoke, he concentrated on the delicate job at hand, then glanced up at me. He was growing into a physically powerful lad and, although he had never set foot in a school, he possessed an enquiring and observant nature. His unsophisticated but sharp sense of humour became very much the Tsuro trade mark as we grew up together, and I enjoyed the way he always found the lighter side of life or came up with a wisecrack in a tense situation.

"Is school food good? Better than my cooking?" he enquired, an impish grin warning me of some devious thought.

"No, I hate their food. See how thin and weak I am," I replied.

He chuckled. "Yes. So how much money will I be paid to make you fat?"

"A hundred pounds."

"Not enough. But I will do it. You just have to stop hunting elephants and playing with girls for one year," were his words of wisdom. Impudent rat!

"Watch out, you're burning my fish. You've just lost your hundred pounds for that," I told him as I reached for my tin plate and piled it up with *sadza* and gravy.

Two hours from camp on the fifth morning we found signs of a herd of cow elephants which had passed by during the night. I was certain that they had been responsible for the D.C.'s call for assistance and we took up pursuit, anticipating they may not travel much further. They were already far from the nearest villages so hopefully were feeling secure.

We soon established that the herd numbered nine or ten animals and, sure enough, they were crop-raiders. Pumpkin seeds in the fresh dung were the evidence. The excitement welled up in me as I realised that here I was with Tsuro on our first 'solo' elephant hunt. All the decisions were mine and mine alone; no one around to call on for help. A novel experience for a schoolboy!

Tracking the elephants was straightforward over the burnt areas, but after a few miles the herd had entered a small, flattish valley covered with acacia trees, scrub and thatching grass. The bushfires had extinguished themselves in the granite hills surrounding the valley. Following spoor weaving through the tall grass and clumps of thicket was slow work, and the wind was becoming dodgy as the mid-morning temperatures rose.

Decision time. "Tsuro, these elephants have stopped in this area. Their dung is fresh. The wind is going with us, so if we go to the high ground on the left of the valley we might hear them or see them before they get our

scent. Not so?"

Tsuro agreed, so we worked our way out of the thick bush up to the ridge several hundred yards distant. No sooner had we reached a rocky outcrop from which to survey the broadening valley below when the sound of a tree breaking reached us. We reckoned the herd was at the far side of the valley, maybe half a mile away, and promptly decided on our plan of attack which was to get ahead of their direction of travel and thus downwind.

A half-hour later we were closing up with the feeding herd. Visibility was very restricted in the head-high grass and clumps of thicket. I moved ahead of Tsuro, rifle ready, heart pounding with nervousness. Right then, I was struck by the responsibility of it all: what if I bungled things and failed both myself and Paul in the eyes of the District Commissioner? 'What ifs' tore through my mind and I turned to Tsuro for moral support. He just grinned and shook his ash bag which comfortingly showed the wind still steady from them to us.

Judging from the sounds, the herd was spread out a little and moving towards us slowly, obviously still feeding. Suddenly there was movement twenty yards ahead under a big acacia, and a couple of quick paces to the left gave me a view of two elephants standing there: a mature cow facing our way and a young bull broadside on but behind the tree trunk.

Steadying my rifle against a sapling, my decision on the placement of a brain shot was instant, and the big cow collapsed in a mighty cloud of dust as simultaneously the shock waves from the rifle's muzzle-brake vents hit my ear. Chambering a fresh round, I raised the .458 again.

The young bull had barged off into the long grass so Tsuro and I ran to the edge of the clearing under the tree, stopping a few yards from the downed elephant. The rush of blood from the end of the trunk was proof of a successful brain shot. As I recharged the magazine, reloaded and felt the first flush of elation, an angry cow elephant screamed nearby.

Like a couple of monkeys, Tsuro and I leapt onto the dead elephant, as much in fright as to gain a height advantage. Seconds later, head down and at speed, the attacking elephant burst through the bushes ten paces away, immediately receiving my shot; too low as it transpired. It did turn the big cow which then swerved off behind the tree. As she passed across the little clearing I had a broadside heart shot and she disappeared from view.

Other elephants were crashing off in the same direction, so we stayed where we were standing atop the dead cow while I reloaded and wondered if my shot would be effective. A quietness descended now on our little scene but it was an uneasy peace.

"Tsuro, do you think the second shot was good?" I enquired of my friend.

I had a horror of losing a wounded jumbo anyway, but this could also ruin my chances of being allowed to hunt by myself on elephant control.

"No, I thought you missed. You just shot the tree!"

Aghast, I studied the tree but saw no bullet mark.

"Where did I hit the tree?" I asked, panic rising, turning to Tsuro standing next to me, but still unbelieving of what he was telling me.

"There," he said, pointing. I still could not see a mark so slid down off the elephant and walked over to the tree.

"Where," I demanded, looking back at Tsuro sitting now on the peak of the great, grey mound, his legs drawn up with hands and chin resting on his knees. A big grin creased his face.

"So you even missed the tree and it was standing still! Anyway, I think the elephant is dead. I heard it fall down while you were playing about putting bullets in your gun."

My nerves began to relax as I swore at Tsuro but he just giggled all the more. We decided to wait a little longer before starting on the trail of the herd. If the elephant was dead, well and good; if it had not expired, then give it time.

We soon found the blood trail in the trampled grass, and there was the dead beast, not fifty yards from the first cow. My relief and excitement at the success of the hunt were overwhelming; this was the greatest day of my life in fact! I pointed out the heart shot to Tsuro, to which he replied, "I saw it was a good shot, but as you did not hear the elephant fall I wanted to see you worried in case you think shooting elephants is easy."

We were back at the Austin by mid-afternoon and immediately drove to the farmer's house. From there I telephoned the D.C., explaining the area where the elephants were, knowing he would get the message to the villagers to collect the meat. I requested that the local headman pull out the tusks after a few days and get them sent to the D.C.'s office. I would collect them some day as I hadn't enough petrol for the long trip there this time.

That evening Tsuro and I sat up late, reliving every moment of the day and laughing happily as we shared the excitement and triumph of this, our best hunting adventure to date. It was certainly as good a time as any to celebrate so out of the back of the Austin I retrieved six beers, secreted there for just such an occasion. I also gave Tsuro one of my cigarettes. Raised on a tobacco farm, it was natural that I had an occasional smoke, though not in public and *never* at school. Sort of!

"Tomorrow is the day I was born, Tsuro," I announced after my second beer.

"You are here talking to me but you are born tomorrow! What does this

mean?" asked a puzzled Tsuro.

"By tomorrow, sixteen years have passed since I was born."

"Oh. Sixteen years. So now you can drink beer like a man."

"Yes. How many years have you now?" I enquired.

"I don't know. I told you before, my father and mother could not count or write so they did not tell me. These things are not important to us Africans. When we go to the D.C. to be registered for a *situpa* (identity document) we make up the day of being born."

"Yah, Tsuro. Us stupid bloody *murungus* (Europeans) make too many laws, too much government, everybody must do this, do that. Better we stay in the bush and hunt."

We droned on sleepily with our boyish philosophies till, lulled by beer, full stomachs and a loud frog chorus from the stream, we fell silent and slept.

Paul Grobler received my report with obvious relief and satisfaction. His 'schooling' of me had paid off. He proceeded to announce that he would recommend to the game department that I be appointed an honorary officer, but warned that the authorities might stall on the idea till I had my seventeenth birthday.

As an honorary officer I would have opportunities to be called upon by the game department, District Commissioners or even private landowners to deal with problem animals. Pity about school, careers and girlfriends. Such things would have to accept their subordination to elephant hunting, to be pursued when the time allowed, not vice versa!

A day after arriving back on the farm from the Mrewa hunt Uncle Dick summoned me, and without pre-amble announced that he and his brother-in-law, Roy Smart, had booked a fourteen day hunt in the Zambezi Valley. Roy's son, Robert, would be coming along; did I want to join them?

Uncle Roy farmed thirty miles away, and Robert was at school with me, though a couple of years my junior. Both uncles were 'pukkah' settler types: jovial, extrovert and fun to be with. Dick had come out to the colony from London in 1928 as a sickly lad but life on a Rhodesian tobacco farm toughened him up. Within five years he started his own farm, then invited his younger brother, Nevill (my father) to join him. Their elder sister, Betty, also immigrated, and married Roy Smart.

In the 1930s, Dick befriended a cattle rancher in the Sabi river lowveld, Jimmy Whittal of Humani Ranch (adjacent to Devuli), where Dick shot the odd buffalo, waterbuck or kudu during his visits. He also once made a short foray into Portuguese East Africa to shoot an elephant. Walking back over the border he was arrested by Rhodesian police. A magistrate on circuit to

the Chipinga court (a pole and thatch structure) fined Dick £10 for illegal exit and re-entry over the border, and £5 for importing ivory without a licence, but allowed him to keep the tusks. They had, after all, belonged to a Portuguese elephant, outside the jurisdiction of a law officer of His Majesty's Colony!

Dick owned the sweetest 6.5mm Mannlicher-Schönauer carbine with wood all the way up the barrel, which I coveted, plus the 10.75mm Mauser which I had used on the Devuli buffalo, and no longer coveted at all!

Roy Smart outfitted the safari providing a 7-ton truck, two Land Rovers, camp equipment, cooks and sundry labourers. Tsuro accompanied me as usual, along with my .458, .303 and double 12-bore shotgun. The use of the camp in the Rekomitjie hunting area, which was next to Mana Pools Reserve, plus four hunter's licences, each covering two buffalo, nine assorted antelope and two warthogs, cost Roy £252; not too onerous for an affluent tobacco baron!

Permits for elephants, lion, leopard, rhino and sable antelope had to be purchased separately. I bought my own bull elephant licence (£25) and Roy bought one for Robert. Once in camp, Dick offered me a trade – I could hunt his two buffalo in exchange for some of my impala, kudu, warthog or bushbuck. My cup was full! An elephant bull and four buffalo would be a serious amount of big game experience, with the huge bonus of this taking place in some of Africa's finest, wildest game country.

The Zambezi river, a mile or more wide with great sand banks and grassy islands, had changed character in the few years since the Kariba Dam was completed. No longer would the great floods come down this way, the low-lying swamp areas would dry out and no more silt would be deposited over the alluvial flats. But the great river of legend and mystery remained the heartbeat of this vast valley. Thousands of square miles of God's own paradise. Still paradise, because humanity had not yet managed to ruin it. No strings of touristy safari camps or swarms of coloured canoes.

Our camp consisted of a number of thatched huts with half-walls scattered under enormous acacia albida trees right on the edge of the Zambezi's steep bank. Taking a walk through the riverine forest along the alluvial flood plains, I felt my young spirit welling up with that same feeling I experienced in the big game wilderness of Devuli ranch, Luangwa Valley or central Africa. Besides the presence of game animals, the varied scents of broken vegetation, acacia pods, baboon droppings, buffalo dung or wild flowers or fruit added to the aura. Sounds of a group of squeaking banded mongooses busily scratching for food in the leaf litter, a secretive duiker trotting away through the undergrowth, or a hippo grunting down in the

nearby river all added to my feelings of excitement.

Mostly, I was not disturbing them and my own senses were as theirs. A split-second before a covey of screeching, wing-whirring Natal francolin had burst from the bushes next to me, I had already detected their presence and therefore was not startled. The predator should seldom be the object of surprise.

Our first night in camp was enlivened by Uncles Dick and Roy over-imbibing Scotch, Robert falling down the river bank when he went off to relieve himself, and a leopard making its wood-sawing grunts around the far end of the camp area where the Africans were bedded down beneath canvas bucksails. None of them, Tsuro apart, had slept in wild animal territory before, so nervous chatter and coughing was much in evidence. Tsuro, by far the most junior, was a minor hero as he answered questions about the possibilities of waking up dead in the morning from an attack by unspecified creatures. Hyena howls and hippo snorts encouraged the insomnia.

Tsuro and I were fortunate to locate a herd of buffalo, possibly several hundred strong, in the riparian forest belt early on the first hunting day. Although the many clumps of dense undergrowth and groups of big trees were good cover for stalking individual or small groups of animals, a herd of this size was spread out over many acres, and inevitably we were spotted before finding a good bull.

The buffalo thundered off, swerving here and there, stirring up a great dust cloud as they broke into an open, dried-mud expanse on the edge of some mopane woodland. Tsuro and I were right there with them having run along, dodging thorns, creepers and fallen trees, keeping up just behind the mass and obscured partially in the dust. The odd animal which saw us could not communicate with the whole herd, so when they all lumbered to a halt, unsure of the cause of the panic, we were within twenty yards of them.

I had quickly spotted a big bull and as it presented a heart shot I fired, just before a cow leapt into action, cutting off my view. The bull however only went a short way before dropping, while the great mass of beasts erupted into a frenzied stampede.

Within a couple of hours we had collected a Land Rover plus helpers from camp, loaded the bull and arrived back to find Roy and Robert in camp with another buffalo.

We all slept well that night, and spent the following day cutting up, salting and hanging strips of buffalo meat to dry into biltong. Both heads, which represented fair trophies, were cleaned and the hides stripped, salted and folded up prior to stretching. Cooking pots bubbled all day, cheerful chatter filled the camp, and the evening meal was welcomed by all.

Including the leopard!

The uninvited guest first strolled past the kitchen hut just as our cook was carrying the coffee tray across the ten yards of semi-darkness to the dining hut. To his credit, the cook made it to our table in two bounds without spilling a drop, but refused to leave his position under the table without a fully armed escort. He had never seen a leopard before. The cat had meanwhile sneaked off down the river bank into a reed bed and we shortly heard it's grunting call from that direction.

Some minutes later, shouts from the staff's tents revealed that the leopard was up a tree next to the drying meat, helping himself and knocking loads of it onto the ground below. Uncle Roy spoke first, "We'd better shoot the bugger before things get out of hand. Richard, why don't you take your shotgun and see if you can get him." Not a question; an order, which I obeyed with alacrity, collecting my torch and 12-bore loaded with SG shot from my quarters and shouting for Tsuro to come over. Understandably, Tsuro shouted back that he was not about to walk the forty yards in darkness without a gun or torch while the leopard was having supper between us.

I shone my torch across to the meat racks and saw no leopard. Noises in the reed bed twenty feet below me drew my torch beam to reveal the leopard lying down chewing a strip of buffalo steak. Sighting down the barrels while holding the gun into my shoulder with my right hand and the torch in my left, I shot him as he looked up. Tsuro and I brought the cat up the river bank into the glare of the gas lamps. A good sized male showing no wounds or impediments. What about a licence though?

"You'd better go up to the game department at Marongora tomorrow and buy a licence," instructed Uncle Roy. I did not have the fee of £15 and asked Uncle Dick quietly if he would lend me the cash.

High up in the hills of the great Zambezi Escarpment, Marongora, which consisted of an office block, workshops and housing for a few game rangers and African scouts, was a two hour drive from camp. I took Robert with me for moral support and duly received my licence on the mumbled pretext that "we might want to hunt a leopard if we had an opportunity". We sped back to camp, full of youthful joy and expectation.

The next day was a bonanza! Robert accompanied Tsuro and I while the uncles went off together with their tracker to look for buffalo. We shortly drove across signs of four bull elephants, took up the spoor and quickly caught up with them in fairly dense jesse bush. A good breeze allowed me time to scout about and select the one carrying the best ivory, which duly dropped with a brain shot. His three companions took off, smashing through the brush straight towards us. I grabbed Robert and pulled him

behind a nearby mopane tree and the bulls stormed by, oblivious to our presence.

The 45lb tusks were by far my best to date and later financed several more elephant licences. It took two days of hard work to get all the meat, hide and ivory into camp. We wasted nothing; all the meat would be handed out to the farm workers back home. Meanwhile the others collected three more buffalo and a kudu bull in those two days.

Our next trip out of camp found us on the tracks of an estimated thirty to forty buffalo which led us through a seemingly endless mopane forest for three hours. Then they rested. As they dozed in the midday heat, I snaked along through the short grass from one tree trunk to the next. From thirty paces I put the first shot into the classic shoulder/heart position of a fine bull to the right of the herd. His reaction was extraordinary. The whole group stood quite still while the shot animal galloped a full circle around them, suddenly falling over, apparently stone dead.

I saw another bull spot me so dropped him with a brain shot. The herd milled but did not stampede until a big cow with unusually wide-spread horns looked set to take off across the front of the group and she received a shoulder shot. Like the first bull, she ran around the herd, collapsing out of sight on the far side of the clustered buffalo.

This was too much for them and the herd took off at a gallop. Except for one. A youngish bull stopped next to the big cow lying dead, turned and saw me move from behind my tree and promptly charged. I shouted but it had no effect and I shot him at the base of the neck at about fifteen yards. He staggered, went down on his knees and I gave him a finishing round.

Tsuro and I arrived back in camp late in the afternoon, alarmed to find that Uncle Dick and Robert had shot a buffalo each. We were now three over our pooled licences! "Not so much of the 'we'," said the others. They ganged up on me, so guess who had to borrow more money and go to Marongora office to buy three extra £5 buffalo licences.

Two days later a Land Rover arrived in camp. It was Lofty Stokes, one of the Marongora game rangers. Well, I might as well face the music. Someone must have told tales. But no, Lofty simply asked if we had any meat to sell for game scout rations. With guilty relief I told him to take two full sacks with my compliments. As he got into his vehicle I saw a massive-looking bolt-action rifle in the cab.

"What is that rifle, Mr. Stokes?"

"Gibbs .505," he replied.

"Wow!" I exclaimed, wide-eyed. "I've never seen one before."

I could not guess that this rifle and I would come full circle seventeen

years later. Fate, destiny or fortune, I don't know?

Lofty Stokes had also let on that each hunter was allowed to buy two extra buffalo, in addition to the two each on the camp quota. So in fact we could take a total of sixteen! My uncles were happy to transport all the meat back home. At the price it was a give-away and I was happy to do the hunting. So I hunted buffalo and more buffalo.

Our final hunt report showed two elephant bulls (Uncle Roy and Robert took a young one); sixteen buffalo of which I accounted for nine; one leopard; two kudu; four warthog and five impala. All paid for, licenced and legal!

[ACT 5/60

Wild Life Conservation (Urungwe Controlled Hunting Area) Regulations, 1961

12. Any person who contravenes or fails to comply with any of the provisions of these regulations shall be guilty of an offence and upon conviction shall be liable to a fine not exceeding one hundred pounds or in default of payment to imprisonment for a period not exceeding six months.

SCHEDULE I

Species of game animals and maximum number which any one hunter may be licensed to hunt during any one hunting period

Species	*Number*
1. Buffalo	2
2. Bushbuck	1
3. Duiker	4
4. Elephant	2
5. Impala	2
6. Kudu	2
7. Leopard	1
8. Lion	1
9. Rhinoceros	1
10. Sable	1
11. Sharpes Grysbok	1
12. Warthog	2
13. Waterbuck	1
14. Francolin	12
15. Guinea Fowl	12
16. Sandgrouse	12
17. Quail	20

SCHEDULE II

Species of game animals and quota which may be killed in the area during on one open season

Species	*Quota Number*
1. Lion	5
2. Rhinoceros	5
3. Waterbuck	20

An example of the quota of animals allowed in 1961

On Official Business

My appointment as an honorary officer of the Department of Wildlife was an important advance in my elephant hunting career. Still at Peterhouse School, I was aware of the special dispensation by the department, being the youngest person to be nominated. The status carried responsibilities but mainly offered me opportunities for big game hunting. One advantage was not being bound by the designated hunting season, which was roughly the dry months of May to October. I was also entitled to buy licences and thus claim ownership of any animal shot on official business; in effect, elephant tusks were mine for the price of a permit.

Fortunately, economics was a subject at which I was not a total failure, so I set about working out how I could finance my hunting trips based on ivory sales, plus any income from selling the meat or biltong when practical. I was sufficiently equipped, with the S.W.B. Land Rover and BSA .458 being essential tools of the trade. With Tsuro as my friend, assistant, cook and tracker, plus bits and pieces of camping kit, I was organised but for funds to cover fuel, licences, provisions and running repairs to the vehicle.

Paul Grobler had introduced me to Mr. Levy, the owner of Manica Cycle Company in Salisbury, where we sold ivory on previous occasions. I took along the pair of bull tusks from the Rekomitjie hunt, received a good cash payment and added this to the little savings I had from selling snakes to the Salisbury Snake Park. My father also gave me a monthly allowance of £5, mainly to spend at the school shop on Sunday lunches when the dining room was closed. I could save half this, so when the holidays came round I was ready and able, financially, to go elephant hunting.

My phone call to the D.C. at Mtoko was successful. Yes, there were bull

elephants residing in an area near the Mozambique border and he would like them chased out as soon as possible. As he knew me, he advised that it would not be necessary to call at his office for written authority, but I must report back on my return.

The low-lying mopane and baobab country was grey, harsh and dry, and sparsely inhabited by tribespeople. Exactly the environment that made my temperament and physical being change gear. Locating the elephants was a challenge, requiring miles and miles of hard tracking, hour after hour under the searing sun, enduring a thirst that could only be relieved by the water-bag once more water was known to be within accessible distance. The exhaustion, thirst and hunger at the end of the day made the cold water wash and simple meal, followed by the collapse onto my stretcher, seem like the icing on a wonderful cake. The cake? A day in the life of an elephant hunter in Africa!

Our third morning in the area started with a fast walk across miles of arid, open country to search for water to the east; the only water we had located to date had not been visited by elephants for several days. Luck had it that we met four local men on a path which connected far-flung villages and went on into Portuguese territory. They had killed a warthog which was tied to a pole carried on the shoulders of two of them. The others had spears, axes, bows and arrows.

When first sighting us the tribesmen stopped, looking apprehensive, but decided that they could not hide and came to meet us. They relaxed when they saw we were just young lads, not wearing any kind of uniform, and that our greetings were friendly. On hearing we were after the elephants they told us of the concerns of some villages further on, where the sole water supply in the area was not only being reduced to a puddle by elephants but turned into a mud-wallow as well. With a couple of months to go before any rain could be expected, the people had a serious problem looming.

One of the hunters told us he personally had passed the S.O.S. message to a sergeant from the D.C.'s office who had been on a bicycle patrol through the area. He assured us that the elephants, six bulls by his account, were still around although he could not say if they had drunk at the pool this past night. His team had been waiting at the warthog's burrow before sunrise, some distance from the water. When we questioned them, they told us that by beating the ground around the burrow, they had frightened the hogs out of the hole, whereupon one was speared. I was happy for their success, and pleased they had let the rest of the hog family escape. A sensible attitude which is rare today.

Tsuro and I moved on, finding the water in a little river bed with a couple

of native footpaths leading to it from the villages a mile or so distant. The elephants had been there during the night so we followed their spoor, catching up with them by late morning. There were indeed six bulls, four of which were feeding in the mopane trees; the other two were standing in an area of scrub mopane, pulling up clumps of grass. Both were huge animals with nice ivory. With a steady breeze and some handy bushes for cover, I sneaked up closer and photographed them. Putting the camera down, I sat biding my time.

I had already made some decisions. The first was that only one bull would be shot as I was sure there were not enough tribespeople in the area to utilise all the meat, and I had only one licence and therefore could not keep more ivory. My other decision was to try a heart shot for a change from the brain shots I had used on all my previous hunts, apart from one cow shot in the Mrewa district. Once the bulls had shifted a little, a clear view was offered and I fired two quick shots, then watched as they rushed towards their friends in the tree-line. Before long the shot bull fell, while his companion kept going after the other four who were already out of sight.

After examining the big animal and admiring his tusks, we quick-marched through the afternoon's intense heat back to our little camp, where we ate a good meal and then drove through the bush following a footpath to a village. The folk were really excited to hear of our success and immediately sent messengers with the news to a couple of other small settlements.

Next morning we packed our kit and plenty of water into the Land Rover, plus two men from the village to help navigate and open a track when the going became difficult, and arrived at the elephant to find half a dozen people already there. Courteously, they had not touched anything but were eager to start the butchering job. Some had cut sticks to rig up drying racks. I parked the vehicle and pitched our fly-sheet at least a hundred yards upwind from the carcass, knowing what the odour would be like in a few hours!

By mid-morning I counted about thirty folks busy on the job. I watched the heart being removed, satisfied to see both shots had passed through it. Tsuro and I tackled the removal of the tusks; a long, tiring job with axe and knife, done carefully to avoid damaging the upper parts with chopper marks. When the top tusk came free, one of the older tribesmen stepped forward and took it from us. He carried the ivory some way into the bush where he removed the great, carrot-shaped nerve. Throughout the country I found the same superstition – any male who had not sired children must not set eyes on a tusk nerve; to do so renders him sterile for life!

As the setting sun slid the world into darkness, the mass of flickering fires, smells of roasting meat and much chatter and laughter gave me a wonderful feeling of being part of this unsophisticated, unspoilt Africa. The experience, a far cry from chemistry classes, smoking after lights out and rude songs after the rugby matches, started the realisation that I was actually happiest with my own company, or at least, in company that did not impose its will, its problems or its stupid ideas on me. Yes, I must spend as much time as possible where I make the decisions alone, doing what I love without let or hindrance. I realised that the hunting era of Bell, Sutherland, Hunter and Taylor had gone, but I would work hard at creating my own little pockets of Utopia such as I was experiencing now. I fell asleep pondering another thought, a contradiction: I had developed a deep affection for elephants *but* I also loved to hunt them. I awoke before dawn feeling wonderful, ready for anything!

Less than a week later we were back at Devuli ranch on the Sabi river in response to a letter from Don Somerville: I was welcome to reduce the buffalo on the Masapas section provided I had department permits, handed over a couple of hides for the ranch's use and kept an eye out for poachers.

Stopping at the ranch headquarters, I convinced the boss we needed Naison. Though Tsuro and I were becoming skilled trackers, Naison was unequalled in our experience, plus his local knowledge was invaluable. I really liked the man too. He had an impish sense of humour, at the same time possessing a quiet dignity, never servile nor conceited.

I picked up an attitude from Naison which impressed itself on my young mind, namely that hunting dangerous animals should not be considered a solemn, humourless activity. Without showing any flippancy nor disrespect for the hunted, it is not necessary to be too grave, too serious. After all, I personally saw no heroism or brag value in big game hunting. One did it voluntarily, for private reasons, paramount to which may be the challenge of defeating the wild animal on its home ground, or to feed people, or on official business. The excitement, nervous tension and even fear are part of the self-imposed task, but these effects can be controlled and the hunt enjoyed to the full. So while Naison's actions and observant ways were those of a born hunter, he was always relaxed and enjoyed the outing.

Hunting the wary, wild groups of buffalo for two weeks also taught me to accept blank days as quite normal, nothing to get tense about. Being overly anxious spoils the atmosphere of the hunt, creating unwanted nervousness when finally approaching the quarry.

Sometimes a herd kept running downwind and evaded us, even if we made wide sweeps trying to outwit them, until we admitted defeat. On a

48

couple of days we did not even locate spoor fresh enough to warrant tracking, and on others we followed a pair of bulls only to hopelessly lose them when cattle walked in the same direction after them.

None of this mattered. There were no deadlines other than to be back at school on a certain date, nor did I have to shoot a bigger trophy than Smith, or more buffalo than Jones, or tell fancier tales in the pub. Being a loner, I seldom discussed hunting with anyone and only came across these strange, 'competitive' notions when conducting commercial hunting safaris many years later.

We managed to successfully butcher and dry the meat of three buffalo, the three of us working fast before each carcass spoilt in the heat. Four more whole animals were delivered to the ranch with my compliments; my little Land Rover could not have carried any more sacks of biltong back home anyway!

My last term at Peterhouse involved writing exams with sufficient skill to avoid passing with university entrance grades. University life reeked of crowds, discipline, hard academic work, years of living in an artificial, social sort of rat race. No thank you. So I capitulated to my father's wish that I should have *some* post-school qualification by enrolling at Gwebi Agricultural College. The annual intake of students was a mere thirty-five, aged from seventeen to twenty; good natured, hard-drinking country boys with mainly farming backgrounds, very few of whom took life seriously. I quickly planned how to spend the next few months before the new college year opened.

THE DEVULI RANCHING COMPANY (PVT.) LIMITED

TELEGRAPHIC ADD.: "DEVULI, FORT VICTORIA"

TELEPHONES:
HEAD OFFICE -- 00260
MANAGING DIRECTOR 00205
CATTLE STATION - 00304
IRRIGATION FARM - 00231
REGISTERED OFFICE: DEVULI RANCH, FORT VICTORIA
R.M.S. ROUTE 33 - - DEVULI HALT
POST BAGS NO. 9026, FORT VICTORIA
NO. F7426, UMTALI

BIKITA

DEVULI RANCH,
FORT VICTORIA
SOUTHERN RHODESIA

19th. July 1963.

Mr. R.A.N.Harland,
P.O.Box 20.
Rusape.

Dear Sir,

        Further to your request to shoot buffalo
on Masapas Ranch: I have been away for some time and
the matter has been held over. I am told that there
are buffalo there and I am agreeable to your shooting
them on certain conditions. You must be in possession
of the necessary licence and the proper firearms. You
let us have the first two hides after properly
them. Such part of the meat as you wish to
you can have but any residue must be given
Africans living on Masapas. The shooting is
limited to buffalo but if your visit fits in
days when the herdboys would normally be
with meat rations we can authorise you to
impala also.

        You should report at Headquarters on your
having this letter with you in case I am not
here, and also on your departure.

        Since your normal activities as an Honorary
Game Warden will also operate, we will expect you to
keep a watch on the area for poachers during your visit,
and also for the removal of snares and a report on them.

        Yours faithfully,

DEVULI   (T.) LTD.

DIRECTORS D. M. SOMERVILLE, J.P. (MANAGING DIRECTOR), M. C. SOMERVILLE, W. D. BRIDGES, J. M. BRIDGES, V. B. DE LA RUE, I. H. DE LA RUE.

Letter from Don Somerville

Zambezi Valley buffalo and Tsuro, 1961

Author, Dick Harland, Roy Smart, Robert Smart - Zambezi Valley, 1961

Hunting camp, Rekomitjie, Zambezi Valley

"Both were huge animals, with nice ivory."

Bandazi with straw boater advises me on skinning technique

EIGHT

Bandazi & The Straw Hat

Free at last! School days were behind me for ever but my father had pestered me, somewhat half-heartedly, to find work for the months prior to my start at college.

"No job – no money, my boy," grumbled my father. So I rang a few farmers in the district, putting down the phone before anyone could possibly answer.

"No one at home, Dad. I'll go to Salisbury and look around there," I announced. I told Tsuro somewhat different plans. "Pack your bag and blankets, we go to the Zambezi Valley tomorrow."

Why 'work', why have a 'job'? There was plenty of life ahead when I would have to 'do some work', but for now it was hunting time. I was in the money from selling the ivory of the Mtoko and Sapi bulls and the Devuli buffalo biltong. I had also sold the .303 SMLE and replaced it with a very neat, light-weight .30-06 by BSA, the same English make as my .458. I filled the Land Rover's tank and several jerrycans with 'free' petrol from the farm supply, nicked a few jars of my mother's home-made jams and pickles from the pantry, and a fifty-pound sack of maize meal from the ration store. I bought the remainder of necessary provisions in Salisbury on our way to the north.

The tiny settlement of Sipolilo boasted a District Commissioner and his staff, a police station, three or four native-owned stores and very little else. Paying my respects to the D.C. and acquiring written permission to hunt in his area needed only a few minutes, and soon we were on the rough track which wound it's way into the hills of the Zambezi Escarpment.

As we meandered down towards the vast lowlands, the familiar feelings of excitement and anticipation welled up in me. What adventures awaited

us; would we find elephants; where did the scattered tribespeople have villages; which rivers still had water; in fact where were we headed today? For us this was new territory, more than a hundred miles east of the Rekomitjie area we had hunted over a year previously with my two uncles.

I deeply inhaled the hot evening air laden with the turpentine scent of mopane, the smells of dust and dry grass, and said silently: "Yes, *this* is my world." I whacked a tsetse fly sharply where it needled me in the back of the neck and swore with a smile on my face. Absolutely nothing could spoil my euphoria at being back in elephant country. At nightfall we simply stopped next to a baobab tree, cooked food and slept. Hyenas called in the distance, their drawn-out moans lulling me back into a relaxing, half-an-ear-open slumber.

Next morning we arrived at a sandy river bed pock-marked with little wells drilled by elephant's trunks, and elephant droppings scattered around but nothing fresh. While scouting about we found a footpath following the river upstream, so tracked it by vehicle, entering a small village half an hour later. The folks who bothered to wander over to meet us did so with no enthusiasm. After lengthy traditional greetings, they nodded in resignation when asked if elephants were present in their district. We asked who could help us find the elephants and they agreed that a certain Bandazi, who lived in his kraal a little way further up-river, was the very one.

Bandazi turned out to be a thin, rickety-looking old guy, but his greeting was sincere and his handshake firm. Even his two ancient wives came out of their huts to bow and clap hands with respect, followed by an offering of a calabash of *doro* (millet beer). Stools were placed in the shade of a great, evergreen Natal mahogany tree where we sat waffling about life while summing each other up. Eventually I broached the subject of elephants at which Bandazi shook his head in despair saying the villages in the area had lost much of their grain and melon crops to elephant raids. This accounted for the depressed air in the other village, as nobody had come to deal with the problem and now it was too late. The people feared they would starve this year.

Bandazi was pleased to hear we would stay to hunt, suggesting we camp nearby and walk the river early in the morning to look for tracks. That sounded like a sensible plan, so Tsuro and I found a good spot a couple of hundred yards along the river bank where we also dug a little well in the white sand to reach cool, clean water.

After we had set out our camp kit and eaten a midday meal, I decided to have a walkabout. Tsuro picked up the water-bag and his *demo* (African-style home-made axe, the blade usually beaten from a section of broken car

spring). I loaded the .458 and my six-round wrist band, and we strolled along the river bank, not seeing much spoor of antelope due to our closeness to humans, but plenty of old elephant signs. Walking on the river bed was hot work under the sun with each step sinking into the sand, but we saw all the tracks of passing game. It was cooler and easier to walk under the shady trees on the bank but we would miss a lot of information in the thick grass and scrub understorey.

An hour after leaving camp we sat down under a sausage tree for a smoke, watching some Natal francolins pecking around on the opposite bank, and hearing a rowdy troop of baboons having serious domestic disputes somewhere close by. Their noise almost masked the sound of a tree cracking in the distance, but both Tsuro and I heard it and knew it was not baboons snapping twigs.

Using my ash bag continuously we circled into the light breeze in the direction of the sound, shortly hearing the sounds of branches being broken. We were then in the dry, more open country away from the river and soon spotted a bull elephant feeding. A straightforward stalk brought me close up, the bull collapsed to the frontal brain shot, and I heard some elephants crashing away in fright. Tsuro reckoned there were three others in the group.

Bandazi was most excited about the quick success, sending his wives to tell the neighbours before nightfall. The meat would keep, smoked or sun-dried, for two or three months. We slept well and rose early to start the day's work on the carcass.

I noticed Bandazi was wearing a straw boater hat like those sported by the Eton College lads in England, strutting around the manicured playing fields of their levitated institution, but I felt it a little unlikely that Bandazi had attended a highly exclusive British public school. In all the hunting we did together over the next couple of years, Bandazi was never without his boater. I knew it would be bad form to ask him how he came to own such unusual headgear, especially as I later felt he considered it was imbued with magical properties.

After two days we moved camp several miles upstream, almost to the foothills of the Zambezi Escarpment, where we found plenty of elephant activity. Bandazi and a friend of his accompanied us; their local knowledge was valuable and both were natural trackers. We hunted long and hard, with tricky winds coming off the hills giving our scent to the quarry time and again. After three blank days we caught a herd of cow elephants in a densely treed valley where I shot two at very close quarters when the herd stampeded on scenting us.

While Tsuro and I returned to our camp, Bandazi and his companion went west to where they knew of some villages, to tell the people about the elephants. It was mid-morning the following day when the two men arrived back at camp, saying we could go on as someone would bring the tusks to Bandazi's kraal in due course.

Moving to an area to the north-east where a small river, the Kadzi, supported a few tribespeople, we passed a village where the inhabitants told us that lions had killed a woman from a nearby kraal on the previous day. Bandazi told them we would go and kill the lions. Just like that. Simple. No 'by your leave' or 'pardon me'! Well, it was an exciting prospect to say the least, but I questioned Bandazi on his confidence as he wasn't actually doing the shooting around here! He replied that I was a lucky hunter, but I noticed he fiddled with his straw boater as he spoke, something I had observed him doing on other occasions, as if receiving some psychic message from it.

The sad story we received from the woman's family indicated that the lions had killed to eat, not in fright or self-defence. We were also told that three lions had killed and eaten someone from a village in nearby Mozambique two or three weeks previously.

In the local case, two women were collecting firewood and, while the victim was busy tying up her bundle ready to carry on her head back to the village, the lions attacked her. Her companion fled home only to find all the men had gone off somewhere, so she shut herself in a hut with her children, the other wives doing likewise. At nightfall the men returned but could do nothing till morning. They decided to collect reinforcements from a couple of neighbouring kraals before looking for the missing woman. We arrived to find a half-dozen men, armed with spears, bows and axes, awaiting the arrival of others.

After discussions with everyone, Bandazi and I agreed we should get to the scene with just one local to guide us and asked the rest to wait until called. They were very happy to do this. Bandazi carried our water-bag and his axe, Tsuro the .30-06 loaded with 220gr soft-points, and myself the .458, also with soft nose rounds. The guide had his spear and machete.

We eventually found the remains of the woman after hearing the howl of a black-backed jackal, which we saw dash off when we approached a large bush-covered termite mound. Obviously the lions had left the spot as the jackal would not have been in the thicket with them. We could see well enough in the surrounding mopane woodland but still moved carefully, ready to shoot, but nothing else came out. Bits of human body, mainly bones, were under the bushes where large areas of flattened grass and

leaves showed where the killers had lain around. I had read plenty of man-eater stories in hunting books and half-expected what the scene would look like, but felt a cold shock at seeing it for real.

I sat down for a cigarette, my back against an elephant-felled tree with a clear view around just in case a lion turned up for an encore. We found the firewood bundle some fifty yards away, signs of the lions' attack and the drag marks leading to the termite mound. We also located the tracks of three lions going northwards. Our local guide assured us that they had gone to drink at the river which made sense. The tracks appeared to be those of lionesses and, although the animals had travelled during the night, we followed their spoor in the hope of discovering where they had gone after drinking.

We found the tracking slow and difficult because the ground was dry and hard, the grass was flattened by elephants and the sun climbed higher. The sun dries a track, particularly that of a soft-footed animal, and the night's dew keeps the trodden grass blades flat till they dry, warm up and rise, while dead leaves also curl and 'fluff-up'. Early morning sun creates shadows on the edge of track indentations which lessen as the sun climbs. Insects and birds scuffle around on the bare patches of soil, obscuring the light markings of big pads. A breeze also destroys spoors rapidly and this is often more likely in the heat of the day. Luckily we had almost no air movement to cope with, but had of course noted it was in our favour from the north.

It was past midday when the local man stopped to whisper that the river was not far ahead. I rechecked the .458 was loaded and chambered a round in the .30-06 quietly for Tsuro, telling him to be ready. We moved on and saw the green trees which lined the river banks a couple of hundred yards ahead. The cats' tracks started to veer to the left heading for a group of big Natal mahogany trees with their dark green foliage, an obvious resting place for the animals, but I thought it unlikely they would be there as their spoor was probably six to ten hours old.

As we approached the trees the cover became thicker, with patches of tall thatching grass and clumps of bush greatly reducing visibility, and game paths weaving amongst this undergrowth in all directions. We eventually reached the mahogany trees on the river bank and the tracks went straight down onto the sand bed, then turned right. Presumably the lions were going to look for water, but our guide was not sure how far along this might be, unless other animals had opened little wells in the sand.

After a while of trudging along the river bed we were startled by loud squeals some way ahead; a terrified death-cry piercing the stillness of the hot, slumbering African forest. The short screams were followed by a couple

of grunts; unmistakable lion sounds. We all froze. I was briefly dumbfounded at the sudden turn of events. Having never hunted lion, let alone man-killers, and the bloody things were just around the bend in the river! A damn stupid green pigeon suddenly rocketed out of a tree next to us, giving my nerves another electric charge.

Fumbling the ash bag out of my shirt pocket, I beckoned to the others to get up the bank into the trees where we had a quick, whispered discussion. Tsuro and I would stalk the lions, Bandazi and the other man would trail us a few yards behind. There was almost no air movement in the strip of riverine forest so I was not concerned about our scent reaching the cats. Taking some deep breaths to settle my heart rate and relax the tension in my muscles, I glanced at Bandazi who was turning his straw hat around in his fingers. On seeing me watching him, he put the boater back on his head, smiled at me and pointed forward. Right then I had a strange calm feeling along with a focus, or mental fixation, on the job to be done.

Slipping silently, carefully, through the undergrowth, I headed for the bend in the river, soon hearing a few muted growls and crunches of bones breaking. My guess was that the lions had caught a warthog at a drinking hole in the river, but could not yet tell if they were eating it on the sand or up on the bank. Once I could see through gaps in the bushes that I was close to the bank, I crouched down and eased up to the trunk of a big tree. Slowly rising I searched the section of river bed below till I heard the lions feeding again, a little further away than I had estimated.

I moved a short way along the bank, checked the wind once more, and with my heart pounding again, crept up to another tree. A small pool of water came into view on the far side of the river bed, probably forty yards away, over which a leafy tree hung. Three lionesses were lying on their stomachs in the shade of the tree, all pulling at the body of their prey. The excitement and tension took some overcoming, and I was thankful to have the tree to steady my rifle on.

The first shot knocked the nearest one onto its side, but it thrashed around, grunting horrifically, so I fired again. That did not seem to have any effect. I reloaded two rounds quickly, noticing the other cats had disappeared. Just as I aimed at the one still rolling about on the sand, one of the others bounded down the bank and tackled it ferociously, grabbing it by the neck and offering me a shot into the spine between the shoulder blades.

With the body of the second lioness on top of it, the first one subsided and then lay still. I felt movement next to me and found all three of my companions standing close, grinning hugely. Before allowing us to go

across the river bed, I fired another round into the bushes across the river where the third lioness just may have been lurking. Then, reloaded and safety off, I went across to the dead cats, still unable to believe our luck, and mentally replaying the last quarter-hour since we heard the hog being caught. Plonking down in the shade next to the lionesses, I lit a cigarette and let the euphoria soak in and the tension drain out. We all became voluble, laughing and re-enacting the lionesses' antics. One sobering discovery was that my second shot had completely missed the cat when she was thrashing about after the first bullet had broken both her shoulders.

We covered the two bodies with thorn bushes to protect them till the following day when our guide would bring people to skin them. I knew that other bits and pieces, particularly the fat, would also be taken for both medicinal and mystical purposes.

We reached the village late in the afternoon to find the funeral preparations had begun and more people had assembled to hunt the lions. Much fuss was made of the heroes and the crowd "Eeh-ed" and "Aah-ed" in great fashion as their friend and Bandazi went through the whole episode in a blatantly embellished fashion. Even the dead woman's husband was enjoying the histrionics, only remembering to be sad when he came to thank us as Tsuro, Bandazi and I took our leave. We did not fancy sleeping too close to the village where the all-night wailing would disturb us, so we decided to camp somewhere *en route* back to Bandazi's district.

Unfortunately, I never managed to return to the area to collect the skull and hide of my first lion. The village headman had asked if he could keep the other which I was pleased to allow. At least there were no more man-eatings in that district for many years.

G.P. & S. 4552—400-50P.—16-2-59

Z.F. 68. (C.I.).
(Pads of 50.)
Form No. 1.

CONTROL OF GOODS ACT, 1954

IMPORT LICENCE

No. *11 / 2 /65*

IN THE EXERCISE of the powers conferred by the Control of Goods (Import and
Export) (Commerce) Order, 1954 , published in ~~Federal~~ *S.R* Government Notice No. *178* of 1954 .

.... *R Harland,*
...... *Box 20, Rusape*

is hereby authorized, subject to the provisions of any other law, including a Territorial law, to
import into the ~~Federation~~ *Rhodesia* from

.... *Portuguese East Africa*

the following goods, that is to say—

Four Elephant tusks only

This licence is valid until ... *April 30, 1965*

....
(Signature)

....
(Designation)

[stamp:]
Department of National Parks
and Wild Life Management
24 FEB 1965
P.O. Box 8365, Causeway
Salisbury, Southern Rhodesia

Date ....

Import licence issued in 1965

58

NINE

Sightly Extra-Territorial

The rainy season was a wonderful time to be in the Zambezi Valley; so completely different to the cooler, dry months. The intense heat in October was often tempered by the first thunderstorms of the season. By December the vegetation had turned green and lush and the small pans (clay-based depressions) were holding water. From January to March, the rivers flooded, big pans filled up, vast expanses of mopane trees turned into parkland and jesse thickets became impenetrably dense.

Many game species, notably elephant and buffalo, moved into areas away from the perennial water supplies and Zambezi river to utilise the food in more remote parts of their ranges. Conversely, few hunters operated in the valley: sport hunters were legally restricted to the 'open season' of the winter months, and most game rangers or D.C.'s staff turned back at the first flooded river, or having been stuck in a mud patch for a day, gave up and went home.

So I had the marvellous feeling of being the only white man in that vast wilderness, camping and hunting wherever tribespeople were being harassed by game. The little Land Rover was never totally overwhelmed by rushing rivers, ten foot high elephant grass or black 'cotton soil' mud and, if we had to, Tsuro and I simply camped where we were until conditions allowed travel.

While we had the advantage of plentiful water wherever we went, the hunting was often very tough going. The tremendous heat plus the high humidity was extremely enervating, and the density of the vegetation generally made close encounters with big game more frequent and much riskier. Added to this, the tsetse flies and swarms of mopane bees drove one

to distraction; the latter by their irritating habit of creeping into one's eyes, ears and hair in search of moisture. These tiny black insects, which are fortunately stingless, secrete a dark-brown, sharply sweet honey in miniature tunnelled hives made in the hollows of tree trunks.

Bandazi, plus hat of course, usually accompanied us on our wanderings over the district where we mainly hunted elephant bulls who visited the growing crops of the local folk. Other animals included the occasional aggressive lone buffalo bulls, a hyena with an addiction to chicken, and a lion caught in a snare, dragging a log.

Naturally, I played by the rules. Just as well; one day I almost had a head-on collision with another Land Rover on the main track going through tall elephant grass. A severe-looking man got out and, ignoring my greeting, demanded my name and reason for being in the area. I showed him my licences and note from the D.C. Without another word he got in his vehicle and drove away. I had recognised him as being Len Harvey, a ranger from the Wildlife Department. Years later, when I had joined the department, colleagues spoke of him as a rather dour character, which I could believe. Poor Harvey died tragically, killed by a lioness while on honeymoon in Hwange Park in 1972.

We did bend the rules slightly on one occasion, when Bandazi, Tsuro and I tracked three bull elephants from the Musengedzi river in a north-westerly direction for a full day. A long day, enlivened once by a pair of rhino charging us in tandem, fortunately from a distance, giving us time to get up trees! Later, we skirted a herd of buffalo to avoid panicking them as we were not far behind the elephants. At sunset we stopped, determined to continue the hunt next morning. We sucked a lot of marula fruit, roasted and ate a few wild mushrooms Bandazi had found on our trek, and each had a stick of biltong. Mosquitoes harassed us in spite of the smoke from the little fires we had around us, and I definitely did not sleep much.

Late the following morning we caught up with the bulls and I put two of them down with brain shots. Their ivory justified the hard hunt and bad night; I was pleased our persistence resulted in such success. Then Mr. Bandazi dropped a bombshell!

"We are in Mozambique, Bwana," he announced, smiling from under the straw boater. "The Zambezi is not far."

"How come you only tell us now?" I reacted angrily. "I have no licence to hunt here. It's jail for you if we are caught. We must go now, in case people heard the shots."

"Sorry, Bwana." Bandazi looked downcast. "But I know the villages are very far away, so I think nobody will know we followed the elephants here.

My plan is for us to go to the Zambezi, maybe three hours walk. We will sleep there and fill the water-bags. Tomorrow we return secretly to see if anyone has found the elephants, then we go back to our camp. We can collect the tusks when you come next time."

Tsuro and I thought it a good plan. We moved out of there smartly and duly arrived at the great Zambezi river. Sitting around a fire, we finished off our little supply of biltong and biscuits for supper and, while I sat spellbound by the magical sunset, it occurred to me that I was sampling a tiny slice of the life led by the ivory hunters of a past era. A free and unique existence that could never be repeated. Not by game rangers, professional safari operators or sport hunters, albeit those options are wonderful substitutes as I well know, but the independence and the liberty are missing.

I lay back against a tree trunk, listening to the night creatures calling and feeling the warm, comforting, valley air enveloping me. The ambience was conducive to deep feelings. I was an invisible speck on the planet's surface, distant in time and space from all humanity but for my two companions, supremely content with my lonely, remote situation. I drifted in and out of sleep, hearing far-off elephants trumpet, hyenas whooping and a myriad of bird, frog and insect sounds, until a nearby lion duet boomed us into wakefulness as the sky lightened.

We sat around the fire discussing our plans until we could see sufficiently to avoid bumping into elephant, rhino or cats. Later, stopping a short distance from the two dead bulls, I sent Tsuro to check them, thinking that he would not be recognised if by chance anyone spotted him. He soon returned with the good news that nobody had been there. We arrived at camp at eight o'clock that night, starving after an estimated thirty-five mile walk.

I had given the ivory much thought and decided to find out the correct procedure for importing it. Should this prove to be too complex or risky, I could simply register the tusks on my present licences after secretly retrieving them.

Well, I was issued an import licence for four elephant tusks by the Wildlife Department with no awkward questions asked – how or why I should have ivory from Mozambican elephants was of no concern. On reflection, I decided that elephants crossing international borders without passports was really an Immigration Department problem anyway!

Months later, I returned to the valley to collect the tusks. They had been moved varying distances from the skeletons, probably by other elephants, but after several hours searching we collected all four and hot-footed out of

there back to the Land Rover. Weighing between 38 and 56lbs apiece, and not having used my Rhodesian licence, these tusks returned a grand profit. Quite tempting to try an encore, but I decided that would be pushing my luck! Unless of course Bandazi missed the invisible border...

TEN

College Life

The day arrived for admission to the two-year course at Gwebi Agricultural College which, despite my slight misgivings, turned out to be pretty much a reunion with old friends, former school pals and various acquaintances. As freshers we were subjected to two weeks of unmerciful initiation by the second-year students. Surviving that with a sense of humour and thick hide resulted in great camaraderie throughout the community of seventy students; no grudges, no hard feelings.

We slipped quite effortlessly into the farm routines of milking cows, ploughing lands, reaping crops, castrating piglets, sleeping in lectures and playing sport. Having an aptitude for mechanical work from an early age, I overhauled my Land Rover and rebuilt the engine in the student's workshop.

As was to be expected, some of us made extra-curricula activities a serious part of college life. Like frequenting the bars and nightclubs in Salisbury, less than a half-hour away, entertaining lady friends, going to movies, or guiltily leaving a warm bed to drive back in time not to be found absent at reveilles. The hostel warden, a tough trooper named Stan Hodierne, had an intelligence network which no CIA or KGB could rival. He knew every misdemeanour which was perpetrated by his wild charges, but tolerated the harmless ones. More serious offences resulted in being called to his office. With steely eyes staring unblinking through his orange-tinted glasses, the interrogation was short and to the point:

"Harland, you've foggin' well cum 'ome after five in the foggin' mornin' twice this foggin' week, then you go milkin' the foggin' cows wearin' a foggin' weddin' soot or somethin'. No more of this, do you foggin' well understand?" End of interview.

Once I dumped a few hundred pounds of rotting elephant meat in a rocky area way off in the southern corner of the college farm. I had been selling it off fresh to labourers on neighbouring farms, but not fast enough and some meat went bad on me. Stan, of course, discovered it although no one had ever seen him drive to that end of the farm. I did not get too much of a dressing down over it, though he did object to "those stinkin' foggin' tusks" under my bed. Fortunately my room-mate, Graham Harnden, was most long-suffering and never complained.

Another source of my problems was a clique of lads, self-styled 'The Manicas'. The eastern province of Rhodesia, Manicaland, was so named after the major tribe of those parts. A number of us from the region had known each other for years prior to college and became, regrettably, a hard-drinking, slightly unruly bunch.

With associates like these, how could I help but be led badly astray? That old jukebox favourite, "Cigareettes an' Whuskey an' Wild Wild Wimin" was an appropriate theme tune for the Manicas, and most of the other students could not stand our pace. Sometimes we eclipsed ourselves such as the night Jim Meikle, in his Renault car with myself as passenger, took a right-angled road junction in a city suburb with more velocity than was wise. After two and a half rolls into someone's garden, I crawled out of the inverted Renault through the hole where the windscreen had been, and found to my amusement that I was still clutching the stem of a champagne glass.

"You've spilt my bloody champers, Jimmy." I berated him. We righted the Renault, then strolled back to the nearby Quorn Hotel to phone Graham Harnden at college to bring my Land Rover and tow us home.

Somehow we all passed our first-year exams, but I was rather starved of hunting, having only been to the Zambezi Valley on two extended weekends. One trip drew a blank, the other a trio of crop-raider bull elephants, the sale of whose tusks gave my finances a huge boost just in time! Like any African worth his salt, my budget for ladies and liquor was in serious deficit.

The three months vacation between the end of first year and the beginning of second year, was spent working on the huge Hippo Valley Sugar Estates situated in the south-eastern lowveld area, a part of the country in which I later spent some of my happiest years elephant hunting. I quickly spread the word among the section managers that I would be pleased to attend to their problems regarding hippo or buffalo damage in the cane fields. My being a game department honorary officer eased their suspicions that I might just be another wild, irresponsible Gwebi College student who probably had never seen a real live buffalo. Possibly a grain of truth somewhere there.

The Lundi river, a major waterway in those parts, formed part of the Estate boundary and was well-populated by hippo and crocodiles, the former occasionally making nocturnal forays into fields of young cane. The grazing damage was actually minimal in the context of many thousands of acres of sugar cane, but one old bull who liked green cane shoots for dinner also enjoyed treading on the aluminium irrigation pipes lying around; hippo-crimped pipes don't pass water.

Knowing the hippo would see me from a distance if I attempted an approach across the fields through the foot-high growth, I studied the exit paths from the pools in the Lundi river, deciding his tracks mainly originated from two places about a hundred yards apart. The bank had a very dense belt of reeds, so I blocked one of the exits with thorn bushes and looked for an ambush position near the other pathway.

I had brought Tsuro to Hippo Valley to work and keep house for me so we set up our hide, with a spotlight and the Land Rover's battery, behind some bushes twenty yards from a clearing which the hippo path crossed. Tsuro operated the light on my command, a task at which he had much experience. We stayed till around ten o'clock for three nights but the hippo never showed so we gave up for one night, finding evidence the following morning that he had come for a feed in the young cane. Murphy's Law!

The next night he came early, but instead of taking his usual path we heard him moving through the bushes behind us. Knowing we would not be able to see him, we sat tight waiting for him to go on to the lands, hoping he would not scent us. After ten minutes of quiet Tsuro shouldered the battery and we worked our way slowly through the scrub towards the cane fields, stopping frequently to listen or to stare through the darkness at a bush which may have moved. Suddenly I knew we must stop moving and I reached out to hold Tsuro back. We froze for a minute, two minutes, then I felt Tsuro turn slightly to the right. His eyes were better than mine in the dark and, as he slowly raised the spotlight, he whispered, "N*hango*! (There!)."

"Okay," I whispered back, the .458 at my shoulder, as I stepped up next to him, seeing the big black shadow in a small clearing very close. As the brilliant light illuminated the scene, it was a surprise to see a buffalo bull standing with its head raised, not ten paces away. I shot him in the chest at which he stumbled, then turned away and tore off through the bushes. I was highly relieved as I did not fancy being charged under those conditions.

A thunderous splash in the nearby river startled us, then we realised that the hippo must have been on land and rushed back over the six foot high bank into the water. We chuckled at the thought of a sort of slow-motion, two-ton belly flop, probably stunning a few unsuspecting fish. Knowing the

buffalo had run some distance, we felt confident in following his tracks for a short way to check for blood, which we soon found and, being sure the shot would be fatal, we went home. The next morning we located the dead buffalo after ten minutes of tracking and soon had a gang of labourers with a tractor and trailer to collect it.

The old hippo moved elsewhere after this incident and did not return. However, I shot another buffalo bull which, having been caught in a cable snare, had chased odd passers-by on a path connecting two sugar sections. The suffering animal had a couple of yards of wire trailing from a back leg, with a terrible wound where the noose had cut to the shin bone.

My favourite evening haunt was the bar at Hippo Valley Club, the centre of all social activities and sporting events. Quietly sipping beers and chatting to a couple of pals one night, I noticed a hefty, middle-aged man come into the bar and look about, then come over to where we sat around a table. Towering over me, he asked in a guttural voice if I was Harland. His size and aggressive demeanour suggested I tell the truth as he obviously knew who I was anyway.

"Who says you can shoot buffalo around here?" demanded Mister Big Shot, glaring ferociously down at me.

"The section manager asked me to do it, so I thought that was okay," I mumbled, trying to shrink into my chair a little more. After all, I had neither my .458 nor Tsuro with an axe to fend off an attack by a bully at least sixty pounds heavier than me.

"Just you understand, sonny boy, nobody hunts here unless I or Sir Ray Stockil (Chairman of the Company) say so. You kids know bloody nothing about hunting, you just wound everything and run away. You just think it's a bloody game. You keep out of it, okay, or I'll fix you," Mr. Big Shot ranted.

He swaggered out of the room, presumably satisfied he had successfully fended off competition for the local hunting opportunities. And successful he was, as next day I informed my section boss, Laury Coghill, that I was moving on. He was quite happy as he really did not need a casual worker on basic cane-cutter's pay who did not cut cane. With a month to go before returning to college, I had better ways to spend my time than being a dogsbody at the sugar estate.

Tsuro and I left the following day, stopping in Salisbury for a while to buy elephant licences and provisions, phone my parents to tell them of the sensible decision their son had taken, and check my girl still loved me. We were back in the Zambezi Valley four days after quitting the south-east lowveld; back in heaven with Bandazi, elephants and the carefree life of a wandering ivory hunter.

Local folk with welcome windfall

Drilling for water in river bed (Oil painting by Brita Harland)

My wristband held six rounds of .458

Bandazi & friend with Mozambican bull

Lundi river hippo bull

ELEVEN

Big Ivory, Bad Buffalo

September is a wonderful month to be hunting in the low country. The days are lengthening, temperatures are rising, spring is approaching though everywhere is dead dry; greys and yellows are the colours of the season, and the evergreen trees along the water courses stand out in stark contrast. Water itself is scarce, only the largest pans still holding muddy, stale remnants of the long-forgotten rains, with most rivers secreting the sought-after liquid deep in their sands.

Wildlife necessarily concentrates within reach of water during the driest months, giving the hunter an advantage in his quest for game. Knowing the area or having a local tribesman assisting on the hunt can offer short cuts in the pursuit of an animal. Should there be a pan or pool in a river bed ahead, one can dispense with slow tracking and, keeping to the right side of the wind, make straight for the water point. Likewise, at the start of the day the hunter may check known drinking spots to see if they have been visited during the night. Some of my most enjoyable and stimulating moments of the day are those spent circling around a waterhole at dawn, deciphering all the signs of nocturnal activity, studying the tracks in the mud at the water's edge, all the while listening to the sounds of the wilderness waking up with the sun's first rays. A low whistle from Tsuro excited me and I walked over to where he stood looking down at elephant tracks. Bull elephant.

As often happens, the grey, hard-packed soil surrounding the pan was a difficult book to read, and we moved into the tree zone to check every path for the number and direction of travel of the animals. Today it seemed that a single bull came to drink and returned to the bush on the same path. Knowing that the troublesome group we were after numbered five or six, we

walked back to the Land Rover a couple of miles away, and drove on to visit other villages in the district. These bulls were destroying the precious water supplies of the tribespeople by not only consuming vast amounts, but also caving in the stream banks around the few remaining pools and fouling them with dung and urine. However, we received no complaints from the locals for a couple of days so decided to go west through the valley into an area we had not explored.

The pedicle of Mozambique extending up the Zambezi Valley between Southern and Northern Rhodesia terminates in a boundary running north/south, west of which was the almost uninhabited Dande North district. Beyond the Angwa river there were no people except for a few elusive, wandering groups of VaDoma folk. This small tribe gained some publicity when it was discovered that a genetic mutation surfaced amongst various individuals which deformed the feet into a Y-shape, almost like those of an ostrich. The mystery of the 'Two-toed Tribe' was occasionally a topic of our fireside discussions, but I never personally saw an example, though I have seen photographs of the phenomenon.

One night Tsuro and I camped in the Dande hilly country just south of the Zambezi river, coincidentally very near the location where, eighteen years later, I had interesting altercations with both buffalo and leopard on the same day. This particular night was warm and still, with a big moon giving a lovely soft light over the countryside, without which the following events could not have been observed.

We were woken by a loud cracking sound, accompanied by muted thumps, coming from the valley below us. Had the night been dark we would have stayed rolled up in our blankets, but with the moonlight and our curiosity aroused, we put on our shoes and, taking the .458, we walked down the slopes towards the noise. The crashing of bushes being broken, punctuated by occasional sharp thuds as if rocks were being hammered together could only mean elephants, so I shook the ash bag to make sure the wind was favourable.

Out of the trees lining the dry river bed, about fifty yards in front of us, came two bull elephants, head to head, straining against each other. The noises we had heard must have been their tusks clashing together, and not surprising either as I gasped at the great white ivories one was carrying; certainly the biggest I had seen at that stage of my life. Tsuro's teeth flashed white as he grinned back at me, knowing we had to have that bull. Suddenly the big tusker stumbled backwards, which we later discovered was caused by his back foot going down an antbear hole, at which the opponent gave an almighty lunge, lifting the other up and sideways so that he toppled over.

The attacker rammed him in the shoulder and ribs, then swung around and disappeared into the trees.

Before I could move close enough to try a shot, the fallen giant had risen and hurried off into the shadows in the opposite direction to his foe. We stood listening to his progress for some time and thought we heard wheezing noises as though he was winded, but decided we would wait until morning before following him.

I did not get back to sleep for hours thinking about the extraordinary scene we had witnessed and wondering why the fight had been so serious. Later on I learnt that some bull elephants, during their mating season, or musth, become very aggressive towards others, but generally the bulls competing to cover a receptive female have other social mechanisms to avoid severe physical conflict. It is rare that one elephant kills another. I was also very excited about the possibility of catching up with those massive tusks, the image of them going through my mind over and over.

Before dawn, Tsuro and I packed our things into the Land Rover and drove across the open hillside to the little valley, hiding the vehicle in a thicket as we did not know how long we would be away from it. We had a look around the area where the struggle had taken place, finding the spot where the tusker had put his foot into the hole, upsetting his balance. Taking up the spoor, we had not followed far when we found some dark-coloured dry blood showing the bull was actually injured. How badly hurt was he, would he be aggressive, how far would he travel? The Chewore Hunting Area was westward and technically out of my jurisdiction for game control, but I satisfied a twinge of guilt with the decision that the bull was now wounded and it was my duty to end it's suffering.

Spooring became very difficult over the flattened grass on paths criss-crossing through the bushes, but the blood trail helped to keep us on track, and after an hour I felt sure that we would catch up as the elephant had lost a lot of blood. We almost bumped into a rhino as we moved slowly and silently amongst the thickets encircling a dry pan, and only when we were a few yards from the animal did we disturb some oxpeckers sitting on it. The sudden alarm calls and whirring wings startled both us and the rhino, which luckily rushed off away from us. We then heard a short, angry blast from an elephant, probably disturbed by the panicking rhino. Tsuro and I looked at each other, then moved quickly out of the dense bushes towards the more open mopane woodland, spotting the elephant bull less than a hundred yards away.

Using the ash bag continuously and sneaking carefully from cover to cover, we stalked the big tusker which we had observed to be facing our way;

the ivory looked even better in daylight, and I could see the dark stains of blood on the left side of his body. Working up to close range, I stood next to a tree trunk, steadied both my excitement and rifle sights, and fired at the heart as I was worried about hitting a tusk with a frontal head shot. The bull promptly came straight for us at full speed, only crashing down to a brain shot when ten paces away and toppling over onto the side which had been holed by his opponent. I was disappointed not to see the damage and could only guess that a tusk had punctured his internal organs, probably the liver or large blood vessels. Blood had been running down the body and dripping off the chest behind the front legs, and the fact that he only travelled a couple of miles since the fight indicated he was doomed. I felt a sudden, rather childish, surge of sadness for this magnificent animal, sad that he had been defeated and mortally wounded by another elephant. It seemed so unnecessary.

I sat down in the shade and admired the great curves of ivory, wondering how long it would take the two of us to cut them out. After some discussion, Tsuro suggested that we get the Land Rover to the elephant so we at least had our water, food and equipment close at hand, and could sleep there if necessary. We finished the job by sunset and slept well after the previous night's excitement and the hard day's work under a hot sun. We left the nerves in the tusks as Tsuro was determined that neither of us must remove them, and I agreed to wait until we passed a village where we would ask someone to do the job for which we would present him with a piece of elephant trunk in appreciation.

In fact, we drove back to Bandazi's village near the Escarpment the next day and gave him the whole trunk; a huge windfall for his family. He had not heard of any elephant problems in his area but word came that people living near the foothills of the Escarpment were being harassed by a buffalo which had commandeered their water supply, so that all the villagers had to go *en masse* to draw water, some banging tin cans and shouting to frighten the beast away. On several occasions the aggressive bull had sent women fleeing for their lives, and once almost caught a man who just got away up a tree where he spent some time before the buffalo went off.

I asked Bandazi to find a couple of men to accompany us as porters for the journey to the village, knowing it was several hours of hard trekking from our camp and that we may spend a couple of days there. Meanwhile Tsuro and I spent a quiet day cleaning rifles, clothing, the Land Rover and the pair of tusks. When I eventually sold them in Salisbury they weighed 79 and 88lbs, which translated into a large sum of cash. A lot more than an eighteen-year-old student could earn washing dishes or picking fruit, or

even cutting sugar cane!

We were ready to travel the following day, Bandazi having rounded up three men, all older, more wizened and decrepit-looking than himself but enthusiastic with the anticipation of lots of buffalo meat. Leaving the Land Rover in the care of Bandazi's wives, we headed south-west towards the hills, arriving at the village by midday, passing tracks of elephant, rhino and buffalo in addition to the occasional signs of kudu, zebra, impala and waterbuck. The local tribespeople did hunt these animals but not to excess, and appeared to visit their snares at least regularly. We seldom came across snare-lines and only once did I have to shoot a wounded animal, the lion mentioned earlier that was dragging a log.

Having arrived at the village we cooked lunch while the men gave us details of the dangerous buffalo's activities. With one of them as a guide, we set off to the spring in the hills, occasionally seeing the old bull's spoor of recent days. When we were a few hundred yards from the water, I took the lead and slowed our progress, indicating to Tsuro and the others to watch for fresh tracks while I searched the thickets ahead. The afternoon breeze was unsteady and changeable, with the convection in the hills causing air currents to go this way and that, though we had no choice but go on to check the drinking hole. Unexpectedly, a thumping of hooves and smashing of bushes, accompanied by the 'chirr-chirr-chirr' of oxpecker birds, told us the buffalo had scented us and rushed off.

The local man was astounded, and I suspect relieved, that the bull had not attacked us, but rather run away in fright. I was less surprised, having learnt that often elephants which care not one iota when they scent natives, will flee when they smell a white man, and suspected this buffalo was alarmed by the different message he received through the air. We had a whispered council of war and decided to wait a half-hour then track him. Finding a little shade under a small tree I lay down, thinking of those great tusks in the Land Rover and then dozed off. I woke suddenly to the sound of a bird's wings hitting the leaves above me and felt a wet patch on my cheek. An emerald-spotted dove had taken off in fright and deposited it's tiny 'visiting card' on my face, all of which had been observed by Tsuro who was in hysterics. He reckoned I should sleep with my mouth open next time.

We caught up with the buffalo at around four in the afternoon when the light wind was more steady. Bandazi spotted it lying down amongst some shrubs. Telling my companions to sit tight, I stalked carefully to a good position and shot for what I thought was the chest. A buffalo lying down in short grass and in shade can be deceptive and requires careful shot placement. Seeing the animal lying there unaware that it is being watched

can give you a false feeling of confidence, that it is under your power. You've got it 'in the bag' so to speak.

The bull leapt to it's feet and took off as I got in a second shot, rather high in the ribs I felt, but I had been surprised that the thing didn't just roll over dead with the first shot. Youthful confidence slightly dented! The countryside was sparsely treed and we soon caught up with the buffalo, lying down and just requiring a finishing shot which I delivered with great relief. My second round had been a good lung shot, fortunately, because the first bullet into the reclining animal had gone through the lower chest and out of the shoulder, nowhere near the heart or lungs.

While butchering the carcass with the villagers, I looked closely for any indication of the cause of the bull's aggression but found nothing. He obviously disliked humans continuously encroaching on his water supply and was not prepared to find another territory to occupy. An attitude with which I sympathised.

Killer Elephant

Bandazi, Tsuro and I spent a couple of days at our camp making biltong from choice cuts of the buffalo carcass, and checking the area for elephants. We then moved to a district near the Mozambican border, following a river bed until we found water where a low rock bar created some pools. We saw plenty of elephant sign on the way. The inhabitants of the only kraal we passed confirmed that some bulls had visited them several days previously and done some damage to their mango and pawpaw trees, only leaving when the people threw burning sticks at them.

We hunted through the area and on the second day came across tracks of several bulls which, around midday, got our wind and headed north for Mozambique. Eventually we had to give up, making it back to camp long after sunset – hot, hungry and dehydrated. The following day was much the same, with us trying to catch up to a single bull, but quite unable to track fast enough across difficult terrain and other older spoor to gain on him. Another long, exhausting, thirsty day, but rewarding in other ways, as elephant hunting so often is. We travelled through some wonderful country, wild and remote, stalked a pair of rhino for a laugh and saw a leopard slip away from drinking at a pan. We passed a troop of baboons close by. They ignored us completely, unlike those on the farm who were continuously persecuted and feared humans.

That night two Africans approached our camp, calling out greetings and asking to enter. With considerable agitation they told us an elephant had killed a man in their village the previous night. It appeared that a herd of bulls had literally raided their kraal, ripping the thatched roofs off the grain stores and pushing over the stilted platforms on which pumpkins and dried

produce were kept. The victim had come out of his hut beating a tin plate with an axe blade, when an elephant attacked, knocking him down and trampling him. One of the messengers had dashed out of his hut in a panic and climbed a large mopane tree from where he watched helplessly, fearing he would be discovered if he shouted. From his description we concluded there must have been at least ten bulls, but of course they could have travelled a great distance during the past 24 hours. No matter, we soon packed our few possessions onto the Land Rover and headed into the night.

We battled through tall grass and dense bush following a path, continuously being bombarded by insects which were shaken out of the vegetation, and stopping once to clear grass out of the radiator when the motor over-heated. Four hours later, with much relief, we arrived at the village and, although it was nearly midnight and I was dead tired after the long day, I went to the dead man's hut. My torchlight shone on a mangled and twisted corpse, a gruesome sight I have never forgotten. If I could find these elephants, I felt sure there would be a confrontation of a type I had not yet experienced. Later I lay under my mosquito net, the .458 next to me, thinking of frontal brain shots on charging elephants, eventually falling into an exhausted sleep.

Long before sunrise I sat at the campfire drinking coffee while Tsuro cooked a pot of *sadza* to take on the hunt. We were discussing the plan of action with the two messengers, who were keen to assist as trackers and water-carriers, when our conversation was silenced by a distant trumpeting of elephant.

The villagers excitedly assured me that those were the bulls, but I was not convinced. How did they know that wasn't a cow herd? Because the cow herds were still living in the south, around the foothills of the Zambezi Escarpment, I was told. Well, the elephant we had just heard could be a bull which had no connection with the village raiders. No, the men replied, most of the bulls in the area would have been in this group – a herd of more than ten was not normal here.

Walking fast in the direction of the elephant, an hour after sunrise found us on fresh signs of a herd. We soon deciphered that this was a bunch of bulls, definitely more than a dozen and that they were no longer feeding but heading steadily northwards. Although the slight breeze was unfavourable from the south-east, I was determined to pursue them, being fairly sure that this was the raider group, but also hopeful of some good ivory.

Tracking was rapid and we were only hindered when we passed through an area where the same herd, we presumed, had been feeding a day or so before. We had now worked out that the group could number a dozen or

more and, although there were no seeds of pumpkin or grain in the droppings, I was more sure these were the raider bulls. Anyway, undigested seeds would probably not be evident a day and a half after the plundering.

We pressed on, with the sun beating down fiercely by mid-morning and creating a sauna-like humidity. A trio of old buffalo bulls crashed away into the thicket surrounding a pan where they, and the elephants before them, had drunk. They had picked up our scent a mere twenty or thirty yards away, as by this time there was barely any air movement. I felt a quick, cold shiver of nervous anticipation, thinking about getting in close to the bull elephants under these dangerous conditions.

Our pace of tracking slowed as the animals had begun feeding, spreading out and criss-crossing older spoor. We discovered an unfortunate puff adder, too slow to avoid the huge foot of a passing bull, pressed flat into the hot earth. The two local fellows spoke a few words in low tones, and I asked Tsuro what they discussed. Apparently they regarded the dead snake as a sure sign that the killer elephant would be found and destroyed. Not only was their logic totally lost on me, but they gave me the uncomfortable feeling of being expected to carry out the retribution!

Later, the elephants led us into an area of rocky outcrops and small valleys. I really hoped we would find them in this terrain rather than the far thicker bush country such as we had passed through. The dung and broken vegetation was now fresh, and I glanced over at Bandazi to see him fiddling with his straw boater as he stared at the tracks ahead of him. Was he just letting the light wind cool his head, or was he absorbing some mystical message and casting spells on the unsuspecting elephants? The sound of a tree being broken brought us up short, and I felt a surge of excitement accompanied by a palpable sharpening of the senses and mental focus. Taking the little ash bag from my pocket to check the wind, I led our group down the small, rocky valley towards the sounds of the feeding bulls. I wondered why they had not stopped in a shady area, with the terrific heat causing sweat to run into my eyes.

We soon discovered the reason for the elephants venturing into this spot. There was a pool of clear water in amongst some large boulders, with a small rock cliff bordering one side, and a little sandy beach where the stream entered when in flood. The patch of sand was crowded with eleven bull elephants all jostling for water.

Constantly checking the movement of the hot, midday air, we moved slowly over the bare rock to a point above the path going down to the pool. The sounds of other bulls feeding came from the side of the valley opposite us, and I wondered if they were still to come down to water or had already

drunk at the pool.

The two tribesmen were whispering excitedly and indicated to me that they recognised a bull with a short, thick left tusk and no right tusk as one of the raiders. Good! Just as the thought came to mind that I had given no consideration as to whether I would shoot one or more of the herd, Tsuro suddenly hissed in my ear. Turning to the right I found a bull elephant striding through the trees directly at us, barely a dozen paces away. I put him down with a brain shot.

Pandemonium broke out. Three other elephants came crashing through the trees from behind the dead one and I put in a heart shot as the leader came out onto the rock slab. The other two turned sharply back into the forest, while the first fell heavily before crossing the open area. I saw a piece of ivory spin across the rock as one tusk broke.

The eleven bulls at the waterhole below us were scrambling up the side of the river bank, the gap in the rocky sides being too narrow for more than two to pass at a time. I realised that one dead bull in the exit would trap the rest in the depression. The brief urge to be a one-man execution squad passed as I realised the need to reload both magazine and ammunition band on my wrist. While still a schoolboy I could not afford a cartridge belt for .458, and had made a leather band with six bullet loops. Two leather straps and buckles fastened it around my left wrist. With four rounds in the rifle and Tsuro carrying a spare box of twenty, I found my system quite adequate for the numbers of elephant and buffalo I had hunted thus far.

The first two bulls, both with smallish ivory, had reached level ground and turned away to disappear in great haste into the bush. Another bull came from the river bed and seeing us only yards away, promptly charged, falling to the brain shot with a tremendous crash and snapping off both tusks on the rock.

A big animal with nice ivory appeared behind the fallen one and as he turned I fired for the heart. Another was running with him and kept going when the shot one fell. I was reloading furiously as Tsuro passed me cartridges while more elephants appeared, going in different directions, trumpeting and crashing off into the surrounding trees. Darting around the fallen bulls on the rocky area, I dropped more with brain shots, till the last raider had fled out of sight and sound.

An oppressive silence blanketed the scene. The 100-degree heat, the after-effects of the violent action and firing the heavy rifle suddenly overcame me. I sat in the shade of a tree next to one elephant, drinking from the water-bag and smoking a cigarette, cooling off both physically and mentally.

Tsuro presently came around to tell me, with a big grin, that there were nine bulls down. I already knew that as I had used nine cartridges. The other six elephants would probably keep moving and hopefully stay away from the villages for a long time. There was no way of telling if I had killed the killer, but the district would be satisfied that retribution had been exacted.

Returning to our far-away camp, we followed a river for some miles, passing a few villages and announcing the good news of bountiful meat. On arriving at the cluster of huts and the Land Rover well after sunset, we found a number of men had converged from other kraals. They did not seem particularly surprised at our success. One commented to Tsuro that he had heard about 'Mafana we Chikuru' (the schoolboy) who had been around the area before and who liked to hunt elephants.

Returning to the bulls with the vehicle next morning, we found scores of tribespeople awaiting us. Word seemed to have spread far overnight, and I was only too pleased to have lots of helpers to cut out the ivory while the carcasses were butchered by the enthusiastic crowd. They would camp there for days, cutting up the tons of meat to be smoke-cured.

The family of the elephant's victim presented me with a chicken and the dead man's personal axe, accompanied by profuse gestures of appreciation. They then hurried off to claim a whole animal for themselves. Their recent tragedy seemed soon forgotten as they noisily attacked the bull's hide with knives. Sensible philosophy, I concluded; live for today, that which has gone is passed forever.

Two days later Bandazi, Tsuro and I returned to Bandazi's kraal, the Land Rover laden with ivory and meat, to a welcome couple of days of relaxation. I then made a trip to Sipolilo, handing over to the D.C. all the ivory for which I did not have my own licences, and stocked up with provisions and fuel. With a week left before college opened, there was no reason to head back to civilization yet.

I moved camp westwards to the Doma area, just south of the Chewore Hunting Area, knowing that there was a chance of big bull elephants lurking there while citizen hunters were shooting in Chewore. However, nobody at the kraals we visited gave us any useful information, and although we came across tracks of cow elephant herds, there was no reason to hunt them. We reluctantly left the valley, Tsuro catching the train from Salisbury to return to the farm at Rusape, while I started the second year of Gwebi College.

"I found a bull striding directly at us ... a dozen paces away."

THIRTEEN

Rainy Nights

T he first couple of weeks of the new college year, which began in
October, were busy with subjecting the new intake of students to a
tough initiation, selling ivory and servicing the little Land Rover. I also
sent an official application, for the position of ranger, to the Department of
Wildlife, advising them I would be available after completion of the Gwebi
course. I made much of what a good boy I had been as an honorary officer,
and how much experience I had of dangerous game in spite of my youth. At
the time I assumed every new applicant wanted to be posted to an area
where he would hunt big game – how wrong I was, fortunately! Sure as hell,
if I was accepted, I certainly was not prepared to be a pen-pusher in some
small National Park which catered for hordes of weekend tourists. No Sir!

I had considered my post-college future and saw my options clearly. To
stay in farming was not really attractive, but was there to fall back on if
necessary. Life as an ivory hunter was no longer feasible; that era had
passed, and hunting elephants as an honorary officer did not offer sufficient
opportunities to actually make a living from ivory sales. Besides, a steadily
increasing number of staff in the recently combined Wildlife and National
Parks Department, and petty staff jealousies aimed at honorary officers
would soon result in most control work being done by rangers. So, much as
I disliked the notion of being employed in a government department, to
pursue my addiction for big game hunting meant becoming a game ranger
and trusting to luck that I would be stationed in big game country.

The short vacation over Christmas 1964 found Tsuro and I heading into a
hot, rain-soaked Zambezi Valley to hunt elephants in the tsetse fly areas. We
actually spent far more time digging the Land Rover out of patches of black,

bottomless mud or waiting for flooding streams to subside than we did hunting jumbo. We slept huddled under the vehicle's canvas canopy, which leaked during heavy storms, while every mosquito in the district enjoyed the pure, unadulterated blood of youth.

Lions like stormy nights, but we did not like stormy lions around our camp (i.e. the cloth-canopied Rover) in the dead of night, and felt extremely vulnerable when, one night, we heard them lapping the rain water out of our cooking pots not five yards in front of the car. I was lying across the front seats with Tsuro curled up in the back and, while trying to pick up the .458 as I manoeuvred myself into a sitting position, the creaking and clinking noises alarmed the cats who started to growl with the deepest, most threatening rumbles. A chilling fear is an unavoidable reaction to the sound of irate lions only feet away in pitch darkness. It took me several seconds to collect my wits. I slipped one hand along the top edge of the windscreen and forced the canopy's loops off their hooks. As the canvas flopped into the cab, it dumped a puddle of rain water over me, but I barely noticed this as I stood up, switching on the headlights at the same time.

Four lions were immediately lit up, two of which trotted out of sight into the bush. My attention was on the nearest one, a lioness crouching down just beyond the washed-out fireplace. As my eye picked up the rifle's sights in the difficult light, she half-rose as if to attack, but my shot took her in the top of the head, going right through the neck, chest and into the ground under her. The fourth lion bounded off and I quickly fired another shot into the trees in its direction. Once the ringing sounds in my ears had faded, there was an intense silence around us, occasionally broken by the sounds of fat raindrops falling to earth from the trees. The massive form of the lioness lay motionless and bleeding in the glare of the headlamps, a short leap from where I stood leaning against the steering wheel.

Reluctant to break the spell, I quietly reloaded the .458, left off the safety catch and cradled the rifle. Tsuro crawled over the seat-back and stood next to me. After a few minutes, I switched off the lights and flopped down onto the seat. We discussed the situation and decided to drag the dead animal well away, which we proceeded to do, towing it with the Land Rover and dumping it a couple of hundred yards from camp.

"Bwana, you must teach me to drive the car," Tsuro stated as we settled down again in the damp vehicle, distant lightning and thunder threatening another storm.

"Shut up and go to sleep. Stop dreaming," I mumbled.

"If a lion or elephant kills you, I must be able to drive home. Then I can sell the Land Rover to buy a wife."

"You wouldn't find a wife if you had ten Land Rovers. Anyway, you would spend the money on beer and clothes and your wife would run away. Now stop waking me up," I yawned.

At dawn we climbed out of the vehicle, stiff and clammy, but soon had a fire going which helped to dry our clothes, and hot coffee put me firmly back into business. Ants were scuttling around on the patch of blood-soaked soil a few feet away, where I noticed a neat hole in the ground rather like a spider's tunnel, from which I soon dug the .458 solid bullet nearly a foot deep in the soft earth. I also recalled vaguely hearing lions calling in the early hours and supposed they were trying to locate the missing one, but I had been too sleepy to pay further attention.

Noticing the fresh, white powder from the mopane logs burning at my feet, I took the little ash bag from my shirt pocket, scraped out the soggy mess and propped the bag next to the fire to dry out. I then refilled it from the pile of ash I had pushed aside to cool down. A functioning ash bag is an absolutely essential tool for the big game hunter, and I found a small plastic bag to house it in so my damp shirt or a rain storm would not affect it. Hunters who pick up a pinch of earth and dribble it from the fingers to see which way the dust blows, face two major disadvantages: firstly, there may be no suitable soil to pick up if the ground is stony or rain has fallen, and secondly, the movement when bending down and the taking of one's eyes off the quarry, can be serious mistakes when closing in on dangerous game.

We located fresh tracks of a herd of cow elephants late in the morning after driving down a grass-covered track which I knew eventually ended up at some distant native villages. As usual, we hid the vehicle well even though there was a chance in a million of anyone passing through this area. Besides, crime and theft were virtually unknown among the tribespeople, and many of them knew me personally or by reputation. We took up the spoor of the herd which was easy to follow after the night's rain, and sustained a fast walk for hours in the intense heat and humidity. By mid-afternoon heavy clouds were building up for rain and the light breezes had ceased; the atmosphere was so incredibly dense that we felt as though we were breathing in a cloud of steam, while our clothes stuck to us, soaked with perspiration.

The herd of elephants was feeding in an area of scrubby combretum bushes five to ten feet high, closely spaced and heavily in leaf. We moved slowly forward using our ears and the ash bag for navigation, only seeing the first movement when an elephant appeared on the other side of a low shrub. I shot it in the brain from less than five yards. With plenty of trumpeting the older cows signalled to the herd to stampede away, while Tsuro and I

dashed around the bush to the dead animal to make certain it was down for good. I ran up the foreleg and stood on the great mound of body to watch the backs of the departing herd as they tore their way through thickets. I was sure they did not even know one was missing.

A rumble of thunder suddenly warned us that a storm was almost overhead. We only had an hour or so of daylight left so there was no chance of reaching the Land Rover before dark. Having had little sleep the previous night and a hot, exhausting day, we decided to stay the night with the elephant rather than to start back for the vehicle. We also decided to eat right then, not only because we were famished, but also because our packet of biscuits was about to get soaked by the approaching rain. We settled down against the elephant's still-warm stomach and ate dinner – digestive biscuits plus lots of biltong and plenty of water. The rain came suddenly, as African storms do, and we sat smoking under our hats, joking and feeling the streams of water running down the elephant's hide, soaking our shirts and pants. The night air was warm, but after the storm passed we were forced to sit or lie on the wet grass in our wet clothes. Only cigarettes, matches and ash bag, wrapped in their plastic, were dry. The .458 was propped up against the elephant, muzzle down on a piece of wood, immune to discomforts and mosquitoes.

Over the coming years I spent other nights with dead elephants, but never such a wet night. At least on the dry nights we could make a fire and keep a bit warm, particularly in winter, and the firelight is comforting in the wilderness. Eventually, before dawn on this damp morning, we managed to get a fire going and sat warming ourselves for a couple of hours until the sun rose. It had been about the most uncomfortable night I could imagine, only slightly relieved by the fact that we had no visiting lions!

On the long walk back to the Land Rover we came across a large area of muddy black 'cotton' soil which stuck to our shoes and built up until several inches thick, forcing us to pull it off or scrape it away on fallen trees every few yards. Our leg muscles and tempers were pretty sore after half an hour of that lot! We missed the spot where we had hidden the car and only found it after striking the bush track further on.

Since the elephant hunt, a lot of rain had fallen in the area through which we had to drive on our way to the main track out of the Zambezi Valley, and we sank up to the axles twice which lost us most of that day. I started to worry about getting back to college on time, fearing serious retribution from both Stan Hodierne and the principal, Rodney Mundy. We made it into the Escarpment late at night, ate then slept until sunrise, arriving at Gwebi just in time to avoid trouble. The next day I put Tsuro on the train back to

Centre of attraction - Zambezi Valley pan

The 'Guardian of the Water' is defeated

Checking for elephant tracks, Dande river

Three bulls of the killer herd

Four more of the nine

Rusape, where no doubt he would get on with hunting pigs and baboons in the maize and tobacco at home.

One of the college highlights was a tour around parts of the country, learning how farmers operated their businesses. We ended up in the southeast lowveld, visiting Hippo Valley Sugar Estates and a well-known family business concern known as Buffalo Range. George Style had acquired a huge stretch of country mainly for cattle ranching, but as the district developed, with Triangle Sugar Estates, Hippo Valley and Chiredzi Town all expanding, George and his sons, Rodney and Clive, diversified their business. Government built Buffalo Range Airport to serve the area, while the Style family built a shopping centre including a butchery and a supermarket.

The concept of sustainable harvesting of game animals was taking hold in Rhodesia. Pioneering work on population dynamics of ungulates and culling methods was done on the Henderson brothers' ranch, Doddieburn, in the Matabeleland region. At Buffalo Range I met Brian Marsh who operated the game cropping scheme, and was immediately taken by this tall, quiet-spoken and unassuming character. I'm sure that, unlike the other students, I subconsciously felt an affinity to the dyed-in-the-wool hunter and I regret that, apart from one or two brief encounters, thirty five years passed before I got to know Brian better. With a lifetime in the bush ranging from crocodile shooting in Nyasaland, through all manner of big game hunting, game cropping and safari operations, Brian ranks as one of Africa's living legends of the hunting world. Fortunately, his great talent as an author has given us a partial record of his enormous fund of knowledge and experiences.

The college year ended successfully a few months later, but the Department of Parks and Wildlife had no vacancy for me immediately, asking me to call them once a month as something was expected to come up. I tried to find out where the possible posting might be, but nobody would give the slightest hint. However, I did briefly meet Ted Davison, the legendary 'father' of the vast Wankie Game Reserve. Ted was the first warden, appointed in 1928 and remaining there till 1961. Seeing him sitting in a small government office in Salisbury was somewhat disturbing to me. He looked out of place and really bored, just waiting out his time to be compulsorily retired. Like an old lion I once saw, when I was a child, in a cage with a travelling circus.

I bought some elephant licences then went home to collect Tsuro to go hunting before I ended up shut in an office in a city, too old to face a charging jumbo.

Derek Tomlinson with the five tuskless elephants

FOURTEEN

Moving On

Unsure of what my future prospects of elephant hunting might be, I was determined to make hay while the sun shone, with nothing else to do while waiting for word from the department about an appointment as a ranger. For a change I was financially well-heeled enough to outfit an open-ended elephant safari, and I was hopeful of collecting enough ivory to recover the costs. If not, no big problem; if luck was with me, maybe I would make something, but most important was to be hunting in big game country.

Having phoned District Commissioners in those parts of the north and north-east of the country which were most likely to have crop-raider problems, I made my plan to work from one area to the next in order to reduce the hunting time lost and the travelling.

For the ensuing months, Tsuro and I worked through a large part of the country, hunting elephants in several areas new to us, as well as those parts of Mrewa, Mtoko, Mount Darwin, Sipolilo and Doma districts which we had hunted during the past few years. We walked hundreds of miles, had many successful days and many blank ones, plus lots of excitement and new experiences. The only mishap happened when Tsuro put a foot into an unseen hole and twisted his ankle so badly he could barely stand up. We had left camp only half an hour before, following the tracks of a group of elephant bulls which had drunk that night at a nearby pool. They had done some damage to crops in the area a couple of days prior to our arrival.

I cut a forked stick for Tsuro to use as a crutch and told him to make his way back to camp, rest his foot, but not to forget that supper was still his responsibility. He also took the water-bag and his axe which he could

manage with one hand. I had learnt that by drinking a lot of water during the evening and early in the morning, most days I could last without drinking during the hunt. As the weather was not particularly hot, I took a chance that the water-bag would not be needed. Slinging the little carry-bag, containing biscuits, spare ammunition and two oranges, over my shoulder I took up the spoor. Elephants in this area had not been hunted for a long time, according to the villagers we had met, and by the signs I found, it was obvious these were in no hurry to distance themselves from the humans' habitation. Mopane trees were broken down and much-chewed branches were strewn along the way. Shrubs had been stripped of leaves and roots, first exposed by digging with the great forefeet and then ripped out of the ground and consumed.

The locals claimed there were six elephant but, as bulls are prone to wandering around singly, in pairs or joining up for some days with others, it was not certain if there was still the same number. Criss-crossing each other's spoor as they meandered along made it difficult to decide, but Tsuro and I had thought there were six or seven. It was not particularly important. The main objective for me, tracking alone, was to be careful not to follow one animal which may go off by itself, splitting from the group. Making cross-checks to stay on the herd's tracks slowed me down. This was not really a disadvantage as it allowed me time to keep a check on the wind, what was going on around me and the general direction I was heading. Following steadily for a couple of hours, I was probably gaining slightly on the bulls when I came across a pan where they had drunk. Assuming they had spent a fair amount of time here, I hoped they were not far ahead. My next problem was to find which way they had gone after drinking, as the bush around the pan was full of pathways and broken vegetation.

Carefully circling the waterhole at a distance of fifty to a hundred yards, I eventually found footprints of at least two of them travelling along a well-worn game trail. Further on more tracks appeared, assuring me that I was on course. However, their direction had now altered and was more downwind than before, besides which they had not stopped to feed since drinking. I quickened my pace while the spoor was easily visible, meanwhile mentally rehearsing possible scenarios, in particular a quick circling diversion downwind if I should hear them ahead. The bush was becoming more dense since I had left the mopane country behind, so it was most likely they would be heard before being seen.

I diverted off the path to investigate a pile of droppings. They were very fresh. As I inhaled the strong odour I knew before touching the balls of fibre that the elephants had passed less than half an hour earlier. I once again

checked my rifle and spare rounds, pulled the ash bag from my pocket, all the while listening intently, the familiar feeling of tension and excitement rising. Suddenly I felt completely and utterly alone, isolated from the world, in the middle of nowhere, where no one knew where I was. I looked at the trees around me, stared down at the elephant dung, and my shoes, then up to the pale, hot-blue sky above. My God, what a silent, lonely place I was in. An emerald-spotted dove gently wound down its somnolent call nearby. I was not alone. A rolling, purring, rumble came through the warm, still air. Elephants! My mind snapped into gear, the ash bag flicked to float out its tell-tale puff of white. I followed the same direction; I must get downwind smartly, must not bump into an unseen jumbo while trying to out-manoeuvre the group.

Another rumble, closer now. The bulls were relaxed, keeping in touch with each other using their deep-throated resonant growls, in olden times thought to be stomach sounds; a strange notion considering there is no evidence and certainly no rationale for stomachs to be consciously directed to create elephantine speech. No, the jumbo has a more than adequate range of vocalisation, some below our own range of aural detection, produced by throat and trunk. Bernhard Grzimek even describes how Mr. I. Buss, an elephant researcher from Uganda, was in amongst "rumbling" elephants in Basle Zoo, and felt with his hand "the vibrations in the animal's throat and the concomitant jets of air from its trunk" (*Among Animals Of Africa*, B. Grzimek).

My bulls were close but still invisible in this scrub interspersed by scattered mopane and rain trees where they had decided to spend the hot hours. The heat was intensifying, no leaves moved in the quietness and the little cloud of white powder hung around the jolted ash bag for a moment before sinking slowly to earth. Twenty yards away a branch high on a giant mopane shook slightly, then disappeared out of sight with a loud crack. Wiping my wet palms down my shirt front, at the same time dropping the ash bag into a pocket, I released the rifle's safety catch silently while slipping through the bushes. All the sounds of a feeding elephant were now very close: the crunch of wood, swish of leaves, quiet exhalation of air through the trunk. Try as I might, I could not make out the great bulk through the screen of vegetation, and it seemed the animal would scent me at any moment now, but I was almost too close to defend myself if he attacked, or even panicked and ran in my direction. It was too late to back off and look for a different approach or another one of the herd; my scent was seeping around the vicinity every second.

Holding my breath, pouring sweat and expecting an eruption of bull

elephant to overpower me in an instant, I quickly took three or four steps to a mopane tree on my left, thankful for the moral support and small degree of protection it gave me. My heart was pounding as I stood, rifle raised in readiness, looking up now at the ridge of the bull's backbone a few feet away above the bushes. Like a frightened squirrel sighting a predator, I darted round the other side of my tree, crunching a pile of dead-dry leaves underfoot. Immediately the huge head with outspread ears appeared as the elephant swung around, trunk upraised as he picked up the scent signal for the first time. Before he could decide on his next move I shot for the brain, at which he disappeared with much crashing of the bushes between us. I rushed around the obstructions and saw, much to my relief, that he lay quite still. Waiting with rifle ready to either shoot him again if he moved, or to fend off any attack by his friends, I heard the others tearing their way through the undergrowth, fortunately away from me.

Several minutes of utter silence passed, apart from a gurgle of gas escaping out of the bull's mouth, before I moved around to the head, half-hidden in the bushes, to see the thick slick of blood issuing from the end of the trunk; the typical sign of a frontal brain shot. Looking closer I found two bullet holes through the centre of the trunk, about a foot from the tip, where my shot had gone on its way into the face below eye level, and up to the brain. The ivory I estimated at a bit over forty pounds aside, the best I had collected for some time. As I sat in a patch of shade, peeling an orange and eating biscuits, the scene replayed in my mind, bringing the realisation that I could not recall seeing the upraised trunk in my rifle's sights, nor the position of the eyes or any other features of the bull's face; yet I had known exactly, in that spilt second, where to aim for the brain. This puzzled me for a while, and I realised how relieved I was that the close encounter had turned out this way after the nerve-racking minutes leading up to it. Now for the long, hot, thirsty hours of walking back to camp, which I would reach before sunset, and then return here tomorrow with people to cut up the carcass and remove the tusks. Shouldering the carry-bag and my rifle, I took up my own spoor and set off in good spirits.

Tsuro seemed pleased to see me and hear about the successful hunt, but his ankle was still swollen and painful, so I told him to rest it as we would be staying at this camp for a couple of days while I returned to the elephant with the local people. We had no appointments, no time limits, nobody else's decisions to abide by. We were just a couple of footloose lads, loving the hunting life.

The powerful spell of this specialised genre of hunting once again totally engulfed me, and with the passion came greater understanding of the skills

to hunt elephants under all conditions, but with enough astuteness not to be killed in the process. In particular, the brain shot developed into a precise art which gave me confidence in being able to tackle unexpected situations, or as my favourite golfer, Gary Player, would say "the harder I practice, the luckier I get". I also had a lot of ivory to sell.

A close friend from school days, Derek Tomlinson, had joined the Department of Parks and Wildlife around this time, and was stationed as ranger of Chipinda Pools on the Lundi river, east of Chiredzi and Hippo Valley Estates. Derek sent word via my folks that I should visit him as there were elephants in need of attention in his area. An offer I could not refuse. Taking Tsuro with me we travelled south, through the wonderful bushveld of the great cattle ranches which we knew so well from our school-time buffalo hunts, to meet Derek in Chiredzi town. After a long, liquid evening in the bar of the Planter's Inn we rose groggily next morning for our first rendezvous on a game ranch which had a small annual quota of elephants to crop.

During the evening session Derek had explained his reason for asking me to come down. The ranch owner was not allowed to shoot the elephants as the department felt he had no experience, in addition to which they suspected he might not report any wounded animals or possibly exceed his quota. Therefore he had to call on the nearest ranger to do the job. However, this presented a second problem as Derek was not only inexperienced himself, but did not want to shoot elephants anyway. He was honest enough to admit, after just one elephant hunt in a tsetse fly corridor, that he was frightened by the aggressiveness of the cow elephants. With thoughts of his forthcoming marriage, at which I was to be his best man, uppermost in his mind, he wisely chose to avoid possible suicide by elephant damage. Nor would he listen to my assurances that his gorgeous fiancée, Patricia, would be absolutely safe with me in the event of a jumbo getting the better of him.

Unfortunately the elephant hunt confirmed Derek's opinion that the female is the deadlier of the sexes, putting him off ever wanting to mix with the great creatures on his own. The herd we tracked consisted of around thirty cows and assorted juveniles, including a teenage bull who thought he was quite the bee's knees, like some other teenagers I have met; two-legged ones that is.

Leaving Derek's tracker and Tsuro under a shady tree on a termite mound, I took Derek into the herd, which was standing around amongst mopane trees on the other side of a gully they had just crossed. I showed him a mature cow which, judging by the mammary glands and no youngster nearby, did not have a dependent calf. Derek appeared to have a problem with his rifle, looking down, working the bolt and jamming a round in the

top of the magazine. The mechanical sounds brought a short, piercing blast from a large cow near us, and a charge by a different one on our right, which I put down. The whole herd erupted, trumpeting and growling, and the young bull came rushing up to the dead cow, then saw us and charged. As we could only shoot one for the ranch owner, for practical and logistical reasons, this bull was about to become an embarrassment.

"Go down the bank," I snapped at Derek. We both half-fell, half-scrambled down the vertical drop into the ravine behind us and up the other side. A bunch of cow elephants had come alongside the young bull on the opposite bank, screaming with rage, trunks waving around, mad as hell with frustration at not being able to get at us.

"Let's go before they find a way over," I suggested. We moved back to where the two trackers sat on top of their termite mound. The elephants were still trumpeting and crashing around in the area we had left them, so I told my three companions to wait for me and returned using a downwind route to see what was going on. I watched with interest as several big cows tried to lift the dead one by lowering their heads and pushing their tusks under her body or head. They had actually moved the body several yards until it became stuck between a couple of trees, which seemed to annoy them even more. Meanwhile, others of the herd milled around, trunks up, growling and shaking their heads with much ear flapping.

I wondered if I could frighten them off, so I fired a shot into one of the tree trunks above the cows surrounding the dead animal and yelled a couple of times. The young bull, followed by some cows, promptly came rushing towards me, so once again I decamped into the gully and headed back to my companions, meeting them coming my way. Tsuro later told me that Derek was sure I had been caught by the jumbos after they had heard my shouts following the rifle shot, then the elephants trumpeting angrily. Derek would not believe Tsuro's explanation that elephants generally dislike the human voice and that we often shouted to frighten them; besides, I would have fired more shots if I was in danger. We heard later from the rancher that the herd had left by the time he arrived that afternoon to butcher the carcass.

From the ranch we travelled east to the northern end of the Sabi/Lundi tsetse corridor to look for elephants which were said to have broken the game fence. We camped near a beautiful clear stream in open brachystegia (*mfuti* trees) country, which should have been full of game but was depressingly lacking in antelope and other species like zebra or warthog due to the Tsetse Department's policy of total elimination of all wildlife. This was later modified to cover only six species, but – too late...

We spent a day checking along the game fences and streams but found

only old spoor and droppings of elephant and one place where a single bull had passed through the fence by simply pushing against the high strain wires till all the two-inch staples popped out of the mopane poles on either side of him, allowing him to force his bulk through. The wires all sprung back into position with not one broken.

Back at camp that evening, while Derek bathed in a pool, I was sitting luxuriously in a government-issue camp chair drinking a cool beer when an elephant trumpeted not far away. With the sun already setting, I hoped there would be enough time to catch up with the animals, so gathering my rifle and ammunition belt I rushed off with Tsuro following me, still pulling his shirt over his head and carrying his shoes in one hand. Ten minutes later, somewhat breathless, we caught up with the elephants, a small herd of five which were moving steadily through the open grassland. Sprinting to get alongside them brought a surprise – none of the three cows or two juveniles had any ivory showing. The matriarch either heard or saw us moving and immediately attacked, head down, ears back and accompanied by the other four, all in a tight cluster. I started shooting when they were about thirty paces away and downed all five.

This was my first experience of the notorious alertness and belligerence of tuskless elephants while hunting them; an experience repeated frequently in future years when I was operating in the tsetse corridors. I learnt to check a herd for tuskless ones as far as was practical, but often impossible in dense cover, because invariably any tuskless cow would attack the instant she detected me. They made hunting in thickets or heavy forest a dangerous undertaking.

Darkness had fallen when we arrived back in camp to find Derek on his third beer, with dinner ready.

"So what the hell was that little war all about? Oh, and thanks for inviting me on your evening jogging session," he complained.

"Your department owes me for mileage, ammunition, camping allowance and a day's wages, but I'll take the pair of eighty pound tusks in lieu of government money. We must start early tomorrow to cut them out," I told him.

"What! Hell, I'll be in deep curds now, maybe they'll sack me. We aren't allowed to shoot big bulls in the corridors. You bloody fool, Rich. In any case, you're not really supposed to be here shooting, and my tracker will talk to the others back at Chipinda. We'll have to make a plan, swop the tusks or something. Maybe say it had been wounded by poachers."

"Stop panicking, Derek, for heaven's sake," I said to calm him down. "You go back to Chipinda Pools and report a tuskless animal shot, I'll get the

ivories, move out and use my next licence to register them. Simple. Now, can I drink and eat in peace?"

Poor Derek was not convinced, and drank several more beers in reaction. I slept well.

As we approached the row of dead elephants next morning Derek's face was a picture.

"You swine, Harland. I'll never forgive you for the ulcers, palpitations and insomnia I have suffered. Eighty bloody pounder! Bastard," he let off steam.

"I'm sorry, really. Couldn't resist it though. Of course, you do realise that nobody is going to believe five out of five were tuskless, not an ounce of ivory. It's unheard of, and there's got to be an investigation of Ranger Tomlinson's activities. You should only get six months to a year inside, and I will look after Patricia so don't worry about her," I reassured him. "On the other hand," I continued, "I'll consider being your witness in exchange for a couple of boxes of .458 ammo, a full tank of petrol and dinner at the Planter's Inn."

On our way back to Chiredzi we deviated to a nearby tribal area to advise the people about the elephants in the corridor, as it was policy to allow them to take any meat not used by either the Tsetse Control staff or the Wildlife Department. From Chiredzi I returned home with Tsuro where my father gave me the news that a Mr. Evans of the Department of Parks and Wildlife had phoned to say he wished to see me. Tense with excitement, I called him back and said I would be in his office the next morning.

Rising at 4am after a restless night, I sped to Salisbury at 40 mph in my old Land Rover, arriving at the department's Head Office in a state of nervous anticipation, and presented myself to Mr. Phil Evans, the deputy director.

"Well, Richard, we have a position for you," the steely-eyed civil servant announced, "but you are a bit young so will be on half pay till you turn twenty-one. There are regulations governing these things. We know you have been helpful to us as an honorary officer, so we decided to take you on ahead of some older applicants."

"Thank you, sir," I stuttered, still beside myself with the big question – *where* was I to be posted?

"You seem to have a lot of elephant hunting experience already, which gave you an advantage over the other chaps as we need a ranger in an area that has a lot of control work; crop raiders, tsetse operations and so on."

My excitement was hard to contain as he spoke. It all sounded as if my dreams of continuing a big game hunting career would materialise. I just could not stop myself smiling broadly, foolishly, as he continued.

"I am sending you to Mabala-uta Field Station, at Buffalo Bend on the Nuanetsi river, down at the southern end of Gonarezhou State Land. As soon as you are ready, pick up a Land Rover which I have allocated to you, and be on your way. Call in at the Regional Warden, Bruce Austen, at Zimbabwe Ruins and he'll direct you on."

Incredible, unbelievable elation! Gonarezhou, 'The Refuge of Elephants', was to be my home!

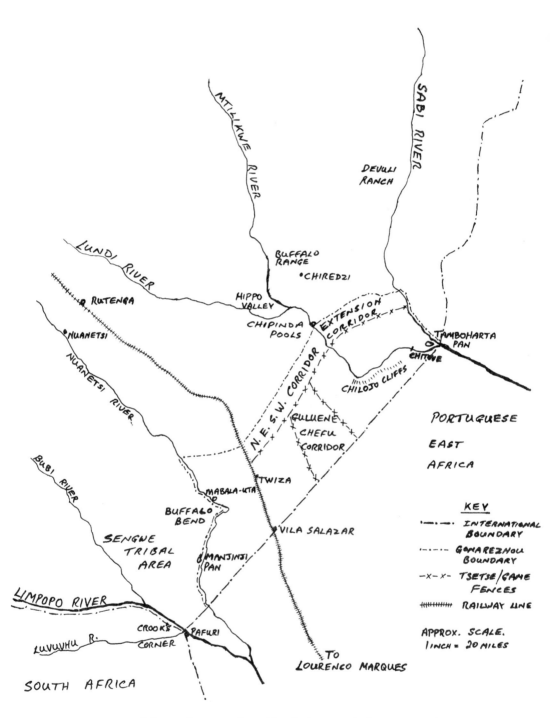

Map of the south-eastern lowveld, Rhodesia (including Gonarezhou)

FIFTEEN

Game Ranger

For my eleventh birthday my mother had given me a book titled *The Ivory Trail* written by T.V. Bulpin, which told of the adventures of an elephant hunter named Cecil Barnard. This rough, tough, wild man was nicknamed *Bvekenya* (pronounced Bveh-ken-yuh, meaning 'walks with a swagger') by the Shangaan tribespeople amongst whom he lived during the period 1910 to 1929 in the great wilderness between the Sabi river to the north and the Limpopo river and Pafuri area in the south. He hunted elephant bulls wherever the fancy took him, irrespective of the artificial borders demarcating South Africa, Mozambique and Southern Rhodesia, but managed to elude the police of all three territories with cunning, a good spy network amongst the Africans, and occasionally by moving the stone cairns demarcating the international boundaries!

The marvellous exploits of Bvekenya really imprinted on my young mind, the vivid descriptions in Bulpin's writing sending my imagination into orbit, absolutely convincing me that I had to be an elephant hunter when I grew up. No ifs nor buts, no analysis nor questions. Just a natural response to the hunting imperative.

Bulpin's descriptions of the bushveld, the animals and the great changes in their habitat wrought by droughts and floods enthralled me. For twenty years Bvekenya roamed this harsh and wild wonderland, much of which was in my own country, and the names, Crook's Corner, Chefu, Pafuri, Limpopo conjured up romantic images of the ivory hunter's life of my fantasies. It seemed incredible, predestined maybe, that nine years later I was going to live and hunt in the very same corner of Africa that already felt so familiar through Bvekenya's adventures.

Tsuro was by now a reasonably accomplished cook, at least by bachelor standards, so I suggested he work for me full-time if he wanted to come down to Gonarezhou where we would also continue to hunt together. His pay would be next to nothing, I warned him, as my own salary was less than the value of a small tusk, at least for the time being until I reached my twenty-first birthday. Tsuro's only question was would we have lots of meat to eat?

My excitement began rising steadily when we turned off the main road leading to Beit Bridge and South Africa at a sign reading "Nuanetsi". Passing the tiny settlement which probably harboured less than a dozen Europeans, mostly policemen or district administration staff, the bush track became more obscure and less road-like as we passed through the tribal area, eventually crossing the 'cut-line' boundary of Gonarezhou State Land. From there on the track wound its way through magnificent mopane areas or rocky outcrops covered in strange msimbiti (ironwood) tree thickets, then patches of grassland, past dried-up grey pans and stark baobabs. Everywhere were trees broken by elephants, wide paths worn into the hard earth by centuries of huge feet coming and going, these highways flanked by the great fibrous dung balls dropped almost daily, it would seem. Tsuro and I were amazed at the sheer mass of elephantine evidence around us as we bumped and bounced our way southwards towards our final destination, Mabala-uta Field Station (*mabala* 'for smoothing', *uta* 'the hunting bow' – the Shangaan name for the shrub *Ficus capreifolia* which has rough-textured leaves used as polishing sandpaper) on the banks of the Nuanetsi river.

I was in the very heart of 'Ivory Trail' territory. Bvekenya had tracked great bull elephants through here thirty-five, forty years before and I imagined him revelling in the solitude and the carefree life, wandering this vast territory with just a few of his Shangaan companions. I was immediately impatient to explore the whole area for myself; to soak up the aura, the spirit, of this unspoilt and untamed piece of game-rich Africa. Apart from the thousands of elephants, there were impala, kudu, nyala, lion, herds of buffalo, giraffe, eland, zebra, sable, waterbuck, warthog and bush pig. Duiker, jackal, bat-eared fox, leopard and hyena all shared their domains with greater and lesser creatures, almost free from human intrusion.

Mabala-uta is situated a couple of miles upstream of Buffalo Bend where the Nuanetsi river kinks abruptly from east to south, in a haven of evergreen trees on a stretch of alluvial soil supporting light riverine forest, full of cavorting impala. The month was May, when the rams competed for their harems, chasing each other madly with occasional physical contact and a hell of a lot of grunting and snorting. Filled with so much excitement on my

first night, the continuous rutting commotion around my little house kept me wide awake for hours. I was in love with the place already.

Probably one of the smallest and most isolated of government outposts in Southern Rhodesia, the station staff consisted of Game Warden Tim Braybrooke, his wife Bridgette and little son Philip, plus six game scouts, a driver for the truck, Tim's tracker and four labourers. Tim generously took Tsuro onto the station's payroll, relieving me of this financial burden. The office was a tiny thatched rondavel equipped with a desk, filing cabinet, firearm cabinet and a two-way radio for communication with other bases around the country. Tim had an elderly Land Rover station-wagon, run on paraffin as petrol was in short supply, and there was the old department Land Rover I had driven down from Salisbury. That was about it!

I had disposed of all my firearms excepting a .22 Hi-Power Savage for various reasons, which in retrospect was utter folly. Such is youth! Therefore my first desire was to get into the gun cabinet and view the treasures therein, particularly the big bores. Regrettably, the promised Aladdin's cave turned out to be more akin to a poorly-stocked auctioneer's reject cupboard.

Tim had his own .375 H&H and laid claim to an oldish .470 double. Beside a couple of shaky shotguns there stood a much-used .375 Winchester, a Rigby double .450, and a .458 by Mannlicher-Schönauer. The gleam in my eye on seeing the Rigby was soon extinguished when I lifted the rifle from the cabinet and tucked it into my shoulder. The stock was so short my right thumb was buried deep in my nostril, guaranteed to cause bleeding and crying with the first shot, a situation highly undesirable when playing war games with Gonarezhou elephants. The weapon was so uncomfortable that I did not even feel inclined to puncture a mopane tree with a trial shot. So *who* had criminally mutilated what was once the pinnacle of British gun-making artistry?

There had apparently been more than a little animosity between the old game department and the National Parks department prior to their recent amalgamation, and the Parks guys were often apt to denigrate their game ranger counterparts as ruffians and rogues. I was told that a certain Tinky Haslam of the latter category had applied something akin to a chain saw to Mr. John Rigby's masterpiece when requiring it during a temporary spell in the area. Of course, I knew Tinky. He was a Rusape boy, as was another game department eccentric, Tommy Orford. Realising the undesirability of being remotely associated with such reprobates caused me to deny, as Judas would do in such circumstances, any association with Rusape and its inhabitants. My home was *miles* from the place, I barely knew the village, or so I airily told Tim Braybrooke.

Tim appeared suitably mollified that I had no links with 'those sort of people'. He was a confirmed National Parks man, a good civil servant who enjoyed administration, report writing, having 'staff under him' and observing the pecking order of governmental structures. We were cast in different moulds. Nevertheless, we got on well together.

My options on heavy rifles were now reduced to zero. I picked out the Mannlicher-Schönauer .458 and looked it over, noting the incredibly long barrel, probably 28-inches or more, and the unusually slim pistol grip. Although a little long in the stock for me, it felt very comfortable in the firing position. Probably the light weight, plus the concave cheek-piece, slender grip and thin fore-end, all added up to a good match for my average height and physique. I studied the action with its unique features, as it was all quite new to me, and liked what I found. The bolt-handle was almost in the centre of the bolt which, along with good tolerances and fine machining of the body and the receiver, gave an exceptionally smooth movement, unlike all the other actions I had used where the handle is positioned at the rear of the bolt, allowing plenty of wobble when the bolt is drawn rearwards.

The magazine was equally unusual, containing a spring-powered rotary spool, around which four cartridges lay snugly, as opposed to the staggered, 3-round boxes found on most big-bore rifles. The feed was silky smooth, positive and with the rim of each case being picked up and held by the extractor, it seemed an excellent system. In particular, I liked the idea of the four-plus-one firepower for my solo elephant control operations. Indeed, subsequent experiences proved to my satisfaction that the five-shot .458 gave a huge, sometimes life-saving, advantage when hunting exceptionally aggressive herds of cow elephants in very thick bush or msimbiti forest.

In truth, along with most big game hunters, I love British-made doubles, and sometimes wonder if a tiny bit of fate stepped in here by forcing the Mannlicher upon me. Would I have ever mastered a double sufficiently well to have put down ten or twenty attacking elephant in minutes and still be around to watch that evening's sunset? Maybe, maybe not. I have recently read Brian Herne's excellent book *White Hunters* (Henry Holt, 1999), and many are the tales of East Africa's professionals whose double rifles were full of empty cases when the elephant, cat or buffalo reached the hunter; and these were single animals. "There wasn't time to reload" is a recurring theme.

My little house stood under the dense, evergreen canopies of Natal mahoganies, overlooking a pool in the Nuanetsi which was otherwise a regular African-looking sandy river bed, about a hundred yards wide and stretching out of sight in both directions. That first evening I took a camp

chair out to the edge of the river bank at sundown and sat drinking a cold beer while spiritually drinking in the wonders of the evening in romantic, wildest Africa. My favourite game birds, Natal francolin, were screeching their way to roost all along the strip of riverine forest, while the snorts and grunts of rutting impala rams gained in frequency as the sun sank, huge and red, into the treetops and gently disappeared. A pair of Egyptian geese flew downstream at tree height, the female's loud blare almost drowning out her mate's weak hiss as they passed the human habitation. They flew on past the pool, where I had been watching a saddle-billed stork march his sedate way around the edges, looking for an evening snack.

Tsuro came down quietly and sat on the ground nearby. We remained silent, each with our thoughts, as darkness brought out a clear sky crowded to capacity with stars, while down on Planet Earth the insect life began its trills, squeaks and chirps, frogs in the pool called sporadically and a distant troop of baboons barked and chattered as they settled down in their arboreal sleeping quarters. A short trumpet blast from an elephant way down river echoed up to us. The sharp alarm bark of a bushbuck sounded from the other side of the river and I wondered what had frightened it.

"Eeh, there are many animals in this place," Tsuro murmured, "more than Rekomitjie even."

I explained to him that one day, maybe soon, this area would be a game reserve but already it was protected from hunting. Even the few remaining villagers awaiting translocation to the nearby Sengwe Tribal Land were not supposed to kill game.

"What is our job here then, if there is no hunting?" he asked, probably wondering if he would be required to dig trenches, make bricks and chop firewood with the other labourers.

"Tsuro, we have been here only one day, so I don't know everything that goes on. We will chase out poachers from Sengwe sometimes, maybe shoot elephants that eat the same people's crops at other times. I know of Tsetse Department areas where we will hunt elephants and buffalo so that tsetse flies cannot live there. Maybe there will be problems with hippo, crocodile, lion or leopard in the tribal area or on the European cattle ranches for us to sort out." I paused to listen to a little Scops owl trill out its sharp call from the tree above us. In the still air, a barely discernible waft of movement passed our heads as a bat fluttered and swooped on its prey.

"What about a rifle," Tsuro enquired next. "Are there some government ones here?"

I told him about the .458 and assured him I would show it to him in the morning.

"Now, I need another beer and you can cook some of that impala from Boss Tim, plus rice and peas. The paraffin light is in the kitchen for you. And keep the doors closed because of mosquitoes," I instructed, not for the last time! A diet of impala, rice and tinned green peas was my standard fare, with almost no serious deviations, for the next few years; the emphasis being on the meat as I was a strongly carnivorous creature. An addiction quite natural for a hunter, I thought.

I also thought about the fact that Tim had not really spoken about what game control was expected of me. Nor was there any query about whether I had big game experience, which I was actually quite happy about. I never spoke about my own hunting activities, probably because of two ideas I held on the matter. Firstly, I did not really have any friends of like mind, so had no reason to discuss my passion with anyone. Secondly, if I was in the company of another hunter, he was invariably much older than myself, and I presumed would be more experienced, so I kept my mouth shut.

A previous experience had also shown me what peculiar jealousies are sometimes stirred in the minds of other people, quite putting me off ever letting on to strangers that I was a hunter. While selling a batch of ivory to Mr. Levy in Salisbury, which included the eighty-pounders from Dande area, a rugged-looking character of middle-age came in, togged out in khaki kit, veldschoen shoes and beard. He carried a pair of 30lb tusks in a sack. As I was leaving the room, I heard this gentleman ask Mr. Levy, "Where did that kid get these tusks?" I stopped behind the door to eavesdrop, hearing the reply, "Oh, he hunts all over the place, I really don't know where." With a loud, derisive laugh, Mr. Big Know-all responded, "That little twit never shot those elephants. He's a bullshitter, let me tell you." Well, stuff you, I thought as I slipped along the corridor and out of the building. I knew the old man would not tell the guy my name. Discreet he was, old Levy.

Sitting with my cold beer while recalling this little episode made me feel wonderfully content and secure in this far-away place. Maybe a bare dozen people knew where I was, and most of those could not care less anyway. A loner by choice, I reckoned being left alone was one of life's most underrated luxuries. And I hold this conviction far more passionately now than I did back then! A call from Tsuro broke my reverie and I tucked into my IRP (impala, rice, peas) supper with great relish, chasing it with a couple more beers while sitting under the trees again. Must get a supply of chilli, and more beer, I thought.

There was, in fact, a system for bringing in provisions. One wrote a letter listing requirements to Meikles Store in Fort Victoria, and left it in a canvas postbag which hung on a tree half a mile from Mabala-uta where the road

to the station met the track from Nuanetsi. An ancient bus passed by once a week to and from Malipati area, collected the post and delivered it to Fort Victoria, almost 200 miles away. Meikles had the goods packed carefully in boxes and delivered to the bus stop in town on the day the transport left for the lowveld.

The approaching bus was audible from Mabala-uta and one of us would drive up the road to meet it at the junction. I was always amazed how our food boxes arrived in such good shape, considering the squash of humanity on board, chickens in home-made stick cages, goats tied up in sacks, kids piddling here and there and vastly proportioned dames waddling up and down the aisle screaming with laughter at their own jokes. A five-pound note and packet of cigarettes for the driver were, I'm sure, the finest insurance premiums I have ever paid. Nothing broken, nothing stolen, not one beer nicked. Should we miss the bus rendezvous, someone would drive to the pick-up point smartly, before baboons found the loot. The following week one sent a cheque off to pay the bill. Simple.

The distorted, high-pitched voice emanating from the radio set was apparently that of Bruce Austen, the Parks and Wildlife boss of the South Eastern Region, trying to tell us that the Nuanetsi District Commissioner had phoned him, complaining about nuisance elephants somewhere down our way. Okay, tell the D.C. we'll check out the report, we called back.

Sergeant Machivana, our senior game scout, resembled Devuli ranch's Naison, although he was much older, with strong features, an un-African aquiline nose, and the tall, upright bearing of many Shangaan men. Mac, as we all called him, accompanied Tsuro and I to investigate the elephant problem. I enjoyed his company on the drive as he pointed out features and taught me names of the dry stream beds we crossed and pools in the Nuanetsi, as well as indicating the almost invisible vehicle tracks leading off to other places.

I asked Mac the meaning of Gonarezhou (more or less pronounced as Gornah-reh-zor) which he explained as 'the rocky hide-out of elephant'; apt in so far as the Nuanetsi river cut through rocky hills in this part of its course, though much of the area north and east of the river is not at all hilly. He answered my questions on some notable trees we saw which were not familiar to me. The beautiful, wide-canopied wild mangoes (*Cordyla africana*), along with the more common nyala tree (*Xanthocercis Zambeziaca*), Natal mahogany (*Trichilia emetica*), African mangosteen (*Garcinia livingstonei*) and apple-ring acacia/winter thorn (*Acacia albida*) lived on alluvial pockets, forming parkland forests, the understorey of which was heavily utilised by game.

The groves of tamboti trees (*Spirostachys africana*) along the dry watercourses interested me, as Mac explained the dangers of the poisonous milk which can irritate the skin, damage eyes, or even poison food cooked over a fire in which the wood is used. It is used as a fish poison and with other toxins on arrow points. Of course, the beautifully grained, hard timber retains its sensuous, sandalwood aroma for years, and not many trees large enough to harvest for timber remain outside the parks or reserves.

Another tree new to me was the msimbiti (*Androstachys johnsonii*), known in the neighbouring Kruger National Park as Lebombo ironwood. Msimbiti (*msimbi* meaning iron or metal in most local dialects, *miti* are trees) grew in colonies, virtually exclusive of other tree species, crowding close together except where stony ground or slabs of rock intervened. With the dark green upper surfaces of the leaves and the drab, rough-textured bark, the groves are very distinctive, even showing up almost black on aerial photos. The timber is close-grained, pinkish-coloured and very hard, though not as heavy as that of another of my favourite trees, the leadwood (*Combretum imberbe*). Msimbiti, like the marula and some others, has 'male' and 'female' trees with quite different and unusual flowers on each.

Elephants feed on msimbiti leaves and branches, and in large forests they often rest up in the shady spots. In due course I was to have many confrontations, some very hazardous, with them in these thickets, and had also to bear in mind that this timber would deflect bullets like no other.

Mac eventually instructed me to park the vehicle under a shady tree as we were to walk to the kraal from which the complaint had originated. Leaving one of our game scouts, brought along for the purpose, with the Land Rover, Mac led Tsuro and I along a path for over an hour before we arrived at a small cluster of huts. I asked Mac where they found water and was told there was a borehole a couple of hundred yards away, complete with hand-operated pump, one of several drilled by the D.C., which was barely drinkable. Most underground water in this district was so heavily mineralised as to be useless to man, and even toxic to animals if drunk for continuous periods.

Mac questioned the two men present about any trouble with elephant. Yes, they asserted, three bulls had been into their plots of melons and millet last night, the third time this week.

"Do you know you will be moved to the Sengwe area soon, because the government is making this a reserve for game?" Sergeant Mac enquired of the men.

"Yes, the *mudzwiti* (District Commissioner) told us, so we are not hunting the animals. But if these elephants eat all our food, we will have nothing to

take with us to the new settlement," came the not unreasonable response. Obviously, the D.C. was aware of this, otherwise he would not have called on us to intervene. Being new around here, I relied on Mac to advise me.

Mac's deep voice announced, "Baas, we should try to shoot one of these bulls, then the others will go far away and these people will have plenty of meat to dry and take with them. They are being forced to move, so they will be happier if we do this for them."

We took up the fresh tracks, heading off through beautiful mopane woodland, crossing last night's spoor of a buffalo herd overlaid with the prints of several lions, which were probably following with the same intentions as we had on our elephant. Tsuro dallied to study the feline footprints.

"*Mdoda imwe ne hadzi mbiri*," he reckoned. One male and two females.

Mac stood staring down for a moment, then nodded. "Yes, that's right. Where did you learn about tracks?" he asked. "I see the baas and you are still young and I was thinking you have not hunted animals like lions and elephants before."

"Oh, *madala* (old man), we were very young when we first hunted elephant. But my bwana is a little bit crazy. He never shoots eland or kudu which are better to eat, so maybe you should teach him about those things."

Mac grinned and moved back onto the elephant tracks, kicking open a dung ball and touching the fresh surface with the back of his hand.

"Sergeant Mac, do you think they passed here at about sunrise?" I asked quietly, sidling up next to him. I had already checked some chewed mopane branches and could smell the familiar acid aromas of dung and urine, by now diluted after three or four hours of sunlight, to make my own assessment.

"Yah, Baas," came the soft reply, "Maybe four hours. I think they go slowly to a pan in this direction. Maybe they are there now. If we see the tracks going on a big path which is near here, then we go quickly to the water." I nodded agreement. Mac's local knowledge and experience of elephant would give us the opportunity for short cuts.

True to his prediction, we soon struck one of the great elephant highways so common in this part of the world, forming a huge network of links between the major waterholes and the Nuanetsi, Limpopo, Lundi and Sabi rivers. We stepped up our pace, but kept a close watch either side of the path in case the bulls had veered off. One stretch held us up where a herd of cow elephants had crossed our course, requiring a thorough check that the bulls had not followed them. The sparse, flattened grass made this very tricky, but we decided the faint traces on the rock-hard surface of the big

pathway further on were those of our quarry.

A distant trumpeting to the east told us that the cow herd had not proceeded to the pan ahead. Good. I certainly did not need complications caused by jumbos who were not involved in this hunt.

Soon, Mac halted to whisper that we were close to the waterhole. Pulling the ash bag from my shirt pocket, I checked the air flow was from east to west, giving Mac the okay to circle to our left while approaching the pan. Minutes later we heard the whoosh of an elephant blasting water over itself. Action time had arrived, the tingle of apprehension coursed through me, tension brought on the wide-awake effect as adrenalin prepared my body for quick-response mode. The mind concentrated, focussing crystal clear on the approaching showdown with the bulls. I inspected the Mannlicher in my hands, checked the sights had no debris or spider webs on them, felt the pressure of the slightly unfamiliar safety catch, raised the rifle to my shoulder and swung it here and there, aiming at odd trees, 'bonding' with my new weapon. It felt good.

I took the lead for the approach through the intervening patch of scrub-like, smashed mopane forest to where we could see the elephants standing in the water, drinking and spraying themselves, not thirty yards distant. The thought had already crossed my mind that I would certainly not shoot an animal in the pan itself, as that would ruin the water for the whole dry season. As the bulls were in no hurry to move out, I signalled to Mac and Tsuro to withdraw with me back into the bushes.

"Mac, Tsuro," I whispered, "go around the other side so they smell you. If you want to, shout a bit but watch out for them. I will wait for them to come away from the water on this side."

My companions moved off quietly. Three or four minutes, I reckoned, before the action starts, as I slipped through the cover towards the waterhole again. The scene had altered slightly as I peered through the leaves and tree trunks. I could see two bulls but not the third. So where the hell was he? I suddenly feared that Mac and Tsuro would walk into him unsuspectingly, or had they managed to check on the pan while doing their circle around it? I waited in suspense; a minute, two minutes, three... The tension built up, the intuitive warning said 'trouble'. That's what it was! Why wasn't I listening to my damn instinct two minutes ago?

Moving quickly along the edge of the bare ground surrounding the water, keeping an eye on the two elephants who still had their backsides towards me, I had covered a good distance along the perimeter when a loud 'whoof' erupted a few yards away in the bush, and in a flash Tsuro and Mac dashed out of the cover into the open just in front of me, the bull's huge mass

bursting forth in pursuit, trunk outstretched, heading for the kill. The Mannlicher was already in the firing position, tucked in snugly and foresight following the unseen brain, the trigger pressed. Not a sound heard nor the recoil on the shoulder felt, but my eyes watched as the mammoth creature collapsed in a great burst of thick dust just behind two little running figures.

The commotion had given the other two elephants a message of no ambiguity – fast-forward or we will be next! Partly to relieve tension, partly to make sure they had no second thoughts, I fired a shot into the water just as they rushed, with their baggy pants and curled-up tails, out of the pan. Like a pair of flop-eared steamrollers they smashed their way through the trees and out of sight. I could not help a giggle. God, I love these animals, came the silly thought while I reloaded the rifle with two fresh cartridges and reapplied the safety lever.

A few paces away, Mac and Tsuro stood next to the dead bull, watching me with grins on their faces. Mac spoke up, shaking his head for emphasis:

"Eeeeh, I was running too fast, but now I am old and Tsuro was leaving me behind for the elephant. I was about to die, for sure. Eeeh, thank you, Baas Richard." With a laugh, I gave each man a cigarette and sat down on the elephant's back foot.

"What happened?" I asked.

"We did not know this elephant had gone into the bush and we were passing between him and the edge of the pan. We were about to come to the open area to look for them, when he came from behind us," Tsuro explained.

I told my companions that I had been concerned on discovering one bull had left the pan, which was why I had come looking for them.

"No, Bwana, you weren't worried about us," quipped Tsuro. "You sent us, with no gun, to chase elephants away with shouting while you sat under a tree to smoke a cigarette. Then you came to look for us because you wanted a drink from the water-bag."

"Of course," I told him, "then when you were running away with my water-bag I wanted to shoot you but this stupid *nzou* was in the way. Now, pass the water please."

The 'last elephant' in typical msimbiti thicket

SIXTEEN

Death In The Corridor

Buffalo hunting is almost always demanding, not least because *nyati* has good eyes, ears and nose and, in areas where he is hunted, tends to be alert much of the time. The challenges, and hunting techniques required to achieve success, vary infinitely according to the circumstances and the objective of the hunter: Is he shooting to feed a labour force; to eliminate the animals for veterinary purposes; to collect a good trophy; to kill a rogue; to follow up a previously wounded animal; or 'for the pot' and some biltong? Is he after a single or several *'dhaka* boys' (old, often lone bulls with a propensity for rolling in mud); a herd of twenty or forty, or is it two hundred, four hundred animals? Is he hunting in riverine forest; dense jesse; open savannah; or on flat, treeless plains?

Tsuro and I had hunted buffalo in many combinations of these circumstances, but were soon to discover an entirely new brand of buffalo: The Galloping Ghosts of Guluene; never seen because they never stopped running!

Not far north of Mabala-uta, in the middle of the Gonarezhou, the Department of Tsetse Control had fenced off a block covering about six hundred square miles, extending westwards from the Mozambican border. Two small watercourses, the Guluene and Chefu rivers, traversed this area, giving it the name, Guluene-Chefu corridor, and along with the adjacent North-east/South-west corridor (almost a hundred miles long) virtually all large mammals had been exterminated to prevent tsetse flies spreading to the west and south.

Shortly after our elephant hunt with Sergeant Mac, I decided to visit the Guluene, having heard the tsetse guys complain of one cow elephant and

seven buffalo left behind in the corridor. Ah yes, the Secret Seven, remnants of the 'shot-to-hell' herds which everyone had had a go at, but which now had been undisturbed for some months. Maybe they had settled down a bit and would not be so wary and wild.

I took Sergeant Machivana along as I suspected the hunting would be difficult and his tracking abilities, bush craft and hunter's talents were first class. Furthermore I had discovered he was a good rifle shot, so we took the Winchester heavy-barrelled .375 for him. Tsuro was keen to take the Rigby .450, arguing that with all three of us armed, we could clean up the little herd in one fell swoop.

"So who is going to carry the water-bag, food bag and axe?" I asked him.

"We can take another game scout with us," was his quick reply.

"No. These buffalo have been hunted by every ranger for the past few years and all have failed to shoot them, because the *nyatis* are more clever than humans now. Four people is too many; even three of us is a crowd for this job. We will be lucky if we even see them. They are *mutakati* (bewitched)."

We spent our first day driving along the game fences, following odd tracks used by Tsetse Control people, and visiting some waterholes which Mac knew, trying to get an idea of the habits and movements of the group. The most striking observation we made was that the tracks we found at various places were always of running buffalo, confirming my concerns that the Galloping Ghosts had not been lulled into a calmer way of life after a long period of non-disturbance. With the thought of them having a third of a million acres to run around in, the possibility of ever catching up with these super-fit, super-charged, demented creatures looked like zero.

We were not happy to come across fresh tracks of a motor vehicle. We followed, duly arriving at a tsetse department camp site with several tents erected and a 7-ton truck loaded with fencing materials. The driver advised us they were in the corridor to repair and maintain the fences, and we should ask his boss for information on elephant and buffalo. Having vehicles and people cruising around was only going to make our buffalo more deranged, if that was possible, so I thought it might be helpful if I could find out how long this crowd intended to stay and which sections of fence they would be working on each day. At least we would know the buffalo would not be anywhere near them.

I walked over to a tent pitched under a large pod mahogany tree some distance from the main encampment, and was astonished to see a lone European man squatting in front of a large fire, hatless under the blazing midday sun, warming his hands, with a crate of beers next to him. As I approached he took a long swig from a bottle which he then placed on the

ground in front of himself near the fire as if to keep it warm! Holy Cow, I thought, is this guy also a nutcase, like the damn buffalo?

"Hi," I called out from a few yards away. No response for several seconds, then a cheerful invitation from the tousle-headed, bearded fellow.

"Pull up a chair and pour yourself a cup."

I glanced around but could see no chairs or tea party laid on. Without shifting his stare from the flames in front of him, he continued.

"Can't offer you a drink right now. Beers aren't cold yet. Never drink warm beer, specially in winter."

"No problem," I replied, relieved that I would not have to stand in the sun, drinking a 100 degree beer, conversing with this exotic chap. "I was passing by and wondered if you can tell me if any buffalo or recent tracks have been seen by your team?"

"Ah, buffalo. Yes. See them daily. All over the place. Dangerous buggers. They tried to get me once but I dodged behind a tree whereupon two of them collided and knocked themselves out cold. So I quickly cut their throats before they came to. Always carry a knife. You never know when it may be needed."

The raconteur had still not looked at me, his gaze fixed on the fire. Even his hot beer seemed forgotten.

"Well, thanks for the advice. I'll be on my way now. Cheers." I turned and walked hurriedly away, fearing he may become conversational and persistent. Maybe he had some rational moments, but I was not keen on waiting around for such an event.

Driving away from the camp I was doubled up in hysterics trying to describe my encounter to Tsuro and Mac. They loved the bit about the buffalo, particularly as the truck driver had told them the white man had not been out of the camp in the ten days since their arrival. Nor had the fence gang seen any buffalo, but they knew a small group still inhabited the corridor. They had seen spoor of a single cow elephant which had been reported to their crazy field officer, known by them as Hungwe (fish eagle), the name being bestowed on him due to his habit of bursting into a high-pitched, screeching laugh when reading his books, sometimes at all hours of the night. I heard later that he left the tsetse department after a bare three months and was not heard of again.

Early the following day we chanced on elephant tracks, those of a smallish cow, which confirmed the accounts from the tsetse people. After half the morning wandering through miles of dry country, mostly grassy savannah or mopane scrubland, the spoor led into a stony area of higher ground covered in dense stands of msimbiti trees. When hearing the animal

feeding ahead, I approached it alone, knowing that the slightest foreign noise would alarm it, and three people in msimbiti cannot guarantee silent progress. I shot the elephant from a few paces when a lucky opening through the tree stems and leaves gave me a fleeting view of its head.

The death of the last jumbo in the corridor was a rather sad event, I felt. The cow, almost a dwarf, it seemed, of under seven feet high with very slim tusks but certainly not a young animal, was living a most unnatural life. On its own, cut off from the herds roaming outside the fences, and apparently unwilling to break through and join others of its kind all added up to a very unusual mentality. I shut away my feeling of remorse with the realisation that she had no future.

We eventually found fresh spoor of the seven buffalo, two days after the elephant hunt. They had galloped across the track we were driving along, a habit they had whenever a road or open space had to be traversed, even though in this case they had crossed during the night. Parking the Land Rover in some shade, we were on the spoor as the sun cleared the treetops and warmed the fresh morning air, promising a long, hot day ahead with thirst, mopane bees, sun-scorched arms and legs and uncountable thorn scratches to add to the certainty of a difficult hunt. The group had kept running for at least a mile before slowing to a walk, then lying down for a pre-dawn rest. They had risen and immediately run for a long way before stopping to graze where patches of 'sweet' grasses grew along the banks of a dry watercourse.

Tracking the seven buffalo was not so difficult where they had run, particularly over dry ground in mopane country, but we were slowed down in areas of thick grass when the animals eased to a walk. The sun was searing out of a white-hot sky, not a breath of wind to relieve the intensity of oven-heat, no shade to hide from strength-sapping temperatures. Persistent swarms of tiny mopane bees tickled as they sought to enter eyes and nose and settled on bare skin to suck perspiration, trying our patience beyond measure. Mac suddenly froze, then sank slowly down to the ground. Tsuro and I followed suit. After six hours of purgatory, we were not going to let things go wrong at this stage. There would be no second chances, at least for today, if not for the foreseeable future.

Mac indicated silently that the herd was amongst some bushes just ahead, with one standing up but partly hidden. Rising slowly to a kneeling position, I searched the scrub before seeing a tail flick from behind a bush, indicating the standing buffalo had moved position so was obviously not dozing on its feet. I looked for an approach route where I could creep up behind small bushes or clumps of grass, then began the slow stalk. Sitting

down with the .458 laid across my waist, I 'inch-wormed' myself forward, feet lifted and placed ahead quietly, body then jacked off the ground on clenched fists to follow. This method means one's head is up, keeping a view on the scene ahead, and the rifle is quickly at hand. The bad news is the number of hard, sharp or prickly objects that place themselves under the backside and hands during progress!

My objective was an isolated bush which I hoped would allow me to stand up without being detected, having a fairly wide-angled view with few obstructions, as I knew I would be lucky if I got off two shots at these animals. The .458 was loaded with solids only, and under these circumstances I was prepared to take shots which would normally be risky. As usual, I had been mentally rehearsing various scenarios of buffalo running here and there, and where I should place my shots accordingly, a practice which I believed focussed my mind to co-ordinate reactions once the shooting started.

Rising very slowly behind my piece of cover, various flicking ears and fly-swatting tails came into view. Suddenly, as if on cue to a danger signal, all seven buffalo were on their feet and instantly into full gallop, an amazingly agile performance for such massive animals. They had not pin-pointed the source of alarm, and fortunately went off at an angle instead of directly away from me. I shot at three different animals before the group disappeared amongst the bushes, leaving a cloud of dust hanging in the still air. Seconds later, a crash followed by a muted bellow indicated one was down. With the Mannlicher reloaded and ready, I walked rapidly on the tracks of the herd, Mac with his .375 on my left and Tsuro behind us. The first buffalo, already dead, came into view and we passed by, following more blood and watching ahead and to each side. A hundred yards further we saw another buffalo standing side-on and both Mac and I fired simultaneously. The animal dropped in it's tracks and was dead when we reached it. We promptly recharged our rifles and searched about for more blood. Tsuro soon picked up the spoor of the remainder and confirmed the wounded one was there when frothy lung blood was seen on a bush.

The group had run in a northerly direction in order to go downwind and this also led them into areas of msimbiti thickets. We were well into one of these, still following blood from the wounded one, when I felt a persistent urge to keep glancing at an extra tall tree thrusting above the surrounding thicket, some yards ahead but to the right of our direction of pursuit. Stepping forward quickly, I tapped Mac on the shoulder and halted our progress. We all squatted down, attempting to peer through the dense leaves and branches of the msimbiti but to no avail. Sweat trickled down

into my eyes, and now knowing my intuition was giving a good signal, I was reluctant to wipe my face in case the buffalo attacked at that moment. Our scent would have permeated through the thicket by now, I thought, and if the animal was indeed waiting nearby, it would be aware we were very close. Mac, now kneeling, looked tense with the .375 gripped tightly, pointing ahead. Tsuro was close behind me, too close really, but he caught my eye and made a small indication with his hand which I took to mean I should move to our right where there might be a small gap to get a better view. From our present spot, we could not see more than two to three yards in any direction.

Rising slowly off my haunches, but remaining bent low to see better, I crept slowly through the wall of leaves; a pace, two paces, three, four, stop to peer around and listen, and look for the next position to place my foot silently. I was already out of sight of my companions only a few feet away, but saw what I hoped was a break in the vegetation. The long barrel of the Mannlicher was a bit of a hazard in these conditions, but by holding the muzzle up, more or less in my range of vision, I kept it from snagging. My attention was abruptly drawn to a quiet wheezy sound, very close, just to my right. The lung-shot buffalo could only be waiting to attack. If it had wanted to escape it would have done so already. I froze, unable to see anything and fearful that I was incapable of coping with the impending onslaught.

An impulsive thought came, and I picked up a fist-sized stone, quickly tossing it over the scrubby msimbiti in front of me to land five or six yards away. The sounds of the rock falling through leaves and landing on the stony ground was instantly followed by tremendous crashes of snapping branches as the buffalo charged the spot. A quick step forward brought me to a gap in the trees and the buffalo, a large bull, seeing me at the same instant, swung his massive bulk around and came, head high with bloody foam covering his nose. The .458 bullet instantly stopped him, passing through the front edge of the boss into the brain, and as the great body fell forward, it snapped a brittle ironwood stem which came down at me, hitting the rifle stock and my left fore-arm with force. I shot the buffalo again through the head, then reloaded magazine and chamber, retired a few yards away and sat down on a rock to massage my arm which was becoming very painful.

"Tsuro, Mac," I called quietly. They appeared and surveyed the scene before asking me what had been going on. Only then did I realise that just two or three minutes had passed since I left them behind; it had seemed ages ago, and the recent tension affected me with a feeling of great fatigue, though undoubtedly the heat had also taken its toll. Between drinking water and smoking a cigarette, I told my friends the recent events, only leaving out

the part when I had momentarily felt helpless and scared.

"When I saw you sitting here rubbing your arm, I thought the *nyati* had knocked you down," Mac said in a concerned tone.

"*Madala* Mac, the bwana has good *midzimu* (family spirits) looking after him," Tsuro interjected. "You saw how they told him when we were close to the buffalo and he stopped us all walking into the ambush. But don't worry about the tree falling on him, that is just a warning that he is not hunting rabbits or springhares."

Old Mac laughed. He had, I think, come to partly understand and accept the unusual relationship which existed between myself and Tsuro; the initial suspicion or even jealousy that I suspected he felt towards Tsuro on our arrival at Mabala-uta had now been replaced with comradeship. He found Tsuro respectful but open and friendly, a hard worker and fearless hunter, and importantly, never a know-all or big deal.

Returning to the Land Rover by way of the other two buffalo, we found they were both old cows. We removed a hindquarter from one, which Mac and Tsuro carried on a pole over their shoulders while I took over Mac's rifle plus the water-bag and axe from Tsuro. Driving past the tsetse department camp, we stopped briefly while Mac explained to the truck driver the location of the three carcasses to be retrieved. I stayed in the vehicle for fear of being accosted by the European fellow with the mental aberrations! We arrived back at our camp at sundown, dead tired, hungry and thirsty. At any rate, I certainly was. While Tsuro cooked supper for us, Mac began cutting the buffalo meat into strips to dry and I cleaned the rifles and enjoyed a wash.

Lying on my canvas stretcher that night, I thought about the day's hunt, the prospects of catching up with the four survivors, and their forlorn existence in this corridor of death. I wondered about this great tract of game country being subjected to the holocaust of the Department of Tsetse Control; there were many questions I needed answered.

For a further five days we pursued the group of buffalo without so much as a glimpse of them. They always seemed to run downwind, and appeared only to rest and graze during the night. We tried sitting at a couple of pans for the night, but the animals drank elsewhere. We gave up and returned to Mabala-uta, tired, footsore, thorn-torn and needing a break from the lifeless atmosphere of the Guluene corridor. I was enormously pleased to hear that shortly after our efforts the buffalo escaped to freedom through the game fence where an elephant bull had damaged it. I hoped they could rehabilitate to a normal life again.

Tsuro with Timoti's buffalo

Mopane woodland with elephant herd

Tsuro with crop-raider bull (photo taken from top of anthill)

Gonarezhou has huge expanses of scrub mopane

Donkey safari crossing the Nuanetsi river

SEVENTEEN

The Buffalo Man

Poaching of game in the Nuanetsi section of Gonarezhou by the tribesmen of Sengwe Tribal Area was not of any great significance during these times. The Mabala-uta game scouts patrolled our area on foot and arrests for killing animals were few and far between. My impression of the local population was of old men, women and kids to teenager size. Working-age men all went away to civilization to find jobs and earn money, which I felt certain was the main reason for the low level of poaching.

One unusual case arose when one of the scouts came to report he had left his colleague with a local man they had arrested for killing a buffalo. Not wanting to leave the evidence in case other people or lions and hyenas damaged the exhibit, the second scout and poacher camped at the carcass while I was summoned. On the long drive south towards the Mozambican border, I questioned the scout about the case, having assumed the hunter had simply snared a buffalo. However, it appeared that he had killed a bull using a spear only; no snare, no dogs, nobody else assisting him! I suggested to my scout that the man had a rifle or muzzle-loader which he had used, then hid it away after shooting the animal, but was told the hole in the buffalo was made by a spear, a whole spear and nothing but a spear.

We managed to get the Land Rover right to the scene of the crime as I intended to collect all the meat for our people back at the station. A heavily-built African wearing tatters of khaki clothing and *manyatella* (sandals made from car tyres) rose from under a bush to greet me. Probably twice my age, I could not help but hold him in respect, seeing the huge buffalo bull which he had apparently killed gladiator-style, lying in the shadow of a tree. Tsuro

and I examined the dead beast, turning it over to check for wounds. The only mark was above the shoulder where the spear had gone into the lungs.

We all sat down in a shady spot to hear the man's story. He told us his name was Timoti, that his home was not far west of the Nuanetsi river, in a kraal near to the one in which the elderly daughter of Bvekenya lived. I had heard of one or two of the old ivory hunter's offspring still living and was intrigued to hear confirmation of this, deciding then to try to meet her. Timoti described how the people were suffering from hunger and sickness (no doubt malnutrition), partly due to a strange disease affecting their millet crops, but also from elephant and baboon damage to both grain and other foods such as pumpkins, melons and vegetables. He had decided to go hunting and duly followed three buffalo bulls from where they drank at the Nuanetsi, into the protected area where he found them and killed one. Such a lot of meat, properly smoke-cured, would last his family for weeks.

"So, Timoti, you just found the buffalo and killed it! How did you get so close to stab it, and where were the other two bulls?" I asked while examining the spear in my hands. The blade was only a foot long, with the short stem fixed into a heavy hardwood shaft about five feet in length.

"There are two animals that a person can get close to: the elephant and the buffalo. It is very difficult to spear a kudu, nyala or impala, unless you have dogs," Timoti explained. "The problem," he went on, "is that a buffalo's ribs overlap each other, so when I am close, I also have to find the right way to stab the animal for the spear to go between the ribs. I found this bull lying by himself in the scrub mopane; the other two had walked on. I moved quickly. The wind was strong so he did not hear me, and his head was facing into the wind. Also, the side on which I came was a good place to put my spear through the ribs, stabbing forwards into the lungs. After spearing him, I ran fast through the mopane bushes to a big tree where I stopped. I heard the buffalo running away, I think all three of them, so I went back and followed. Soon I found my spear on the ground and plenty of blood. That was over there." He pointed towards a group of tamboti trees growing along a dry river bed fifty yards away.

"Okay, you have told me only half the story," I interrupted him.

"No, Baas, that is all."

"No, Timoti. You have spoken as a hunter who has done these things many times. You have speared buffalo before this one. Tell me about them. I will not tell the police because it does not concern them."

Tsuro spoke up, reassuring him that I was not trying to trap him into making a confession. To put him at his ease, I asked the two game scouts to start butchering the buffalo where they would be out of earshot.

A tale of incredible daring unfolded, and I believed every word of it. This Nimrod of Nuanetsi, a fellow hunter whose skills and courage were way ahead of my own, had single-handedly killed eight buffalo bulls, plus a lion which had commandeered one of his kills. No dogs, no snares, no poisoned arrows; just his trusty spear. He hunted only to feed his community, never for profit, and as most of the animals were killed in the area before it was designated as a wildlife preserve, the only real technicality was that of hunting dangerous game without using the legal minimum rifle of .375 calibre! A minor detail about which he was totally ignorant of course.

I asked Timoti how he killed the lion, as it presumably was not fast asleep when he speared it. He related how he had returned to his village to organise porters to come and collect a buffalo he had killed at a pool in the Nuanetsi river. He returned ahead of his friends to start cutting up the carcass, only to find a young but full-grown lion eating the buffalo. From a safe distance he shouted and threw a couple of stones at the cat which departed up the river bank with a few grunts of annoyance.

A short while later Timoti looked up from the job at hand, probably his hunter's intuition at work, to see the lion watching him from the top of the ten foot high bank. The youthful lion must have momentarily been at a loss as to its next move, by which time Timoti had hurled his heavy buffalo spear at it, the blade going into its neck. The lion went mad, thrashing around roaring and gurgling till it fell down the bank, landing next to the buffalo, at which Timoti promptly rushed *up* the bank to watch the death throes of the lion from above! The approaching villagers, hearing the commotion, came running to save their hero from the lion, only to find Timoti calmly straightening the blade of his spear in the fork of a tree.

I had decided on our next move, so after loading the bits and pieces of buffalo on the Land Rover, we set off for Timoti's kraal, arriving there late in the afternoon. I lectured the people on the illegalities of poaching game on State property, and then unloaded pieces of rib cage, the neck and offal and presented them to the old headman. Leaving the game scouts with the Land Rover, I told Timoti to take Tsuro and myself to the village where Bvekenya's daughter lived. We found her sitting alone on a log under the eaves of her thatched hut, an elderly woman, clearly of mixed race or 'coloured' to use the southern African term. She was not particularly interested in discussing her father, but said she remembered him passing through the village on occasions, when her family lived further down the Nuanetsi in Mozambique. He always left meat and either money, a blanket or some food with the young girl's mother.

I told her, using Timoti as interpreter as she only spoke the Shangaan

language, that many people knew of her father from a book that had been written about his life as an elephant hunter in this area. I did not attempt to explain how, as a boy, I had been besotted by the adventures of Cecil 'Bvekenya' Barnard, and to meet one of his direct descendants was almost a historic moment. She would not have understood the romantic thoughts of a young white man.

We left some buffalo meat with her for which she seemed genuinely thankful and bade farewell to the small group of tribespeople who had gathered around. Having kept Timoti in suspense I told him on the walk back to his kraal that I was not going to hand him over to the police for prosecution, but would be taking the rest of the buffalo meat as punishment for poaching. Secretly, I disliked the idea of one day having to drive all the way to attend a court case at Nuanetsi Police Station. What a waste of time, I thought, and my sympathies lay with this intrepid hunter anyway. The poachers I hated were those who set scores of steel wire snares and then left the trapped animals to die and rot.

Shortly after the Timoti episode I was called by the District Commissioner's staff living at Malipati, a small outpost on the river downstream of Buffalo Bend, to deal with a buffalo said to be a danger to them and the local inhabitants. Taking Tsuro along, I visited the Malipati post where a district messenger described how, the previous day, he had been pursued by a buffalo while cycling along a path to a village. Apparently the villagers had also complained that several of them had narrow escapes from this buffalo over the past couple of weeks. The D.C.'s man described the area a mile or two down river where we should visit to look for the miscreant.

I had brought the short-stocked Rigby .450 double with the idea that, if the opportunity arose, Tsuro should use it to shoot the buffalo while I backed up with the Mannlicher. He had been pestering me since we had arrived at Mabala-uta about the necessity of him becoming accustomed to the rifle so that he could assist in difficult situations, such as shooting elephant or buffalo that were about, or had just managed, to turn me into a has-been. I strongly suspected that he also wanted to be a notch or two up the pecking order of the African staff at the station and by shooting some big game he would gain a little acceptance amongst the others, all of whom were of a different tribe so he was definitely the odd man out.

We found fresh spoor of a single buffalo crossing the vehicle track and immediately saw the left front hoof was dragging. We had been told the aggressive bull ran with an unusual gait which, coupled with the fact that he was too slow to catch up with his intended victims, meant there was

something wrong. To be more certain we were after the right animal I told Tsuro we would try, if the conditions allowed, to get him to charge us. With both of us armed, there was no real danger from a single, half-crocked buffalo, no matter how viciously he might attack.

We caught up with him within half an hour, actually hearing him ripping up grass as he fed before seeing the great black bulk moving through patches of combretum scrub. Checking the slight air-drift with my ash bag, I indicated to Tsuro that we get upwind of the animal and see what his reaction would be. We circled ahead and waited on the edge of an open area where we thought he was headed. Tsuro was ready with his double .450, both chambers holding solids. A sudden crash in the bushes twenty paces away revealed the bull coming at full charge through the scrub. However, on reaching the clearing he stopped, head high, glaring at us. The Rigby boomed, the buffalo staggered a few steps to one side, Tsuro fired the left barrel and the old bull collapsed.

"Reload," I prompted Tsuro who wore an ammunition belt with enough rounds to take on a whole herd.

Tsuro's shots were good, the first going in at the junction of neck and chest, the second through the shoulders, maybe a little high. We discussed the possible reasons for the bull stopping his charge on seeing us, and decided either he could not understand why we did not run away or else he scented me, a white man, which flustered him. Elephants frequently react with fear or aggression on scenting a white person where the same animals completely ignore black folks, so there is no reason why buffalo should not also distinguish between the two races.

We called on the district messengers to help us with the carcass, and while skinning it we found pieces of a copper-jacketed bullet inside the knee joint of the left front leg which we had noticed looked swollen. Although an old wound which had healed well, I felt anger at the man who had done this thing, a stupid damn thing, to this fine animal.

Manjinji Pan, a bird paradise

EIGHTEEN

Elephants Here,
There, Everywhere

It took the whole day to find the little Venda kraal hidden in rugged, rocky country near the Bubi river, not far from its junction with the Limpopo. We had visited the Crook's Corner vicinity where the borders of South Africa, Southern Rhodesia and Mozambique meet, a favourite haunt of Bvekenya and other dubious characters. The magnificent riverine forest captured my imagination; huge evergreen trees, including sycamore figs by the hundred and an understorey of dense shrubbery interwoven with game paths which was home to a host of birds, monkeys, bushbuck, impala and nyala. And bull elephants. Big tuskers, whose vast ranges would include the Kruger National Park, Mozambique and my Gonarezhou, just as in the days of *The Ivory Trail*.

Turning north, we left the green belt of plenty and drove into the rough country overlooking the Groot Vlei expanse of grassy plains, probably once the course of the Limpopo river. The Land Rover stumbled and crawled along stony elephant paths which eventually led us to the isolated kraals of the community of Venda people, most of whose tribe lived in Northern Transvaal, situated to the west of the Kruger Park. A small spring in the little valley provided the people and wildlife with water, so we set up our simple camp a short distance away, not wanting to disturb the animals nor prevent them from drinking. As the sun settled over a hazy horizon in a blaze of African reds, yellows and oranges, a group of Venda men came to greet us and ask us to chase away the elephants which were eating their crops.

"We are here to hunt the elephants. We had word via Chief Sengwe about your problem," replied Luke, the game scout I had brought along with Tsuro. This drew nods of approval and words of gratitude, then came an odd

request. I could not understand a word they spoke, but Luke, rather embarrassed, interpreted.

"They say some of the children in the village have never seen a white man and ask the baas if they can be brought tomorrow to meet you."

My first reaction was to burst out laughing, but I quickly realised that the elders may think that ill-mannered or feel humiliated, so I cheerfully told them that as we would be gone early to look for elephants, they must bring the kids to our camp when we returned. Out of the corner of my eye I saw Tsuro taking great pains to light a cigarette, 'displacement behaviour' he often resorted to when desperate not to burst into hysterics. Once the Vendas left I studiously ignored Tsuro, knowing full well he was dying to pull my leg about this, although I was also most amused with the thought that I was to be a historic event for some fellow human beings!

I sat in my government-issue chair (camp: folding, rangers-for-the-use-of) at my government-issue table (etc.), writing my diary in the light of a quietly hissing gas lamp, listening to the night birds and insects all around. The water at the spring was the centre of attention for many creatures from miles around. A warm, mellow evening and a feeling of relaxed contentment brought back memories of many wonderful nights spent in the wilds, the majority of which had been preceded by days of equally superb big game hunting. Once again I was in another world, far, far from that considered the norm by my family, friends or acquaintances, but living the life I craved and which no money could buy. Thank heavens that, although only twenty years old, I was able to fully appreciate and steep myself in the ambience, for I think that sort of life has become extinct.

I watched Luke and Tsuro sitting ten yards away in the flickering firelight. Each was cooking food; Luke for the two of them and Tsuro doing my supper, quietly discussing something or other which occasionally brought a chuckle of amusement from Tsuro. He certainly had a way of getting along with most people, his quick humour being a great attribute.

A plate piled with steaming rice, peas and impala steak was placed in front of me.

"Thank you, Tsuro."

"Bwana, you made a mistake with those people," Tsuro announced, standing back. "When they asked to bring the children to look at you, you should, by African custom, have asked for a favour in return."

"I want no favours from them, Tsuro. What can they give anyway?" I asked.

"Two girls, one for me and one for Luke," was the response.

"Luke is too old and you are too young for girls. But if we shoot an elephant, then you two can go and find your own girls. I don't want Venda

misikana in my camp, thank you," I told him.

"Yes, but I think it is better to be admired by girls than to be stared at by bush-children like a photograph. Think of what they will say about you when they go home!"

"You talk rubbish. Go and eat. We are hunting early tomorrow, and I need to dream of elephant bulls. Maybe we will have luck." I tucked into my welcome supper with a hearty appetite. It had been a long day, full of interest seeing new territory. Now with the promise of some good hunting, I was looking forward to the morrow.

Waking long before dawn I saw a figure hunched near the campfire, coaxing the coals into a little blaze of flame. It was Jecki, a middle-aged Venda from the village who had volunteered to accompany us. Knowing the district intimately he would be invaluable, and would almost certainly be a good tracker. Greeting him, I sat down at the fireside and scraped away some fine, white powder to fill my ash bag, a little ritual I always enjoyed at the start of a hunting day. How often had those tiny clouds of tell-tale ash guided me to success, or warned of a potentially dangerous situation to be avoided? I asked Jecki in *Chilapalapa*, the lingua franca of southern Africa, whether elephants had visited the village during the night. Yes, he replied, and that was the reason for him coming early to our camp. He thought they would drink at another spring some miles to the west, as they obviously had not used our waterhole. According to him, the local crop-raiding bulls tended to drink at night, then spend the day feeding and sleeping before wandering towards the natives' fields after sundown. Sometimes they would go down to the Limpopo for days, living in the luscious riparian forest, or even crossing the river to move south into the Kruger Park, but would return sooner or later.

Leaving Luke to attend to minor camp duties and glean information from the locals about goings-on in the district, Tsuro and I followed Jecki, heading west and by-passing his kraal, until the rising sun cast enough light for us to start seeing tracks. After crossing some older spoor, we found that of several bull elephants which had travelled from the direction of the village. While tracking these animals where they had meandered along feeding off trees, we established there were five in the group, one with particularly huge feet. I wondered if he had tusks to match, but quickly remembered that I was no longer an ivory hunter. As a game ranger there was no point in going for big tusks, rather preserve those bulls for their breeding value.

After a while Jecki called a summit conference. We should now head directly to the spring he knew of, to save time, as he was sure the bulls had

gone there. Tsuro and I had no objections, and two hours of fast walking brought us to the waterhole, complete with elephant spoor, including that of 'Big Feet'.

A couple more hours of difficult tracking followed, only for us to find the bulls had scented us before we knew they were anywhere nearby. They had moved off in a hurry, but not at the run. Long strides, toes dug in a little at the front edge of footprints, but no bulldozing of vegetation. Not panicky but rather a hurried departure. Now close to midday, we decided to have a half-hour rest, a snack and a smoke. By not pursuing the bulls immediately, might also allow them to feel relaxed and stop to rest in the heat.

We caught up with the five during the afternoon in fairly open country with plenty of tall grass and few trees, and with the distant dark belt of Limpopo forest visible to the south. The immense body of Big Feet was instantly recognisable, his massive, thick tusks also very distinctive with *both* being broken off three to four feet from the lip, jagged but somewhat worn down. Definitely way over 100 pounds a side at one time, probably down to sixty or seventy now. And nearby, two nice tuskers with fifty pounds a side or more. The other two, both standing under a tree, were youngsters and I put them down quickly with brain shots. To my surprise, the three big bulls rushed away to the north-west, almost the direction we had come from, instead of heading for the Limpopo and the sanctuary of the Kruger Park.

We trudged wearily into camp late in the afternoon, Jecki turning off earlier to spread the good news to the villages. I had decided to move camp quickly to the spring where the elephants had drunk so that we could hunt further west and north than was possible from the present camp. While Luke, Tsuro and I packed our bedrolls and cooking utensils into the Land Rover, several men, women and half a dozen children, aged about three up to six, arrived and sat quietly under a tree watching us. A couple of the men spoke to Luke, thanking him for the elephant meat they were about to receive, while the kids watched my every move: fuelling the Land Rover; folding my stretcher, shaking sand out of my shoes; drinking coffee etc. Of course Tsuro enjoyed passing snide remarks. He shut up when I told him to lead the way!

Fortunately we found a good elephant path for most of the way, driving at jogging pace and arriving at the spring just before dark. Not bothering to unpack table, chair or flysheet, I put my stretcher under a tree a few yards from the Land Rover while the two Africans made a fire and prepared supper. They laid their blanket rolls down between the fire and the Land Rover, and we all turned in after a wash at the spring, twenty yards away on the stony slope of the little depression. Guineafowl chattered with alarm,

probably frightened by a hunting eagle owl. Nightjars on silent wings hawked insects around us as the moon rose over the rolling countryside, and I fell asleep contentedly.

The moon was high when I awoke suddenly, all my senses fully alert and intuitively feeling danger. Slowly raising my head and simultaneously picking up the loaded .458 with my right hand, I looked about but saw nothing moving in the moonlight. I propped myself up on my left elbow and turned to look behind me just as the towering bulk of an elephant appeared between me and the spring. The sight of the great moonlight-white stubby tusks momentarily shocked me. It was Big Feet. He stopped, broadside on, his trunk down, fiddling with something on the ground not more than ten or twelve feet from my head. I was petrified. He was so close that I felt there was no escape, nothing I could do. A brain shot was not only impossible but if successful, he would fall on me. Beyond his legs I saw more legs, those of the other two bulls at the waterhole. The absolute silence was unnerving. I suddenly thought the bull was remembering my scent from the hunt and was contemplating which of the three bedrolls held his enemy. The hated scent of the white hunter. Why did he not go and drink water, why come near me and the Land Rover? Still he stood, casting his vast black shadow towards my bed, the trunk still now, the right tusk gleaming in the sky, menacing, intimidating.

I swallowed hard to moisten my fear-dried throat while inching the Mannlicher forward to point towards the bull, my right thumb easing the safety catch off. I then spoke very quietly in a low tone to the bull.

"Nzou," I rumbled softly, "go away, go away." I swallowed again, sweating and breathless, and repeated the words. I cleared my throat gently, as black folk do when they are nervous. The elephant, obviously aware that he had been detected, turned away and strode to the water to join his friends. Slipping off my bed, I crept to the Land Rover and stood next to it, feeling shaken but highly relieved to be unhurt and now in control of the situation. These animals were unpredictable, unlike those living around camp sites like Mana Pools. The bulls drank in silence for a long time, then moved off in single file, disappearing into the trees like grey ghosts.

I sat down next to the coals of the campfire, lit a cigarette and put the coffee pot on to heat up.

"Tsuro, Luke. Wake up." They stirred, then Tsuro sat up and stared at me.

"What's wrong? Why are you holding your rifle?" he asked.

"That giant elephant was here with his brothers. Just now he was standing next to you, watching you."

"You had a bad dream," Tsuro replied. "No elephants have been..." He

stopped mid-sentence and sniffed; "Eeh! Sure, I can smell them now."

Luke sat up smartly when he heard this. I laughed at the look on his face as the flickering flames lit up the scene.

"You're too slow, Luke. They have gone because I told them to leave us alone. I told them Jecki shot their friends."

I recounted the events of the past twenty-odd minutes, then went with my torch to look for whatever it was the big bull had been sniffing in the short grass. I found my face flannel, which I had dropped when coming from my wash at the spring, twisted in amongst the grass stems as if he had tried to tie it in a knot with grass. Well, I thought, I'm glad it wasn't me tied in knots. The bull probably disliked my brand of bath soap anyway.

We walked the area for two more days but found only one other group of kraals; Shangaan people who had not seen elephants for some weeks. Once we crossed the tracks of Big Feet and his two accomplices heading south. I was certain they were going down to the Limpopo after finding us still hanging around these parts.

Having collected our ivory from Jecki's village, we headed back to Gonarezhou, stopping to visit one of the most beautiful spots in the whole south-eastern lowveld, Manjinji Pan. A flat, alluvial flood plain, probably a couple of thousand acres in extent, lay along the west bank of the Nuanetsi. A beautiful parkland of lush grass, shrubs and huge trees; the biggest leadwoods I have ever seen covered the plain, in the centre of which lay the half-mile long oxbow lake, Manjinji. The scimitar-shaped stretch of water, only a few feet deep and eighty to a hundred yards in width, supported an incredible mass of life. Lofty acacia albidas, fever trees, sausage trees and Natal mahoganies towered over the jungle-like thickets that ringed the water. Millions of water lilies flowered in the warm, clear lake. The bird life was astounding. Thousands of weaver nests of various species hung from thorny acacias and open-billed storks sat around near their untidy nests in other trees. Egyptian geese, pygmy geese, white-faced ducks, spurwinged geese and knob-billed ducks flew back and forth calling, splashing down and taking off in a non-stop frenzy of activity. Waders, herons, egrets and jacanas all added noise and motion along the water's edge. Coucals, louries, parrots, several species of dove and all manner of smaller birds were in abundance in this paradise. A few native settlements were scattered around the area and their cattle and goats drank at the pan, as did occasional herds of elephant. Although the people tilled patches of land, there was little degradation of the habitat at that time. The ghastly scourge of Africa, human over-population, was yet to begin its destruction of this jewel of nature.

NINETEEN

Wanderlust

The hankering to explore the proposed game reserve on foot had been growing in my mind since arriving in Gonarezhou, particularly as I had the perfect means of transport for an extended safari. The station owned five donkeys and proper pack-saddles to go on them, ideal for wandering through the wilderness, totally self-contained and independent apart from water requirements. This simply meant planning my moves to find water within the range of the donkeys' walking abilities. I took along one of the game scouts who knew something about the area, plus a map which was already marked with several of the major pans. Besides, the Nuanetsi river held permanent water at many places even at the end of the dry season, so there should be no difficulty in finding sufficient water.

I looked forward to getting into the least accessible parts to find out what game lived there, whether there were waterholes as yet unknown and any sign of poaching or old roads which could be opened up for future access. I had also planned to make a sortie or two into the tribal lands, not only to check on poaching and 'show the flag', but possibly deal with any problem elephants. The main reason for my enthusiasm to go off on this trip however, was simply to disappear from 'civilization' for more than just a few days, and live the free life of a 'Bvekenya' in unspoilt, wild Africa.

Although we had five donkeys, only four were saddled in case one had a mishap or suffered from saddle-sores, then we could keep going without dumping kit or provisions. We loaded up maize meal, dried and canned vegetables, tins of bully beef and some cooking oil as our basic foodstuffs, intending to shoot birds or small game as needed. The luxuries of coffee, tea and sugar, plus cigarettes, were added. Clothes, a spare pair of shoes,

cooking pots, blankets and the flysheet of my little government-issue tent were divided out amongst the pack-saddles, a job that John, the game scout accompanying us, was adept at.

Besides John and Tsuro, the fourth member of the party was a young Shangaan named Willie, who had come to work as a general labourer at the station, but soon became Tsuro's pal and was often called upon to help around my house doing odd jobs. Very quiet to the point of being shy, Willie was an unassuming character who made up for his academic under-achievements with the brute strength of his stocky, muscular build and, as I later discovered, fearlessness and excellent tracking skills. He had a great smile when one could be coaxed out of him. Something to do with a total lack of imagination maybe, but it was pretty difficult to detect any emotions stirring the soul of our Willie. This, I decided, also accounted for his zero perception of danger, as opposed to being courageous in the face of peril. To stand unmoved, as he did many, many times, armed with a water-bag and small axe in the face of an onslaught by screaming, angry cow elephants, often in impossibly dense forest, while dead bodies crashed down and my rifle became too hot to handle, required a delightful obliviousness to the possibility of personal harm. Willie was indeed a star; not a supernova of course, more a star whose light has not quite reached Earth. A good guy to have around in my little world anyway.

Besides the .458, I took along a recently acquired .22 rifle, for which I had traded a .38 revolver with the aforesaid Tinky Haslam. I promptly fitted the tiny Browning 8-shot repeater with scope and silencer, and to this day it ranks as my most used weapon. It was ideal for doves, guineafowl, francolin and sandgrouse; all of which were plentiful in the various habitats through which we travelled. The heavy rifle was necessary in case of hostilities from elephants by day or night and lions by night, as well as the possible need to go after crop-raiders in the tribal areas. The Mannlicher and I had become inseparable by now, and I never left home without it.

We dawdled out of Mabala-uta the first day, travelling gently so that the beasts of burden could become accustomed to their pack-saddles and the sounds and smells of the strange surroundings. Besides which, we did not have to be anywhere at any time, to do anything or meet anyone. In other words, we had successfully dropped out of the 'rat race'. Crossing the Nuanetsi's sandy bed at Buffalo Bend, we meandered downstream for a couple of miles then set up camp amongst big Natal mahoganies next to pools in the river.

After lunch, John oversaw the donkeys while they drank and grazed along the banks, and I went downstream with Tsuro and Willie, criss-crossing the

river bed to stroll through patches of alluvial soil supporting beautiful groves of tamarind, nyala berry and sausage trees inhabited by kudu, impala, nyala, baboons and monkeys. Later in the afternoon the herds of elephant began arriving along the river.

We spent several days in this idyllic existence, wandering from the river into drier country where we camped next to large pans, exploring the surrounding areas, locating unmapped waterholes and making notes of major elephant highways and game animals we had seen. At night, the donkeys were tethered to trees in a close group with a fire or two burning on one side, while we slept on the other with the saddles and food packs laid on branches or broken trees, also as close to us as possible. Most nights we heard lions, usually distant, but on a couple of occasions visiting us to investigate the possibilities of a donkey dinner, forcing me to stay alert, .458 in hand, stoking the fires until the cats moved on. Much the same procedure for inquisitive hyena, but I thought leopards were no threat to us, the donkeys or our belongings. Unlike many of their brethren living in Africa's National Parks, these leopards were still wary of humans and again, maybe the even less-familiar scent of a white man helped keep them at a respectful distance. Of course there was no shortage of prey for them, and I did not hear of any cases of man-eaters while living in the district.

The herds of cow elephant were a different matter, and I had experienced first-hand the much-discussed aggressiveness of these animals, both towards people and motor cars. We took great pains to avoid them as an attack would have scattered the donkeys, with possible serious consequences, and I certainly did not want to kill any elephants in this area of the future game reserve.

A week into our safari we visited the tribal area west of the Nuanetsi, camping next to some pools in a small but perennial stream, and then searching out the little kraals scattered through the countryside. We cut across the spoor and droppings of bull elephants loitering in these parts so were not surprised to receive complaints from the locals that their food supplies were being depleted by the same animals, and that none had been shot. Although it was already late morning when we found their previous night's spoor, I decided to track the bulls, hoping they were locally resident and undisturbed.

We caught up with them in a couple of hours during the heat of midday, finding all five elephants clustered under a shady tree next to a massive termite mound. Tsuro and Willie followed a little behind as I approached the bulls with a view to selecting the smallest. One had enormous, evenly matched tusks of at least 80lbs each, another almost as big, probably a 65

or 70-pounder. Two others had their backsides towards me, while the fifth had smallish ivory and was close to the termite mound, offering the best target. Making a quick advance before the uncertain wind gave us away, I scrambled up the mound and brain-shot the bull, then fired off another shot into the air and yelled at the fleeing elephants. They would not give any trouble for a good long time.

Back at the village I instructed the headman to pull out the tusks after a week, and keep them safe until I returned to collect them. The people were jubilant at the prospect of so much meat, as well as knowing their crops were safe, hopefully for the rest of the season. They presented us with watermelons and a pumpkin before setting off to butcher the carcass.

Our wanderings then took a more easterly direction back across the Nuanetsi into the dry country, much of which was a 'Kalahari sandveld' type of vegetation extending over large areas into Mozambique. We knew of a few permanent pans and hoped to find others by following the elephant paths. We spent several days camped near one of the largest waterholes, Manyanda Pan, enjoying long walks over the surrounding country, seeing more of those species which favoured this habitat such as eland, sable, giraffe, bat-eared fox and duiker, besides the ubiquitous elephant.

Our camp was a few hundred yards from the pan, far enough away not to disturb game visiting the water, and for us not to be kept awake at night by noisy elephant herds. One night, lions came up close to inspect our donkeys, keeping us all awake for a couple of hours as we sat around the built-up fires, drinking tea and talking. Waking early, I sat at the fire waiting for my coffee to heat up, when the three Africans began arguing over which day of the week it was: Sunday or Monday. Tsuro opted for Sunday, saying he was going to the bar to drink beer all day, while Willie and John thought it was Monday. I dug my diary out of a pack and settled the discussion. It was Monday, our eleventh day since leaving home. As I wrote up my notes, Tsuro leapt out of his blankets with a shout. A huge centipede had stung him on the leg, which soon swelled up, giving a lot of pain for a few hours. He stayed in camp for two days, after which his leg was quite recovered.

Willie and I found a dried-up pan some miles south of Manyanda with the skeleton of a bull elephant embedded in the dry, cracked basin, but both tusks were missing from the skull. We spent an hour or more searching the surrounds, eventually finding one tusk, still in good condition and weighing around 50lbs. We hid it well in some dense scrub to protect it from the sun and other elephants, who make it their business to scatter bones and ivory of dead comrades, carrying the objects away with their trunks for considerable distances. I planned to return with the Land Rover someday to

Msimbiti forest with a fortuitous open patch

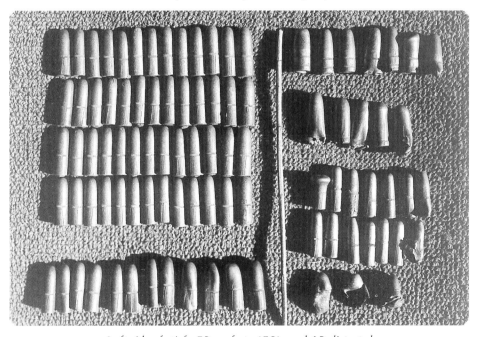

Left side of stick: 52 perfect .458's and 12 distorted
Right side from top: 7 x .505 Gibbs; 5 x .450/.470; 14 x .375; 3 x 10.75
(All from elephant, except 10.75 from Devuli buffalo)

My dog Bvekenya with his crocodile

Tsuro supervises removal of hippo bull

Dry-season causeway across the Lundi, Chipinda Pools

collect it, but never did so. I wondered, of course, what had caused the bull's death, as he obviously had not been shot at the pan in view of the ivory not having been chopped out. Like everything else, elephants get sick or old and their teeth wear out, and they die. But, it was quite possible this bull with reasonable ivory had been wounded by a hunter, maybe in a tsetse corridor or Mozambique or on someone's ranch, and it fled to this place to die.

Leaving Manyanda Pan, we meandered southwards for three days, passing through beautiful mopane country alternating with sandveld areas covered with scrub and large mukwa and mahogany trees. Depressions and grassy vlei's held pans, mostly dry at this time, but with a larger one now and again holding water. Using the network of major game trails, we simply chose those going roughly in the direction we required, arriving at the Nuanetsi once again not far from where it entered Mozambique. Camping under shady trees, with cool, clear water to hand was a luxury and a good opportunity to clean our kit, wash some clothes and let the donkeys fill up on green grass. We had found no signs of poaching at all; no spoor, old fireplaces, snare lines or cut trees, so there was no reason to go into the villages to the west of the river. Although we heard distant drums throbbing in the night, we did not see anybody during the couple of days we camped there.

Making our way north along the east bank of the river, we took two days to reach a point where we crossed over to Manjinji lake, the avian paradise, and set up camp near the northern end. The Nuanetsi District Commissioner, Alan Wright, had asked that elephants be discouraged as often as possible from using Manjinji for drinking because they messed up the lake to the detriment of the local people and their livestock when the water level dropped during the dry season. Sending Tsuro and Willie around the water's edge to check for elephant sign, I went the other way with the silenced .22, shooting a few doves and green pigeons for the pot. We had fared well on sandgrouse, francolin, guineafowl, doves and a hare, collected with the little Browning, and had only used a few tins of bully beef over the past couple of weeks.

My two trackers arrived back to say elephants had not been to Manjinji for more than a week according to some locals they had met bringing their cattle to water. However, just before sundown on our second evening, a herd came to the lake barely a hundred yards from our camp. Tsuro and I crept through the thick undergrowth to find about twenty elephants, cows and youngsters, drinking, playing and splashing, enjoying themselves as they usually do at water. I felt quite guilty at ruining their evening, but they could drink at the nearby river, so I fired the .458 into the lake just near them. A

nuclear explosion could not have caused more pandemonium! The elephants erupted out of the water, trumpeting and growling and crashing off through the dense jungle in a mad panic. At the same time, thousands of birds up and down the lake rose in alarm with a deafening cacophony of noise. We stood dumbfounded for several minutes, watching the kaleidoscope of countless waterfowl flying about, yelling their heads off. After a while the world around us gradually returned to normal and I suggested to Tsuro we follow the herd to check if they had crossed the Nuanetsi.

Once out of the strip of forest, we crossed an area of more open bush, but nearer the river we again entered thickets which caused us to slow down, particularly as the evening light was fading fast. I was sure the herd had already crossed the Nuanetsi, judging by the flattened vegetation we had followed, but we still could not see the river bed through the curtain of greenery until we came into a small open space overlooking the sandy expanse. And there was the herd of elephant, crowded close together, heads and trunks turning this way and that with nervousness.

Before I could decide whether to fire another shot to urge them on, the sound of smashing branches right behind us gave me a heart-stopping moment. A big cow elephant had waited in the bushes, presumably to check if the hated humans had followed, and we must have passed her seconds before she decided to attack. Swinging the Mannlicher up as I whipped around, I accidentally hit Tsuro across the head with the barrel, then fired into the elephant's face which was mostly covered with leaves and branches collected during the charge. She crashed down into the little clearing and I quickly gave her a finishing shot through the top of the head. Looking over the river bed, I saw the herd decamping back to Gonarezhou in the falling darkness.

"Hey, Tsuro! This was a cheeky elephant," I exclaimed. Turning to him I noticed his bleeding ear and laughed.

"Bwana, you were frightened by the elephant, so why hit me?"

"Because you were dreaming of those Shangaan girls instead of looking out for the elephant," I replied. "Now it is dark and you have to cook my supper, so let's go."

The tribespeople were overjoyed to have many weeks supply of meat, and we were given eggs, sorghum meal and vegetables in gratitude before packing up camp to trek back to Mabala-uta. We arrived home two days later all in one piece, including five good-as-new donkeys, after dodging herd after herd of elephants and resisting the urge to just disappear back into no-man's land for another few weeks.

TWENTY

Msimbiti Experiences

D istrict Commissioner Alan Wright had once again requested help to put a stop to crop-raiding elephants, this time in Sengwe Tribal Area north-west of Malipati Bridge. I had heard it said that only bull elephants raid crops, never cow herds; some of my colleagues in the Parks and Wildlife Department being adamant on this matter. They were wrong, but I saw no point in arguing, particularly as I was the youngest ranger present, so could not *possibly* have any experience of these things. I had long learnt that when two or three are gathered together in the name of hunting, the Silent Power quotation is frequently most apt: "Those who know do not speak; those who speak do not know." No matter that most crop damage is caused by bulls, it does happen on infrequent occasions that female elephants will break the rules, and as I left Mabala-uta with Willie, Tsuro and the game scout named John, I had no idea that the even more unusual experience of *two* different groups of guilty cow elephants awaited me – and on consecutive days!

On the way, I noticed an overgrown track leading off our road, so stopped to ask John where it led to, and was told a tale of yet another unusual experience. Apparently the D.C.'s road grader was working here when an aggressive elephant charged out of the bush at it. The driver took fright, leapt off the other side of the big machine and aimed for the distant horizon, leaving the grader, engine running and in low gear, to fight off the jumbo and carry on wherever its fancy took it. The blade had not been lowered, so with little resistance the machine followed the road uphill, but after reaching the top, it steered itself off into the bush, down into another valley, straight through a patch of small msimbiti trees. Its route then took

it through scrub mopane and on towards a deep ravine almost half a mile ahead. Yards before it reached the steep-sided gully, a front wheel struck a stump or rock, causing the steering to jump nearly 90 degrees, and the lumbering giant missed the little canyon by a few feet!

It moved on up the hillside again for several hundred yards, not far from the road now, until a wheel hit another object, swinging the grader round to head down the slope towards the same gully. Unbelievably, yet again the front wheel was deflected by a stump and the grader just missed going into the head of the ravine, returning back up the hill, through the msimbiti forest again and to the top of the rise about fifty yards from its original point of departure off the road, where I had left my Land Rover, to follow this incredible journey on foot.

The grader's path circled round and then went directly downhill towards the same gully, bashing for a third time through the msimbitis, missing the gully and carrying on uphill, where it met a big marula tree head on. The tree stood its ground while the rear wheels of the machine made trenches into the soil till the chassis rested on the ground. The fuel eventually finished and the engine stopped.

The half-hour we spent following this track was worth every minute. Not only did we all have a good laugh, but I would not have believed it had I not seen it myself. Although it had happened a few years previously, the passage of time had not quite obliterated the passage of the grader.

Continuing into the Sengwe district, we followed a barely visible track originally made by borehole drill-rigs, stopping at the first kraal to enquire about troublesome elephants. The people confirmed that they had a visitation a few days previously, and that they had heard of other raids in the area more recently. They said the elephants were many and had young ones. So, a cow herd this time – very unusual! They were apparently moving around at random, so I decided to camp at some water in a nearby stream, the Mauze, and work from there by foot or vehicle, whichever was practical.

We footslogged to far-flung villages that afternoon and the next day, eventually locating the most recent damage where the herd had visited for three nights during the past week. They appeared to have returned east towards the Nuanetsi each time, possibly because they felt secure there and it was certainly part of their 'home range'; the case with most elephants of southern Gonarezhou.

We decided to pack up camp and move nearer the scene of the latest action, which we completed by sunset after a difficult drive, skirting numerous patches of msimbiti trees that were impossible to drive through. The weather turned cool and windy, and the following morning was overcast

with a light drizzle blowing over us from time to time as we checked the kraals in the vicinity. No visits by elephant were reported, so we spent the rest of the day making jelly from the many marula fruits we had collected, and doing a bit of maintenance work on the old Land Rover.

During the night we heard the distant throb of drums which both Willie and John said indicated the elephants had put in an appearance, so we planned an early morning start with John staying at the camp. Willie would carry the food bag, water-bag and axe, and Tsuro the double .450.

We woke to a drizzly, dark morning and were soon soaking wet as we tramped through the long grass and dripping bushes on our way to the kraals we thought had been raided. We met with fresh elephant signs going the same way and shortly arrived at the damaged millet and pumpkin patches scattered through the bush between the clusters of huts. The villagers were most amazed and excited to see us arrive so promptly, when I had expected to find them in tears over the great loss they had suffered to their food supplies. I also realised that they were envisaging huge quantities of meat being available at any moment, putting me right on the spot!

The three of us moved off along the tracks of the herd, having decided we were six or seven hours behind, and being a cool, overcast day, the elephants may travel far before resting. The tracking was rapid through the damp vegetation, and it appeared that the herd felt insecure, trying to retreat back to their normal domain before light, judging by the fairly straight course and dug-in-toenail spoors. Zigzagging behind my two trackers as we traversed an area of bare ground in mopane woodland, I totted up that there were well over twenty animals. I decided, should we catch up with them, to only shoot one or two adults, preferably not lactating mothers or the herd's leader if I could avoid it. I wondered if this would be one of the notoriously hostile herds. The government-issue canvas ammunition belt I wore held twenty rounds, there were five in the Mannlicher and Willie carried a full box of twenty in the biltong-and-biscuits bag, more than a safe margin for even the most ferocious assault.

We moved fast, enjoying the cool, moist conditions, so different to the vast majority of big game hunting days I had experienced. With no mopane bees, no tsetse flies (they did not exist here) and no burning sun, this was a really enjoyable 'walk in the park'. The pace slowed up somewhat when, after several hours, the herd started meandering through a series of msimbiti thickets, feeding now that they were on home ground.

Our estimate of numbers had risen to around thirty, so it was not surprising that we heard them well ahead of us, snapping the brittle hardwood branches of the ironwood trees. Pulling my ash bag out of its

waterproof plastic wrapping I checked the wind then set off, with Tsuro and Willie following, in a wide arc to avoid our scent reaching the elephants. We were still in open woodland, but could see a belt of msimbiti along our left flank, stretching ahead, and that was the forest from which the sounds of the feeding animals emanated.

A shrill blast of trumpeting pierced the peace and quiet of the bushveld; just an irate elephant cow reprimanding a junior, but always a spine-tingling, primal sound, full of the grand fury of Africa's giants. It certainly caused me to stop mid-stride, the catalyst for an adrenalin overdose and the realisation that we were about to start a conflict in highly unfavourable circumstances.

With the wind in our faces and knowing the elephants in the msimbitis could not see out, we moved quickly up to the edge of the thicket to seek a path through the densely packed trees and work our way in towards the herd. Creeping quietly along, weaving between the msimbitis with almost no visibility apart from small gaps where we crossed other paths in the maze, I started feeling vulnerable and losing confidence. I was putting all of us in a situation where I could fail to stay in control should the elephants attack *en masse*, or even stampede in our direction. Meanwhile, the sounds of the herd were coming closer. I knew that if we backed out now they would soon reach our scent and probably run for Gonarezhou, but may well return to crop-raiding later.

I had never been in so large an expanse of such impenetrable ironwoods; in fact I had no idea of the extent of this forest or what lay ahead. The only slight plus we had was the light rain which had fallen on and off, softening the leaves underfoot and allowing us to proceed silently. The brushing of msimbiti leaves and twigs against our clothing was also muted in the damp atmosphere. I stuffed the ash bag in my shirt pocket. We were now committed. The confrontation inevitable.

I desperately needed to find a clearing where I could at least see a few yards around. A hiss behind froze me stock-still, then a faint whisper from Tsuro. Turning to him, I saw him indicate we should turn right down a nearby path. He had seen a break in the treetops close by, and thought it indicated an open area. We quickly zigzagged along the path for twenty-odd paces and came upon a heaven-sent mini-arena formed by a large oval slab of rock about ten yards long and elevated like a whale's back, two to three feet above the surrounds.

Although still fully alert and ready for action, I felt a massive relief after the past quarter-hour of intense concentration and the strain of heading into danger. The ash bag came out again to confirm the light wind was still

in our favour. All over the forest in front of us were the sounds of elephants but with the trees crowded right up to the rock we still could see nothing moving until, only yards away, the head of a large cow briefly appeared. The boom of the .458 finally released my tension and the dispassionate mode returned. My autopilot, born of experience, took control. As the elephant dropped to the brain shot, I reloaded the Mannlicher's chamber with a fresh round from my belt, knowing that at every opportunity I must replenish the rifle's complement of five cartridges in case several individuals charged simultaneously – which they proceeded to do – time after time.

The first one to smash its way onto the scene fell to a frontal shot which did not kill it, and it thrashed about, roaring and trying to get up, this being a signal for the whole herd to converge on us. My next shot put it down just as it tried to stand, then my attention turned to dealing with offensives by several others who had seen us, while still more were gathering around the two dead ones. The whole place became a seething mass of trumpeting, enraged elephants, with the next few minutes just a blur of noise and furious action of shooting, reloading, elephants falling, trees crashing, tusks smashing, more elephants charging, and the odd explosion from Tsuro's .450 as he finished off anything that tried to get up after my shots.

The cartridges in my belt were running short and I called on Willie to put more in quickly. Out of the corner of my eye I saw him bend down next to me, and glancing down, I saw he had dropped the ammo box into the one and only pool of rainwater on the rock! I kept shooting as he methodically broke open the wet carton and stuffed the rounds, right-way up thank heavens, into my belt's pouches.

Quite suddenly, the few remaining elephants had had enough, and as if on cue, they went crashing away through the trees, the sounds of their retreat fading away to be replaced by a strange quietness. The tempest had passed, leaving death in its wake.

Once more, I reloaded the Mannlicher's magazine and chamber, accidentally touching the shimmering-hot barrel with my left thumb which promptly blistered and was quickly relieved by putting my hand into the same puddle of water into which Willie had dropped the ammunition. Our next move was to check the twenty-plus bodies piled up around the slab and to look for any sign of wounded animals that may have run off. Four or five elephants had fallen onto the rock and some tusks had shattered. There were a few chips of ivory actually lying amongst the empty .458 brass strewn about where I had been standing.

The sun was struggling to break through the thinning clouds, which helped brighten my mood as we finished our investigations and returned to

the rock slab to smoke a cigarette and relax. I was still feeling the effects of the mass shooting. The depression at seeing most of the herd lying dead around me, my sympathy and great admiration for the elephants' courage in attacking us, and the relief that we had survived, brought conflicting emotions.

"This was war, Bwana," murmured Tsuro, sitting with the Rigby propped up against his shoulder as he rolled a cigarette of newspaper and raw, crushed, native-grown tobacco. I watched him moisten the edge of the paper tube with his tongue, press the creation into final shape and admire his handiwork before reaching for his matches.

"Tsuro, take the bullets out of that rifle, or there will be more war," I told him. As he unloaded the double I enquired how many shots he had fired.

"Three: at that elephant over there when it was getting up behind you; at one of those in that heap of six, and at that one on the other side of the rock which you did not see coming."

"Yah, Tsuro. These Gonarezhou elephants are different animals. They are not afraid, but also they do not understand danger. They are too hostile, and make war when they should run. What do you think, Willie?" I turned to him, interested to hear his opinion.

There was a pause as Willie studied an empty .458 case he was fiddling with where he sat, slightly apart from us.

"These elephants wanted to fight," Willie duly pronounced with furrowed brow. Ten out of ten for stating the obvious I reflected, rather unkindly.

"Why, Willie?" I persisted. One could not hurry Willie.

"Because we are in their homeland. Perhaps if we shot them near the people's villages they would run away, because that is land for people, not elephants. They know they cannot chase us out of the tribal area. But they don't want us in the elephant's area, so they make a fight."

Well, I thought, Willie's erudite speech made a lot of sense, the problem being that the elephants were nocturnal raiders, and shooting them at night would be difficult, with a high risk of wounding and of being run over. Maybe it would be more practical, though, with a few bulls in the crops rather than a herd of cows. I was sure we would find an opportunity to try a night assault sometime.

Meanwhile we had to return in some haste to the African villages to spread the word as fast as possible to get maximum use of the huge quantity of meat, and we only arrived back in camp at sundown, much fatigued from a long, eventful day. We found John entertaining a man who had come to report further crop-raiding in his area, a few miles south, and I was somewhat sceptical when told that female elephants were the culprits.

I was sure it was the same herd we decimated that day, but the messenger was certain there were only a few animals. Okay, I told him, we will check the area in the morning.

After a solid night's sleep I woke to find my right shoulder feeling very stiff, and beautifully 'rainbowed' in blacks, mauves and yellows! Well, more than two dozen shots totalling around 130,000 foot-pounds of energy exiting the front end of the Mannlicher in quick succession, I mused as I dressed, just had to have some effect on the fool hanging on the other end. My clothes felt damp, and I stepped out of my tent to find yet another dark, drizzly morning, accompanied by a cool breeze. Standing over the campfire with a cup of hot coffee in my left hand, I tried swinging my right arm around to loosen up the bruised muscles.

Tsuro, being inquisitive, asked what on earth I was doing playing windmills so early in the morning.

"Those elephants of yesterday are having their revenge. They cause me pain, so today I will be afraid to shoot the rifle when an elephant charges us."

Tsuro's infectious giggle was followed by a typical rejoinder. "Why don't you stay in camp and cook marula jam like a woman. Willie and I will shoot the elephants, as that is a man's work." Even Willie's impassive countenance creased into a broad grin as he shot me a glance, not sure how I was taking this impertinence.

"Your mother should have named you *whari* (francolin) instead of *tsuro* (rabbit)," I told him. "Rabbits are quiet, francolins chatter and screech before sunrise. And the eagle owl hears them so he catches them to eat. Now let us get moving, or are you afraid of getting wet in the rain?"

We reached the first kraal, the home of our guide where his people informed us of drum-beating at a village further on, definitely a signal of elephants' raiding. Half an hour on, we arrived at the scene, with the strange discovery that two big cow elephants plus three younger ones had done the damage. This was unusual as they were obviously nothing to do with the big herd of the previous day, having been around these parts for some time. We left the local man and set off immediately on the spoor.

As usual, the elephants made fast progress away from the village for a while, but cunningly went downwind continuously, not stopping to feed, nor loitering in any of the msimbiti forests they passed through. At one point we found they had put on speed, either from detecting a whiff of us or just their leader's intuition warning of danger. Do elephants have such a sensory ability? I wondered if we would catch up with this ultra-wary little group. The clouds had thickened, the cool dampness was conducive to non-stop

travelling. I had also noticed how, in the most dense patches of msimbitis, the visibility was severely reduced by the gloomy light, as if dusk had fallen.

Around midday, after six hours non-stop tracking, we again found they had run, but this time only a short while ahead of us. I decided to have a break, so we sat down to our snack of biltong and biscuits, quite sure the elephants would now go far and fast, possibly leaving the tribal area altogether. At least, Tsuro and I thought so, but Willie, with unexpected candour, spoke up with his predictions. Not far ahead were villages, he said, and the herd would have to change direction and thus no longer run downwind. He also had the strange idea that they would stop the fast pace soon, enabling us to catch up again. Willie's power of positive thinking was encouraging, I felt, though Tsuro looked unconvinced as we got to our feet to continue the hunt.

Some miles on, we discovered that the elephants had split up while going through an area of thick grass, so we found ourselves on the tracks of just two, one of the adults and a half-grown youngster; quite weird really. This slowed us down, with spooring becoming particularly tricky in areas of flattened grass, but at least we no longer pursued them downwind. Soon we found signs of them feeding, as they slowed to a more normal pace, rather giving the impression that they felt safe, completely at odds with their behaviour thus far.

We were approaching a large stretch of msimbiti trees when the thought of them possibly being holed up in the forest quickly turned to certainty, the 'sixth sense', or instinct, was unmistakable. Interestingly, at that moment, Tsuro turned to look at me, grinned and nodded in the direction of the looming, dark mass of ironwoods, then cast his eyes back to the spoor. The tracks shortly veered left, heading directly to the forest fifty yards away, luckily not quite downwind.

The two elephants entered the wall of closely-packed tree trunks on a path so hemmed in that I was amazed they passed through. We were in single file, Tsuro in front and Willie behind me. In the poor light the spoor was all but invisible, even on the rain-moistened soil, while vision through the leafy trees was reduced to mere yards, other than a patch here and there where a tree had fallen over or an elephant path crossed our passage. Worse than yesterday, I thought, because of the darkness in here. Damned lucky it's only two animals! The attack was very sudden, unexpectedly from our right where the big cow had waited undetected.

She came down at us with an almighty smashing of brittle timber, barely discernible in the semi-darkness and dense vegetation. There was nothing distinctive to shoot at, just a black, oncoming mass. Almost falling over

Tsuro who ducked out of the way of my rifle as I swung it around to the right to face the charge, I got one step forward when the elephant spun around the remaining tree trunks onto our path, towering over us and still festooned with branches. I fired into the face, momentarily seeing the white of ivory, not more than a few feet from the rifle's foresight. The great bulk collapsed, fortunately sideways and not forwards on top of us, though one of the msimbiti trees that smashed down with her hit the Mannlicher's barrel, almost wrenching it from my grasp, then hitting Tsuro across the ribs.

Regaining my balance, I shot the elephant three times into the heart before reloading the magazine and forcing my way through the mangled vegetation to reach its head. Seeing the blood slick at the end of the trunk was the tell-tale sign that the first shot had, miraculously, hit the brain. I found the bullet had entered the left tusk socket near the trunk base, travelled up at a steep angle to reach the brain, but did not exit the top of the head. In one of those unbidden moments of fleeting emotion, I gave the big cow a couple of pats on the flat of her great ear; a sort of "Farewell, but I'm glad I won!"

We all sat down on the elephant's legs, breaking out the standard fare of biltong, cigarettes and slightly dust-tainted water from the canvas bag.

"What happened to the other elephant," I asked my two trackers, having completely forgotten about it in the rumpus.

Both Tsuro and Willie shook their heads, agreeing that it had never put in an appearance, nor had we heard it running away. Another little mystery to add to a day of highly unusual elephant behaviour. Except of course, for this cow's attack.

"That was scary," I announced. "That was very close." To my surprise Willie shrugged it off, though I later learnt that he was incapable of comprehending the word 'danger', while Tsuro simply said, "It's only one elephant. You've killed plenty of charging elephants. What about yesterday? *That* was a big *hondo* (war)." As an afterthought he enquired about the state of my bruised shoulder.

"It is fine. I shot the elephant, didn't I?"

"Well, just. You took too much time thinking about the gun hitting you again. Perhaps you were thinking you should have been cooking marulas in camp."

We reached camp after sunset, ending one of my most memorable hunting experiences; a long day, a long trek, strange elephants and a nerve-racking finale. The weather had changed during the afternoon, and by sundown the disappearing clouds gave way to a deep-cobalt sky, the Evening Star shortly being joined by the uncounted multitudes of greater

and lesser stars as night fell to the light sounds of insects, fruit bats and frogs. I sat near the campfire, feeling the still-damp, cool air around me as I wrote in my diary by the light of a paraffin hurricane lamp:

> Elephants crop-raiding in Machisanga area. Tracked 2 cows & 3 sub-adults 6½ hours. Found two of the group in very dense Msimbiti forest. Shot large cow at close range. Informed villagers of whereabouts of carcass. Gonarezhou elephants, especially in msimbiti terrain, are different animals to any others I have hunted.

I listened to the soft murmurs of the three African men discussing the day's events as they sat hunched around their fire, cooking their supper and mine. What did Willie and Tsuro really think about this hunting as an occupation? What were their inner feelings when that elephant was feet away from killing or maiming them? Were they telling John about the drama or simply how much ground chilli should be put into their pot of simmering buffalo hash? I had discovered over the years that while Tsuro and I actually hunted as a team, many of our observations and feelings on various subjects were reflections of our widely differing cultures. Our separate psychologies, born of diverse historical origins, were moulded by far deeper and more complex influences than simply disparate levels of scholastic education. We saw the world differently, but without discordance.

I felt sure that Tsuro's and Willie's casual responses to being in what I called a life-threatening situation, were genuine. I supposed that they had unquestioning trust in me, an almost blind faith that I would not allow harm to befall them, but it made me think hard about the responsibility of putting them in such situations as we had faced yesterday and today. Hell, I was far from infallible! I lay on my camp bed, tired but unable to sleep, pondering the question of whether my confidence had taken a blow, but after some positive thoughts that the necessary attributes for survival were still with me, namely my ability with the rifle, experience, temperament and intuition, I felt better. Definitely, more days of elephants and ironwoods lay ahead I decided, as the distant sound of drums lulled me to sleep.

A Patchwork Of People

Life at Mabala-uta was extremely pleasant, in fact close to Utopian for an anti-social lad whose dreams of living in the wilds and hunting big game were already, and continued to be, fulfiled to the highest degree. Considering the epoch of unfettered hunting had passed decades before, I was incredibly free of interference by humanity, living in a corner of what little remained of raw African wilderness still unsullied by the gaggle of safari lodges, safari camps, safari operators, safari hunters, safaris for photographers, birders, anglers, canoeists et al. who converge *en masse* wherever the ghastly words 'Tourism Potential' are written across the map. The mass tourism industries have even spawned Railway safaris, Elephant-back safaris, so-called 'taylor-made safaris', safari clothes, safari shoes and no doubt will soon market safari sex, safari drugs and cyber safaris.

I suppose we were a little guilty of being at the thin end of the wedge of invasion in so far as we made roads, built a workshop, horse stables, more staff houses, and generally 'showed a presence'.

I returned to Mabala-uta in 1996, thirty years after leaving the station, and was heartened to see only a modicum of development there, and a reasonably discreet set of lodgings for visitors down at Buffalo Bend itself, delightfully deserted. Long may it last. But it won't, of course, because the talk now is of combining Gonarezhou, Kruger Park and a chunk of Mozambique into a contiguous, vast game reserve. That will be fantastic for the game, particularly the elephant populations which need big country. But as sure as the sun sets, those that delight in the artificiality of thousand-roomed hotels with casinos, indoor waterfalls and plastic palm-trees will press a few million of the folding stuff into the grasping palms of Earth's

most corrupt creatures – human despots – and erect such structures across the thousand-year-old elephants' trails. Looking back, I thank Destiny for the fortune in non-material wealth that I reaped from my Gonarezhou days.

We got thoroughly lost one night; quite a miserable night actually, but we had a good laugh at ourselves next day. One of the game scouts came to the station late in the afternoon to report that he had heard a shot fired in the area across the Nuanetsi river which needed investigation. Calling on Tim Braybrooke's tracker, a half-Bushman named Johnny Mulupi, and the scout to accompany me, I jumped into my Land Rover with my rifle and water-bag and we set off across the river, heading west through thick bush. Stopping after a couple of miles, we continued on foot, following game trails here and there, trying to pick up human or vehicle tracks before sundown. We found no sign of intruders but did see a leopard sitting on a branch of a tree, watching us with idle curiosity.

As the sky clouded over we turned back for the Land Rover, reaching it in the dark just as a light rain started falling. With the infallible Bushman, Johnny, sitting in the cab with me, we set off home and as I wove our way through the bushveld, he indicated when I should go left or right or keep straight. After half an hour I felt uneasy as we had not passed through any open mopane areas which we had crossed between the river and our stopping point. The three of us got out of the Land Rover to discuss the matter. I lit a cigarette while the two Africans debated the direction of Mabala-uta, but eventually none of us could agree, so I decided that Johnny had lived here the longest and was full of Bushman instincts, so we must go his way.

We continued driving for nearly three-quarters of an hour in the rain when a shiny object showed up in the headlights. Curious as to what it was, I stopped and got out, only to discover it was the foil from my 20-pack of cigarettes which I had opened at our previous halt! Now, this really threw us. It was a chance of millions to one that we should find this spot in the thousands of acres of dense bush and trees we had covered, on a dark and rainy night. It is a well-documented fact that people who are lost in the bush will *walk* in a circle, but how on earth did this phenomenon become transmitted from Johnny Mulupi sitting in a vehicle? Getting lost at night, with no landmarks, moon or stars to navigate by, is easy enough. But why *drive* in a circle?

There was no sign of the cloud cover breaking, so we had further consultations on our predicament, and I smoked another cigarette. Once again, Johnny was keen to try the direction he had in his mind, so off we drove on a different bearing. I tried to more or less alternate my left turns

and right turns circumventing thickets, rocky areas and trees, doing my bit to keep on the straight line Johnny's little hand indicted in the dimness of the cab. Occasionally we passed a tree or slab of rock which was unfamiliar, giving me hope that we were on a new route towards home. However, after driving for nearly an hour I became certain – certain we were still lost! Minutes later, something glinted in the grass just in front of the Land Rover. I stopped, got out and picked up the piece of cigarette box foil! This was unbelievable, and I just burst out laughing. It was now ten o'clock and I was quite prepared to sit out the night in the discomfort of the vehicle, confident that with dawn we would easily reorientate. The three of us stood silent, each no doubt wondering how the hell we managed to make ourselves look so idiotic. The distant sound of a dog barking came from behind us. My dog! I knew my Labrador's voice. And it came 'from behind' us, because we were mentally facing the wrong direction. Suffice it to say we were home in twenty minutes, cold and tired and very sheepish. I was quite pleased to find the sun had the decency to rise in the right place next morning.

I had hijacked Bvekenya from the Braybrookes intentionally. They owned a Weimaraner and two black Labrador-type dogs: Ganyana who was thin and sickly; and Bvekenya, a big, lovable hound. He and I fell for each other and Tim soon saw the hopelessness of trying to break the bonds, as we all lived on the same five-acre fenced plot, so he did the honourable thing. The dog's food dish was officially moved from the Braybrookes' house to mine, completing formalities of the hand-over.

Bvekenya was the first dog I had all to myself. Growing up on the farm I was amongst several hounds of various shapes and sizes, but all family owned, and since leaving home I had no opportunity to keep a dog. Bvekenya became a wonderful friend and companion to me, and being totally acclimatised to the sight, sounds and smells of game, he only gave warning if certain animals such as elephant, lion, leopard or hyena came within his discomfort zone. He also hated crocodiles, barking furiously if he smelt where one had been lying on a sandbank or when he saw any croc-like object floating in the water. One of about six feet long took up residence in the pool in front of my house until I shot it when it tried to grab Bvekenya as he stopped for a drink while we were strolling about the river bed. He never forgot that lesson.

Neither Tsuro nor Bvekenya were impressed by my sense of humour one night when, using the garden watering can as my amplifier, I called in a lion which was roaring its lungs out across the river. He came over and walked around the fence for a while, delivering the most thunderous rolls of hair-raising sound I have ever heard. Tsuro was most put out as he wanted to go

to the staff compound to cook his supper and retire to bed, but the compound was outside the fence, a couple of hundred yards walk in the dark. After that occasion, whenever lions were heard during the early evening, Tsuro would hide the watering can and, if I asked for it, would say Tim's gardener had borrowed it.

Generally, we kept ourselves in meat by cropping a couple of impala when required, with the occasional change if I shot a buffalo on control work. Thousands of impala lived in herds all along the Nuanetsi river and around the large pans, easy enough to pick off using my silenced .22 Browning with the help of a spotlight at night. Besides meat, our African staff received weekly rations of maize meal, a couple of pounds each of peanuts and sugar beans plus a pound of coarse salt. They also grew their own vegetables in a small fenced area, and were taken at the end of each month for shopping to Chikombedzi, a small village on the road to Nuanetsi, which boasted two little stores, one fuel pump (hand operated) and a missionary hospital run by an American, Dr. Paul Embree.

Visitors to Mabala-uta were rare. One of the D.C.'s staff or a policeman might drop in for a meal or spend a night, and occasionally friends of the Braybrookes would spend a weekend. A surveyor or borehole drill-rig foreman may stop to ask directions or request help in repairing a vehicle. My old school pal, Derek Tomlinson, who was ranger at Chipinda Pools on the Lundi river at the northern section of Gonarezhou, would visit every couple of months, arriving with two or three crates of beer and leaving with a serious bout of shakes from 'malcoholaria'. One of the National Parks Research Division staff, Tony Ferrar, came from Head Office to carry out a quick survey of the Buffalo Bend area habitat; elephant damage and so on. He set up his camp downstream from Mabala-uta, accompanied by his little terrier-type dog. Naturally, everywhere Tony went, the hound was sure to follow, or more likely, to lead. One day Tony turned up at the station, a paler shade of pink and a little disjointed in his telling of how his dog had done a David and Goliath with some cow elephants, with the result that both Tony and the terrier only just escaped whole and unblemished. Obviously the professors at Tony's university had omitted to advise their wildlife management students that elephants kill people, but Tony was later to learn!

Some years later I heard that Tony experienced a second incident under almost identical circumstances when he approached one of the Gonarezhou elephant cow herds accompanied by his faithful terrier and a lady companion. The dog raced in to demolish the nearest cow which showed its displeasure in the usual way – by chasing the dog which ran straight back to

Manjinji lake

Bull elephant at Manyanda Pan

The leopard who came for dinner

Tamboharta Pan near Sabi/Lundi junction

Tony. His friend ran back towards the Land Rover but Tony was knocked down, his pelvis broken and tusked in the abdomen and back, fortunately being pushed against the trunk of a fallen tree which gave him some protection until the elephant left him. With great presence of mind the girl marked his position by pulling a branch into the road before speeding back to Mabala-uta to fetch help. Tony spent weeks in hospital but happily recovered and married the nurse who had seen him through the bad times.

For a short while I had good company in the form of a new cadet ranger named Barrie Duckworth. We became firm friends, and Barrie spent many years in the department before leaving to run his own business as a safari outfitter. We had a couple of good elephant hunts together which obviously stuck in Barrie's mind, prompting him to relate the episodes to Ed Matunas, author, hunter and expert ballistician who hunted with Barrie three decades later. Ed Matunas, in his excellent book, *Modern African Adventures* (1998 E. Matunas. Moosup. C.T., U.S.A.) tells, in Barrie's words, about some exceptional bulls we tackled down near the Limpopo, not far from the area where I had hunted Big Feet's group and met the Venda people. Barrie was eighteen years old when he joined the department, and I quote him from the book:

> "Almost immediately, I am sent down to the Gonarezhou (which means the place of the elephant). It is a wild, wild place, a beautiful area with very aggressive elephant. Please understand, at this point in time, I have zero elephant experience. The only elephant I have ever had contact with were the ones I had seen in Kruger and Hwange National Parks. I know nothing about elephant.... At Gonarezhou, I am fortunate enough to meet an experienced hunter by the name of Richard Harland. My very first elephant hunt is to be with him.
>
> The district commissioner calls Richard into his office and tells him there is a bunch of bull elephant down in the tribal area that are marauding at the cattle water supply, and in general are causing havoc. He instructs Richard to go down there and try to sort them out. The commissioner also tells him to take me along for training. Because I have absolutely no experience with large caliber rifles, the warden also suggests to Richard that he is to have me fire a few shots with a F.N. 375 H&H before we actually go into elephant country. Richard does so, allowing me a couple of shots at a tree, about seventy-five feet away. I do not mind the few practice shots, but this is

certainly not much of a training schedule.

We arrive at the tribal area and waste little time, immediately starting into the bush. We soon make contact with the elephants. As we close with them, I cannot help dwell upon the fact that I have never before hunted elephant. To date, my total game experience includes an impala and a kudu, which I shot at about seventy and eighty yards respectively.

There are eleven elephant in the group, all big bulls. We come up to them, in some heavy scrub mopane. They are milling about contentedly. I look at them thinking they are huge. I mean, they look enormous! We do an approach on them; actually Richard makes the stalk, I simply follow. Richard is using a Mannlicher 458. He has delegated his back-up rifle to me, a 450 double. I have never used a double; but I know enough about them to recognise that this one isn't a very good rifle and that it does not fit me very well. As we approach the jumbo, in order to keep the wind in our favour, Richard makes a wide semi-circle behind them. We silently approach to within forty yards. Richard now sees that I am very nervous and says to me, 'Listen, if you want to stay back, do so; I'll go and shoot these elephant'.

I think to myself that if I do not go with him now, I'll never, not ever, hunt elephant. I show my willingness to continue and we walk in closer.

We are only twenty-five paces away from the nearest one, a big bull. Richard says softly, 'When I shoot, if it doesn't go down, shoot it in the shoulder'.

He shoots, and the elephant fails to go down. As it swings around, I pull off two fast shots, doing no better than hitting it in the guts. The elephant begins to stagger around and Richard brains it. The bull goes down instantly to this shot, with its legs folded under it. I will later learn that this position is a sure indicator of an elephant that is truly brain shot and dead. If an elephant falls with its legs outstretched – watch out!

It is a seventy pound bull. I'm learning that the ivory in the Gonarezhou is just unbelievably large.

Due to my inexperience, Richard feels it is best that we now head back to the vehicle, to give me time to calm down. On the way back, we again bump into the herd; the ten bulls are moving quickly. For some unknown reason they have executed a big

circle, allowing us to again meet up with them. They are travelling single file on a trail that crosses directly in front of us, with the smallest elephant in the rear.

Richard runs up, with me running right behind him, and he shoots the last bull in the head. He fails to knock it down, so he shoots again, this time going for a heart shot. The elephant turns to run off and I pump two rounds into its backside. It spins around again, and comes right for us. This time, Richard ends the affair with a proper brain shot. Now this is the smallest of the bulls, and it's ivory weighs fifty pounds. Some of the bulls in the herd are carrying ninety to a hundred pound ivory. I mean the ivory is going right down to the ground! Beautiful stuff."

Barrie certainly had reason to be impressed with the tusks we saw that day. When I eventually got the ivory of the two bulls back to base, the heavier pair were an even 75lbs and 74lbs, the smaller ones 48lbs apiece. I wonder how often hunters have seen such a sight as eleven *big* tuskers together; so much magnificent ivory in one spot. I had learnt to judge tusk weight 'on the hoof' with great accuracy, as proved by weighing many tusks of those shot and seeing plenty of weighed ivory at Mr. Levy's store. At least two of the bulls topped a 100lbs aside, one maybe going 110. Three others were in the 75 to 85lb class, three more carrying 60 to 70lbs. The smallest weighed out at 48lbs, so I reckoned the other two were in the 50 to 55lb range. This meant a total of somewhere between 1560lbs and 1600lbs of big ivories, giving an *average* of over 70lbs per tusk. Probably even Bvekenya Barnard did not see a similar sight for he assuredly would have told of it in *The Ivory Trail*.

Poor Barrie was completely put off double rifles forever, quite understandably as the Haslam-mutilated Rigby .450 was a bad fit for me, and Barrie is much taller. It was definitely a 'Tsuro-occasional-back-up' weapon, and I am sure I did not foist it upon Barrie for laughs. Not forgetting I had only been a junior ranger for less than a year, and barely a couple of years older than Barrie, I certainly had not assumed the mantle of elephant-hunting professor! In short, I was not yet a Paul Grobler grade of mentor. Barrie, of course, soon picked up the skills as he is a born hunter; he has the right genetic cocktail.

The two occasions when my head shots did not put down the bulls were cause for discussion, in view of the frequent debates on the .458 supposedly failing in penetration. This was blamed on compression of the powder which then burned erratically. Certainly it was proven that the velocities were not up to the makers' claims, but stories of solid bullets barely

penetrating elephant or buffalo hides were really disturbing. If, as sometimes happened, my brain shots did not drop the elephant, I always assumed it was error on my part, not bothering to spend time trying to trace the path of the bullet. Either the animal had fallen on the side of the shot, or there were several carcasses to deal with, or we left the tusks in the skull to be pulled out later by the local headman.

As talk of the .458's failures began to filter through to me, I speculated as to whether some of these shots which I took for granted as being my misplacement, had actually been due to faulty cartridges. Fortunately, I never lost confidence in the Mannlicher .458, and I burnt a lot of powder in that rifle. Possibly I was lucky to always have fresh cartridges that did not contain compacted cakes of powder. Another factor could be the exceptional length of the Mannlicher's barrel, giving late-burning clumps time to add their pressure before the bullet exited. I rather like that theory! Whatever the failings of the factory loadings, the construction of the 500-grain solid bullet with its thick steel jacket and long, non-tapered shape was, in my opinion, unbeatable and streets ahead of any of the nitro express heavy calibre projectiles of the day. Long live the .458 Winchester Magnum (at 2150 feet per second, of course!)

Touched By The Sun

Summers in the lowveld were a fantastic mix of heaven and hell, the months of October and November marked by quite unbelievable temperatures, both day and night. After long nights of tossing and turning in the discomfort of continuous sweating on a damp sheet and rising frequently to drink water, the unremitting, burning heat of the day sapped one's energy, ability or desire to eat, and left one feeling worn out both physically and mentally, only to face another restless night. I had a maximum/minimum thermometer hanging on the verandah of my little shack which once registered 100°F at ten o'clock at night! That same October, I happened to stop at the D.C.'s sub-office at Malipati Bridge, not far from Manjinji lake, where one of the staff showed me Alan Wright's entry in the log book that 165°F was the sun temperature at the flagpole a few days earlier. There was no escape from the ovens of hell.

Not quite true though, for one such as myself who not only *loves* the intense harshness of big game country in the dry season, but finds a bit of heaven in the hour of sunrise, the hour of sunset, and the gradual change in the atmosphere when, in late October or November, the super-heated air becomes thick and humid with the build-up of the first great thunderstorm of the season. The morning wake-up calls of the Natal francolins are slower, more subdued as if their watch-springs needed winding up; baboons sit around doing very little most of the day; elephants are quieter at drinking time, more interested in sucking the buried water out of their little holes in the river sand than fooling around. The herds of impala cluster in the black shade of Natal mahoganies along the river banks, watching us pass by instead of leaping away in a red-and-white panic.

My main problem with elephants at this time of year concerned damage to water supplies for domestic livestock, both in the tribal areas and the European-owned cattle ranches, and the perennial tsetse-corridor-fence breakers. I felt sorry for the game animals that lived with the hardships of the dry, hot season, particularly in drought years, and the elephants became especially desperate with their need for large quantities of water coupled with the necessity for them to search over huge areas for sufficient feed. One could not blame them for seeking fresh territory to find life's essentials, and I avoided killing when possible, usually firing shots, shouting and chasing them for a while. As Willie had suggested on a previous hunt, the elephants generally took flight back to familiar grounds because they were probably outside their home ranges. However, any aggression was, of course, summarily terminated.

Derek Tomlinson radioed from Chipinda Pools to advise that the tsetse department wanted action against a couple of bull elephants that had broken into the corridor and overstayed their welcome.

"It's too bloody hot for hunting, Derek. Anyway, you're closer than I am, I'm saving petrol," I replied.

"Sorry, friend. My Land Rover's waiting for a new half-shaft. Can't make it either," was his lame excuse.

"Go to your vehicle, get in it, press the yellow knob down and drive to the corridor. Front-wheel-drive will do fine. In case you hadn't noticed, the last mud patch dried up six months ago, and you do not have any sand rivers to cross. Or is it something to do with the expected visit of one blonde beauty this weekend? Okay, Tomlinson, I'll go. But in between your frolicking with the fräulein think of your pal suffering in hell. Over and out, you lucky sod," I grumped as I switched off.

Knowing the bulls could only drink at two pans, all else having dried up, I did not foresee much difficulty in locating them. Theirs would be the only spoor in the corridor which would facilitate tracking them, so we should have the job done smartly; a day, two at the most. Willie was on leave, and with all the game scouts out on patrol, Tsuro and I threw the bare necessities into the Land Rover and left home before midday. The thermometer on my verandah registered 108°F, the cab of the Rover was hotter, the plastic seats slippery with sweat, and my thoughts of the idle Tomlinson turned highly uncharitable.

Our first stop was at a fence guard's camp. The fellows assured us the two bull elephants had not left the corridor and we would see they had drunk at the pan some distance in from the fence. We drove on, stopped and walked the mile to the pan and confirmed the story. Deciding to simply make camp

right where the vehicle was parked, far enough from the muddy waterhole not to frighten the animals away but close enough for a pre-dawn start in the morning, we turned in early and sweated the dark hours away. Tsuro sounded restless, and I simply thought he was uncomfortable in the heat.

Dawn light crept in around four-thirty, so I put on the coffee pot, drank a lot of water and readied rifle, ammo belt, ash bag and biscuit bag. Tsuro groaned as he sat up on his blanket.

"Eeeh, Bwana, I am not well. I have a bad stomach and I was sick in the night. I think that fish I cooked was bad," he moaned.

Concerned that he would suffer serious dehydration if he came hunting, I decided he must stay behind, at least while I checked the pan for elephant sign. Slinging the food bag over my shoulder and picking up a water-bag and the Mannlicher, I left immediately, arriving at the waterhole before sunrise. The bulls had been there, and before long I found their tracks departing to the east, the first droppings indicating they had left the vicinity several hours before me. Might as well follow them, I thought. With a bit of luck they might not go far, specially in the heat, and they certainly would not expect to be pursued here as no hunter had visited this area since I shot the lone cow elephant and the three buffalo some months previously.

The huge, red, shimmering orb crept above the horizon straight ahead of me, rapidly shrinking to a white-hot disc by the time it cleared the tops of the scattered mopane trees standing like stark, grey skeletons across the mirage of black-earth flats. I tracked the two elephants steadily as they meandered across the open expanses of sparse yellow grasses and scrubby bush, through rocky areas covered with msimbiti trees, in and out of leafless patches of woodland, while the sun climbed higher, burning down on me fiercely.

By ten o'clock I could resist the water-bag no longer, my thoughts turning more and more towards the thirst and heat I felt, and less on the job of tracking with concentration. Spotting a baobab tree ahead, I thought to continue and see if the bulls had gone that way before I stopped to have a drink. It turned out they had actually rested at the great, prehistoric tree, standing around for a while on the shaded west side. I did likewise, slipping the food bag off my shoulder, leaning my rifle against the smooth grey monster, then drinking deeply from the tepid contents of the old canvas sack. The exceptional evaporation had also taken its toll on the water level, but I was not sorry to have a lighter load. After nearly six hours of non-stop walking since leaving camp, I was fatigued and sweating profusely in the great heat. I ate a few biscuits, smoked a cigarette and had a small sip of water before circling the baobab. One bull had tentatively stuck a tusk into

the tree and levered a small wedge of the fibrous tissue off. He must have eaten it as it was not dropped anywhere nearby. They had both kicked up earth with their front feet to throw over their bodies, leaving some grains of sand still resting on little knobs of bark on the tree. As I circled further from the baobab, hoping to find a clue as to when they had moved on, a double-banded sandgrouse startled me when it flew up from almost under my feet and hurtled off with its chuckering alarm call.

Returning to the tree's shrinking patch of shade I gave thought to the options facing me. It was nearly midday and the heat was oppressive, both physically and mentally. I was miles from the Land Rover; the tracking would become more of an effort in the full sun and the trail would fade in the glare. Was I doing this crazy thing, on a Saturday afternoon, for love (of the tsetse department?) or money (joke!) or ivory? Damn right I wasn't. Wiping the stinging perspiration from my eyes I tightened my cartridge belt a notch and picked up my paraphernalia, a wave of confidence coming over me as I set off on the spoor again. Now certain the elephants would not have travelled far in the past couple of hours, I also considered the undesirability of going through all this again the following day, even if Tsuro was in shape to hunt and carry the food and water-bag. Shuffling along under 150°F sunlight with a heavy rifle over one shoulder and a few pounds of water hanging from the other hand is tedious.

I lost the spoor several times over hard ground or where the grass was flattened into resilient cushions, and the elephants' feet left no impression or signs of disturbed vegetation. Bulls feeding while on the move do not walk in file, so I was actually following one set of tracks most of the time, an exacting and slow process under these conditions, the sole advantage being that there was no other elephant spoor in the area to distract me.

I found the two bulls at around half-past two, almost nine hours since leaving the pan where they had drunk. They were standing in a grove of tall msimbiti trees, which offered some shade as they are seldom completely leafless. The small eddies of hot air were insignificant, so putting down the food and water-bag at the base of a big marula tree, I walked slowly up to the dozing animals and shot the first, reloaded and fired for the heart of the other as it swung away behind the tree trunks. Feeling unsure of my shot, I ran after the bull, reloading both magazine and chamber as I went, then seeing him well ahead of me when I broke out of the patch of ironwoods. I doubled my efforts to catch up, and was fortunate to find he was veering to the right in an arc, allowing me to gain on him by short-cutting across the scrub-covered plain. I was tiring fast and beginning to weaken in the heat, but the thought of losing this bull spurred me on, for I had never knowingly

lost a wounded elephant. Not yet.

He either saw me out of the corner of his eye or heard me clumsily staggering through the stunted shrubs, for he turned and came for me. Heaving with breathlessness and exhaustion, I could not steady the rifle, my shot for the brain having no effect at all as the bull lumbered on, looming like a great, grey apparition through my sweat-distorted vision. By the time I had sat down and steadied the Mannlicher, with elbows resting on knees, the towering giant was barely twenty paces away. Again my shot did not reach the brain but the elephant staggered, turned broadside on and took a step when my next bullet finished him. I simply sat where I was, gasping for breath, wiping the salt out of my eyes, trying to hold back the nausea brought on by over-exertion in the intense heat, until, after at least ten minutes, I felt better and the drumming in my head had subsided.

I rose on slightly shaky legs and walked over to the big bull. He carried evenly-matched fifty pound ivories which I coveted. As he had fallen on the side of my first shot, I could not judge why it had missed the heart but thinking back to how he had slowed down before turning on me, I suspected he had been mortally wounded. I spent some time inspecting the body for any old wounds before leaving to find the first bull in the ironwood trees, and to collect my food and water-bag. This elephant was younger and not so large, with tusks barely thirty pounds each, but showing an old scar completely encircling his left back leg above the foot; the result of a steel cable snare.

When I reached the marula tree to retrieve the two bags, it was with some alarm that I saw the water-bag lying on its side, and a patch of wet earth under the stopper. It had leaked where the canvas was sewn up to the wooden spout, which does not always create a seal, even if the cork stopper is water-tight in the spout. Hundreds of insects, mostly little black mopane bees, were busy sucking water from the damp canvas and the moistened earth. I was devastated to find the bag held only a few ounces of water when I picked it up and brushed off the little thieves. I cursed myself as I figured out what had happened. When I had dropped the bag against the tree trunk, it landed on a small dead branch lying half-buried, which I had then stepped on as I went to the elephants, causing the far end to topple the water-bag.

Desperately thirsty after chasing the wounded bull, I was worried about the long trek back to the Land Rover which I knew I could not reach before nightfall, forcing me to spend the night, roughly an extra ten hours without water, before walking on to camp, an unknown distance away. The fence guards' camp was even further, and I had no idea how far or the exact direction to the other pan which, in any case, was probably just mud at this

stage. I agonised over whether to have a sip of water now, or to save it for as long as I could stand it, while thinking that it was also slowly evaporating through the canvas. It was a no-win stalemate. Suddenly I realised the danger of my state of mind; the sun had touched me and depression could cloud my ability to make the right decision which was to walk in the right direction and reach camp.

I set off immediately chewing on dry biscuits, battling to swallow them with a parched throat, but with raised spirits as the sun's heat slipped from unbearable to uncomfortable. It was very difficult to shut out recurring visions of condensation-covered glasses of iced coke, beer, water, anything. Or floating in a pool of cool water in the Nuanetsi, or standing next to the garden sprinkler on the green lawn as we often did on hot days.

When the sun finally sank out of sight, I stopped and sat on a log, smoked a cigarette, ate the last couple of biscuits and finished my water supply of about three warm swallows of ecstasy. I hurried on then, knowing there would only be another half-hour of sufficient light to walk by. There were too many tree trunks, stumps, thorn bushes, rocks and holes to make walking in the dark a proposition.

With the greying light of dusk the last doves called their good nights as the Mozambique nightjars zigzagged low on silent wings or sat quietly trilling their drawn-out ratchet sounds. My ears picked up a distant but unmistakable call, sending a shiver of anticipation and excitement through me. The sound of the Land Rover's horn! Elatedly I said, "Tsuro, you're a bloody hero, you are." The .458 boomed in answer. Thirty minutes later I yelled, and was answered from a hundred yards. I staggered through the black night into the firelight, a wreck, lifted the other water-bag off the car door hinge and drank. Long and slow.

We filled both bags from the twenty-gallon container I always kept on the vehicle and I had a wonderful, cooling splash in my little canvas bath then ate hugely of rice and curried bully beef, much salted, and chased with more volumes of water. I collapsed onto my stretcher, still hot and perspiring but very, very contented, and slept soundly. Tsuro, fully recovered, also slept well.

Back at Mabala-uta, I called Derek Tomlinson on the radio, telling him to advise the tsetse department people to go down to the corridor and recover the elephant meat; their fence guards would give them directions. I asked him if his weekend had been as strenuous as mine.

"Probably not," came the crackly reply over the airwaves. "Bit hot for much of that sort of thing. However, Patricia and I want you to be best man at our wedding in three months time."

"My pleasure, Derek. Be assured, I will drink every last drop of your champagne after what I endured this weekend."

"Please do, and thanks. By the way, Rich, has Bruce Austen told you about the new tsetse corridor?"

"No," I replied. "Tell me more."

"There's talk of them fencing off all that hilly country from the Lundi river right up to the Sabi, as they reckon it's prime tsetse-breeding territory. But it is also prime elephant country and I suspect tsetse control are going to ask our department to send you up here for the jumbo work. They seem to think you know something about dealing with difficult cow herds in difficult country. There's a little iron pre-fab house on the river bank here at Chipinda Pools. I'll clean it up ready for you."

Derek was right. A few weeks later, Tsuro and I packed our possessions onto the seven-tonner and with Willie and Bvekenya (my Labrador) in the back of the Land Rover, I drove away from my beloved Mabala-uta, waving sadly to the Braybrooke family and Barrie Duckworth who was replacing me. However, I soon cheered up with exciting thoughts of new country to explore and hunt, and being left to my own devices with the elephants of the proposed 'Extension Corridor'. It was promising to be an interesting challenge as Derek had once told me, "Don't expect me to go there. Those cow elephants are mad!"

My tin house, Chipinda Pools, Lundi river

TWENTY-THREE

New Territory

Chipinda Pools station, on the Lundi river, was not entirely unknown to me although I had never visited the place before my move to live there. Derek had told me a lot about the whole set-up, the people, and the rather strange relationship between the staff of the Department of Tsetse and Trypanosomiasis Control (a division of the Veterinary Services Department which was part of the Ministry of Agriculture) and the local ranger of the Department of National Parks and Wildlife Management. All very long-winded, civil servantish and 'who's who in seniority' etc. etc. Personality clashes, petty jealousies, back-biting, taking sides, and a whiff of adultery at times, gave character to the resident population of white folks, which numbered ten adults and two school-age boys.

The lone ranger was outnumbered by the tsetse fellows, which comprised one senior officer and four field officers, some of whom had wives, so Derek welcomed my arrival not only on account of our long-standing friendship but to help quell any incipient uprising by the one department against the other. He generally coexisted most amicably with the neighbours and managed to avoid, by and large, being dragged into any inter-familial disputes, but it took tact and diplomacy.

Anti-tsetse fly campaigns have been waged over parts of Africa for a long time. For example, in his book *Last Chance in Africa* (Victor Gollancz Ltd. 1949), Negley Farson writes:

> "... Southern Rhodesia, (which) shocked world opinion some years ago when it frankly announced that some 320,000 head of game had been killed in its tsetse-fly campaign of 1922-45 ..."

But not only have great numbers of wild animals been killed, huge areas have been bush-cleared and untold tonnages of synthetic insecticides sprayed around millions of acres, and thousands of miles of game fences erected; all in the war against the tsetse. And as is the case with most wars, much of the effort, certainly with hindsight, was misconceived, misguided and a huge waste of time, money and fauna.

Take for instance the assumption that the fly obtained its meal of blood from any mammal, so all game was killed. Later, tsetse research found that in fact the fly had 'preferred hosts', namely kudu, warthog, wild pig, bushbuck, buffalo and elephant. Too late for the 12 rare Livingstone's suni, 500-plus grysbok, 160 nyala and many other species shot in Gonarezhou. They thought tsetse did not bite donkeys, but discovered this was wrong. In later experiments, they found that the fly actually did not favour bushbuck at all! Too late for the 360 killed in Gonarezhou, and 8000 in the other tsetse areas of Rhodesia.

On the other side of the coin, and to be fair to the tsetse department operating from Chipinda Pools in my time, the new Extension corridor game fence was well-constructed; no mean feat through much rocky and densely-treed country. The old fences of the Guluene-Chefu and North-east/South-west corridors were well maintained, the roads kept open and the hunting gangs closely supervised. Each field officer spent twenty-five days per month camped in one of the corridors with his twenty African hunters armed with .303s plus three cartridges each. Known universally as *magotchas*, they usually hunted in pairs for the kudu, hogs, pigs and bushbuck which were to be eliminated from these demarcated areas. The word *gotcha* (gor-chah) means roast, and roast meat they did! Little groups of cattle were kept at several strategic points and herded along the fence lines regularly. Their blood was sampled for the trypanosome organisms in addition to the catching of any tsetse flies by their herdsman. When no 'tryps' was detected and no flies seen, then the tsetse population had died out in that area at least.

The spraying operations were not confined to the game-free corridors, and indeed covered the whole of Gonarezhou from the Sabi river down to the Chefu fence and eastwards into a vast area of Mozambique. The objective being to eventually eliminate the fly and thus the danger of it penetrating into the tribal and ranching areas west of the Gonarezhou, or south to the Kruger Park and northern Transvaal.

During the dry months, a group of supervisors from the South African tsetse department would arrive with their trucks, chemicals (D.D.T.) and knapsack sprayers, recruit a horde of locals to work with, and head off to pre-

selected camp sites. The workers, each loaded with a sprayer, were directed in a series of grid-like patterns, and as each man passed a tree with dark-coloured bark, an evergreen bush, an antbear hole or fallen tree trunk, he would give it a squirt of insecticide. As tsetses need dark, cool or shaded locations, any fly settling on the poisoned area would be killed, the long-life D.D.T. remaining potent at the site for months. This was very effective over several years of the programme, the big plus being the relatively tiny fraction of the habitat contaminated by the chemical.

So where was I going to fit in with all this? Derek was quite busy enough running the station, with the various administration duties, repairs and maintenance, resupply trips to Chiredzi and Buffalo Range, chasing odd poachers or some crop-chomping hippo or buffalo or baboon. The construction of the game fence for the Extension corridor started from the Lundi river some miles downstream of Chipinda and would run parallel to the existing North-east/South-west Corridors, up to the Sabi river nearly thirty miles distant, effectively doubling the width of the original corridor. This belt of rugged, rocky terrain, full of msimbiti and mountain acacias, with pretty areas of little grassy plains surrounded by *mfuti* (brachystegia) woodland in the northern section, was the home range of many cow elephant herds. My job was to continuously harass these herds in order to frighten them out of the area ahead of the fence being erected, so that, hopefully, there would not be too many on the wrong side of the fence upon its completion.

My quarters at the station consisted of an old, galvanised-iron 'pre-fab' cabin with a large living-cum-dining room, two small bedrooms and a bathroom. From the back door a flight of brick steps led up to a small tin rondavel, five yards behind the house, which housed a wood-burning stove, table and wash basin. The house was empty. I provided my own paraffin-burning fridge, bed and paraffin-powered Tilly lamps. The station had a spare camping table with folding legs and a couple of metal-and-canvas folding camp chairs that I commandeered, supplemented by my own camp chair and table, to furnish the main room. Great! I could at least entertain two folks to dinner. Any extras must bring their own chairs, plates, cutlery, and drinking glasses. But – never their own food and drink. Booze was the one commodity, along with hospitality, that every household was never without. Mostly brandy, beer and gin, all of which I enjoyed, sometimes together and frequently in excess. It was fortunate that there were only five days, at the end of each month, when everyone was at Chipinda doing the social rounds!

My house, situated halfway down the bank, was overshadowed by

towering nyala and Natal mahogany trees growing on the narrow band of alluvial soil supporting dense capparis thickets and riverine forest. The quarter-mile wide Lundi river was a maze of channels and pools amongst the extensive reed islands. Hundreds of hippo, scores of crocodiles and a good stock and variety of fish lived along this stretch of the river, from the well-known 'Governor's Pool' a mile below Chipinda Pools settlement up to the nearby boundary of the corridor.

During the rainy season, with luck the Lundi would rise in flood, five or even ten feet, allowing the aquatic creatures to move up or downstream according to the migratory instincts of each species. Two tsetse officers had their houses on the south bank of the river while everyone else lived on the north side. During flood time, people, supplies and equipment had to be ferried across the water in craft powered by old and temperamental outboard motors, and inevitably hippos threatened the safety of boats and their occupants when passing through the channels and gaps in the reed beds. Reluctantly I shot the occasional one which would take up a part of the route as its own territory. Shooting from a small boat wobbling about on the swirling currents, aiming at the brain of a hippo which exposes its ears, eyes and nose for only a few seconds, is very tricky, and I kept wondering if the animal might just take it upon itself to capsize or attack the dinghy. If there is anything that terrifies me more than the thought of cleaning the windows of Trump Tower in New York or sky-diving, it is the vision of floating down a flooded river full of hippos and crocs, all the while half-drowning and trying not to let go of the heavy rifle pulling me under the water. Well, it didn't happen, and I pulled off a few fluke shots. Hippo meat is one of the best of all wild game so there was some compensation in addition to the removal of the danger.

Apart from an occasional buffalo I shot in the corridors, I did not kill any game for the pot while at Chipinda, relying on the tsetse guys for fresh venison and biltong, otherwise eating fish or my favourite stand in, bully beef.

At one period a leopard took up residence in the environs, killing someone's dog, another's domestic ducks, and chickens in the workers' compound, but evading attempts to kill it. One of my friends gave me a kudu hindquarter late one afternoon and Tsuro hung it from a branch of a tree, intending to cut it up for refrigeration the following morning. That night Tsuro brought in my supper with the story of having just seen the leopard walk past, illuminated by the light shining out of the dining room window, and reminded me of the venison hanging from the tree, less than twenty feet from the house. Bvekenya's nose rose into the air and a deep grumble came

Sometimes I used abandoned Tsetse Department camps

Tsuro and Willie work under the supervision of Derek's terrier

Big game country, Nyahungwe area, Lundi river

Willie repairs kraal, Tsuro skins elephant cow

forth. Leopard confirmed.

The only weapon I had in the house was my baby Browning .22 autoloader with the scope and silencer, everything else being locked in the armoury at the office a hundred yards away. Shutting the lamps off, I settled into my chair at the window with the rifle and torch, giving Tsuro and Bvekenya strict instructions to keep silent. Shortly I saw a shadow rear up against the tree trunk, so steadying the .22, I switched on the torch, and was ready to shoot. As the beam lit up the cat, it dropped to a crouch facing me and snarled aggressively. Aiming between the brilliant orbs which stared at me down the scope, from what seemed like a few feet away, I fired. The tiny 'pop' of the under-powered cartridge sounded hopelessly inadequate, and the instant whining noise of the bullet ricochetting startled me. With a sideways bound, the leopard disappeared down the river bank, followed by absolute silence. Idiot! Now I've buggered things up, I thought.

"Tsuro, light the lamp and shut the doors and windows so Bvekenya doesn't get out. I'm going to get a shotgun."

On my return we searched cautiously around in the clumps of thorny capparis and undergrowth but saw nothing, and I was not prepared to go right down the bank into the reeds below the house. The next morning we found the leopard, an average-sized male, lying dead in the reeds just out of sight of where the torch beam had been able to penetrate. When the head skin was removed the path of the bullet was revealed. Entering between the eyes it had hit the sloping bone and slipped along between skin and skull, exiting behind the head then moaning off into the night. The impact had however resulted in severe haemorrhaging of the brain, causing death within seconds, even though the skull was not fractured. Lucky me! I thought it might be a very good idea to stop potting away at dangerous game using subsonic .22 squirrel-loads with immediate effect. The results can be almost as hair-raising as falling into a river full of things with big teeth.

At the first opportunity, Derek, myself, Tsuro and Willie packed the Land Rover, put Bvekenya on top of the kit in the back and went on a reconnaissance of my new domain, heading straight into the range of hills which extended past Chipinda Pools in a north-easterly direction. The stony, eroded track wound its way up a few hairpin bends from the flats of Chipinda, continued on through the dry, rough terrain for several miles, then descended back to the Lundi. The river, in cutting through the hilly country, flowed over the Chiviriga falls, which is a barrier to the upstream progress of some species of fish. Thus, tigerfish, black bream and Hunyani salmon do not occur in the upper Lundi system above these falls.

Leaving the main track which followed the Lundi downstream, we turned north, back into the hills again and followed an even rougher trace line, cut by a team of Africans in some places, and by a bulldozer on the flatter sections in preparation for the new game fence. I marvelled at this countryside, so different to that of the Nuanetsi area. Little valleys were covered in dense stands of mountain acacias; beautiful trees which are common on the granite *kopjes* of the highveld, but seemed strangely incongruous in the hot, dry lowveld. Not true acacias, but brachystegia, they are thornless but have small leaflets and pods, thus slightly resembling the acacia family. On the higher areas, there were thickets of tangled scrub and jesse, interspersed with large and small patches of msimbiti forests. Elephant trails went in every direction, and when we stopped to eat a snack lunch, we heard trees being broken by a feeding herd.

We took other routes through the area, passing the place where I had shot the five tuskless elephants in the old corridor more than a year previously, and eventually arrived at the Sabi river where we camped for the night. The countryside was far more open; grassy savannah with occasional areas covered with *mfuti* trees, one of the elephant's favourite browse species. These conditions are completely opposite to those of msimbiti forests or Zambezi Valley jesse as far as hunting is concerned.

We spent the following day driving through the wonderful bushveld lying between the corridor and the Sabi/Lundi junction and then along the Lundi's north side, with the great, picturesque, pink sandstone Chilojo cliffs coming into view off the south bank. We saw kudu, zebra, nyala, waterbuck, reedbuck, impala, duiker, baboons and a small herd of buffalo. We crossed spoor of other buffalo including that of a very large herd. We met a couple of elephant herds, but everywhere was evidence of a big population throughout the district, and I could imagine there would be continuous movements of these herds between the low-lying riverine and mopane areas, up to the hills of the Extension corridor.

A few Shangaans still lived along the Lundi river in small, scattered kraals near the junction of the Sabi and Lundi at the point where the border with Portuguese East Africa met the rivers, and also further upstream at Chitove pools and around Fishan's ford where the Chilojo cliffs abruptly ended up against the Lundi's south bank. These folk subsisted on fish, foraging for foods in the bush and trading such items for maize meal at distant stores or with Mozambicans who lived in areas where wildlife did not destroy their crops. They were on notice to be transferred out of Gonarezhou to the Matibi or Sengwe tribal areas, having been advised of the proposed change to make the area a National Park. A year later I had the

rather depressing job of burning down all their deserted villages after their evacuation.

Some parts of the riparian forest, particularly from the Pombadzi river junction to beyond the Fishan's crossing point, had the most magnificent wild mango trees (*Cordyla africana*) I had ever seen, in amongst the other evergreen species and riverine shrubs and creepers. Nyala, impala and baboon were resident in this habitat in great numbers, along with a wonderful diversity of bird life, particularly where the water was held in permanent pools. It reminded me of the Mabala-uta area but on a much grander scale.

That evening we stopped to camp where the track passed near a series of pools formed by a rocky intrusion across the Lundi, a few miles upstream of Fishan, and we heard lions and hyenas calling sporadically through the night plus numbers of elephant coming to drink. A leopard's rough-throated grunting call came from over the river. Yes, I said to myself, this is *my* scene; this is where I could live. Pity about the station being in the corridor at Chipinda, but with judicious planning during my elephant campaign in the Extension, I could camp all over this fabulous area.

On our arrival back at the station we found two items of news: Derek's application for transfer to the Research section was approved and he was to move to Sengwa Research Station in Chirisa Safari Area in a couple of months' time, and secondly, could I attend to elephants damaging water tanks on a cattle ranch?

I was disappointed at Derek's imminent departure. Our friendship went back to school days when we had built up an exceptional collection of birds' eggs, spent school vacations at each other's homes raising hell and misbehaving, and keeping up our accustomed rate of smoking and drinking while back at school. A slight diversion was an intense, secret infatuation I had for his elder sister, Anne, the goddess of my teenage dreams. My unrequited love fortunately faded when Anne left Salisbury to work elsewhere. With Derek's move, I would also have to do the station duties which was not to my liking, but hopefully someone else would take his place. I would have the excuse for not completing office work by laying the blame on tsetse department's demands on my time! Meanwhile, I told Willie and Tsuro to be prepared for an early departure in the morning, we had problem elephants to deal with once again.

Barrie Duckworth: "It happens so fast ... elephants crashing into the earth."

The Good,
The Sad & The Scary

Weddings are joyous occasions. In Africa, friends who never see each other for years at a stretch will gather together to ensure the newly-weds take their vows, that traditions are perpetuated and that the happy couple get away on honeymoon with the greatest possible difficulty and maximum ribald advice. That done, the guests feel constrained to show full appreciation of the event by partying on till they drop. And so it was on Derek and Patricia's happy day. Old school pals and game rangers, relatives and family friends created an atmosphere that only weddings can muster. Anne was there, more radiant and delectable than ever, instantly melting my resolve to keep passion at bay, and reducing me to the same stuttering, blushing fifteen-year-old idiot of six years back.

The Tomlinsons subsequently spent some years at Sengwa Research Station, where Derek assisted Dr. Dave Cumming with work on warthogs, tsetse fly and habitat monitoring. Derek also studied a course on ecology, and eventually he, Patricia and their two sons left Rhodesia for Natal where Derek had a job with the Parks Board. We remained in contact, corresponding once or twice a year, until one day a letter came from Patricia. It was a shock; unbelievable. Derek was killed, apparently by an accidental discharge from a shotgun he was cleaning in the house. Why, brother, why?

The fence of the Extension corridor was moving ahead and I began spending most of my time there, hunting and harassing the herds of elephants, both bulls and cows; at that stage shooting very few, usually only in self-defence. I often used thunder flashes, or fired shots, to frighten the animals and followed them for a while, making more noise if they stopped too quickly. As expected, in many instances some individual or group would

come charging down on us and be shot, but I tried to keep the number of deaths to a minimum. I figured that with the loss of habitat behind the new fence plus the present large elephant population, a reduction in numbers was no bad thing, but I still wanted to see how things stood once the fence was fully completed. There may or may not be a lot of animals to hunt down once that happened.

Barrie Duckworth came up from Mabala-uta on a couple of occasions to gain more elephant experience, and we had good hunting together. To quote again from the aforementioned, *Modern African Adventures* by Ed Matunas, Barrie describes his first corridor hunt as follows:

> "As we stepped from the vehicle at Lupoche [*Note*: my camp on the Lipoji river in the Extension] Richard's head tracker says he hears an elephant trumpeting. Richard cocks his ear and listens. Trumpeting is still a foreign sound to me and I don't hear it well. Obviously, the others hear all they need as we are immediately back in the vehicle and heading off in the direction of the trumpeting.
>
> We are close to catching up (on foot) with the elephant when Richard instructs me to just stay next to him and to watch what he does. I am told not to fire even a single shot.
>
> We soon make contact with the herd; it consists of eleven cows [*Note*: my diary records twelve]. As we cautiously approached, one big cow peels off and wheels across our front. Richard doesn't want to shoot it because he isn't in the right position to make good work of the main herd. He instructs his tracker to watch the cow. He feels she is just going to move forward and turn back into the herd, but, he wants to be certain she doesn't surprise him by doing something unexpected. Well, before I have a chance to really begin to observe the proceedings, there are ten elephant lying dead on the ground. It happens so fast that, in my mind, I cannot untangle the sequence of events. It was simply a mass of trumpeting, shooting, and elephants crashing into the earth."

I photographed Barrie, still slightly bemused, among the bodies before we settled into a thorough discussion on the details of the final approach, shot placements and anatomy. Having the elephants in different postures helped Barrie familiarise himself with the animals.

The Extension, with its diversity of vegetation types, rocky areas, grassy

vleis, deciduous woodlands, jesse-type thickets and permanent streams, became one of my favourite parts of Gonarezhou in spite of the anti-tsetse operation going on there. I found a pair of magnificent crowned eagles nesting in the Masasanya river valley. The open grasslands held good numbers of the little oribi antelope, and occasional reedbuck. Less common sightings were eland, wild dog, lion and leopard, though the three predator species moved out once the fence was completed and teams of *magotchas* were eliminating the kudu, bush pig and warthog. Interestingly, impala were not common, sable and zebra rarely seen, and I cannot recall ever seeing waterbuck there. Buffalo were also nomadic which was strange considering the grazing, water and dense forests and thickets available to them. Years later, once the tsetse flies had been exterminated throughout Gonarezhou and the adjacent part of Mozambique, the Extension fence was removed and this beautiful area included in the National Park.

The attractions of this tract of country to elephants were obvious, and they loved it as much as I did, which made me feel unhappy at times with the harassment and shooting. After all, they had done no wrong and were already confining themselves to the human-imposed artificial boundaries of their ranges. I was spending half to three-quarters of every month hunting the corridor herds, with the following diary entries being typical of my initial efforts:

> 4th January.
> Left Chipinda for new corridor extension. Just before arriving at camp, saw elephants. Followed up and shot one young tuskless bull from herd of about 10 animals, and fired a couple of shots as rest of herd were at first reluctant to go. Returned to Land Rover, but heard more elephant. Went to have a look and found herd of 40. Shot one cow and herd went off but stopped again. A tsetse department vehicle came along and the herd moved off up the corridor, hopefully to go out. Told tsetse gang of locality of the carcasses.
>
> 5th January.
> Found spoor of herd on fence halfway down to Lundi from camp. Followed them a couple of miles to near Masasanya river. Shot cow and fired other shots. Young bull charged and was shot. Herd then ran, heading up corridor. Returned to Land Rover and drove to fencing gang camp to advise about elephant meat...

These terse notes filled several books, and seldom conveyed the excitement, drama, and 'blood, sweat and fears' I experienced. I think elephants are wonderful, intelligent, courageous creatures and I love them. They can be, and Gonarezhou elephants frequently were, fearsome, awe-inspiring, vindictive and murderous, and I admire them. I was a hunter of elephant and I shot them, not with wanton abandon nor with malice, not for numbers nor self-assertion, but because the hunting imperative destined this, and bestowed on me a natural ability to do the job; a task I found challenging, mentally and physically stimulating, and *never* dull. I am sure that during my control work in the Gonarezhou district, more elephants were put down with frontal brain shots while attacking than occurred, per hundred shot, anywhere else in Africa.

I experienced a more malicious form of attack on several occasions, not as petrifying as a mass charge in thick cover, but proof that a vindictive attitude can be taken by some elephants even though unwounded. Once we had disturbed a herd which scented us and bolted from a waterhole in open grassland, entering a patch of thicket. Accompanied by Tsuro and Willie, I decided to follow up and make certain the herd kept going, preferably out of the area. After a short penetration of the thicket, it seemed obvious to go around it and check if the herd had gone on through it into more open country beyond, so we turned sharp left and walked a couple of hundred yards along the edge of the dense vegetation, weaving in and out of the trees and shrubs. The wind was coming from the direction the herd had taken, so there was no possibility of them scenting us.

We crossed other elephant tracks *en route* and paused to check them out. It looked as though four or five bulls had trekked through the area during the previous night, and I had a discussion with the two trackers about where the elephants may be headed and which sections of roads we would check out later. Something made me look behind, along the edge of the thicket, where movement caught my eye. Fifty yards away several elephant cows were marching along, also weaving their way between the same trees and shrubs we had passed ten minutes previously. They were tracking us down by scent.

Ducking low, we slipped away, going downwind to a large termite mound thirty yards off and waited there, watching the silent hunters approach *en masse*. They reached the spot where we had milled around on the bulls' tracks, when the matriarch soon found our spoor turning off to the mound. With our scent also hanging in the air, trunks started to periscope all around, and suddenly 'Big Mamma' gave the attack command. Leading the charge, she fell to the first shot, whereupon the herd pulled up around and

behind the body with plenty of trumpeting and roaring. We kept hidden on the far side of the mound and watched the confusion for half a minute then I fired off a couple of shots in the air and we all shouted at the tops of our voices. This had the desired effect and the dozen or so animals crashed away in a tight group into the dense bush and kept going.

We tracked the spoor back for at least two hundred or more yards to where they, and we behind them, had first gone into the jesse. The elephants had stopped, keeping absolutely silent, about thirty or forty paces in. They had then retraced their steps to where we had stopped and retreated out of the dense stuff, and followed our scent.

On a similar occasion, during the rainy season when visibility in the leafy msimbiti forests was often reduced to feet or yards, we had discovered a break in the fence where a herd of around fifteen elephant came into the corridor overnight. By eight o'clock we had caught up and heard branches being broken deep inside the almost impenetrable green jungle in which the herd had decided to spend some feeding time. We moved very slowly, easing ourselves between the stiff twigs while trying to avoid stepping on dead wood, our ears straining for the minutest sounds around us as we closed in on the herd. A step at a time, a shake of the ash bag, a searching look for a route through the next group of densely-packed ironwood trees, nerves on edge, and the sweat and high humidity forcing me to wipe both my eyes and palms continuously. The mopane bees were infuriating with their incessant attention, but at least they were silent, unlike the cicada beetles which would suddenly burst into their maddening screeching at all the wrong times.

There was no air movement in this stifling, sauna-like atmosphere, so unless we inadvertently came too close to an elephant, we would remain undetected for a while, but I was beginning to feel very vulnerable and concerned that there were no breaks in this forest. Without warning, the sounds of a great body brushing through the leaves very close confirmed my fear that we were in a helpless situation, and my reaction was to fire off two quick shots with the .458, followed by yelling and whistling. Tsuro and Willie joined in as I reloaded the Mannlicher's magazine and chamber, and the forest erupted in crashes of timber and screams of angry elephants, fortunately apparently going away from us. We could not see anything at all, in effect standing within a three-yard-wide cylinder of greenery, but at least the closest elephants had rushed off. We listened as the sounds retreated for a few seconds, then suddenly all went quiet. An uneasy silence descended like a heavy veil over the jungle, and I did not like it at all. My intuition eased in with a warning so beckoning to Willie and Tsuro to follow,

I quickly zigzagged through the msimbitis back in the direction from which we had come. A few minutes later I spotted a clearing with a big, grass-covered termite mound in the centre; a haven in the green hell.

We all sat down on the summit, ten feet or so above the surrounds, lit cigarettes and held a whispered discussion on what we thought the herd was doing. All was still and silent, shortly to be disturbed by the crack of a twig being broken, followed by the swish of leaves as large bodies pushed through the thickets. This was it. They were looking for us, following our scent left on the leaves along the trails we had used, with the sole purpose of destroying us. This was with the knowledge that we had guns, making their courage and determination all the more amazing. Or am I being childishly anthropomorphic? Maybe!

Three big cow elephants emerged purposefully, trunks still probing here and there. Sitting on the mound, elbows resting on my knees, I was slightly above the animals so I raised the Mannlicher slowly and shot the middle cow, ten yards away. Instead of fleeing as I hoped and expected, the other two charged straight at us. The nearest collapsed to my second shot before she took two more strides, by which time the third had arrived at the base of the mound. The brain shot caused the hindquarters to crumple first, the head being thrown up with trunk outstretched, and as the forelegs folded, blood sprayed over us from the trunk as it whip-lashed down a few feet away.

I stood up and quickly recharged the magazine, but relaxed when the sounds of the herd receded as they stampeded away. Looking down, I saw Tsuro pick up his cigarette from between his feet. It was still alight and he took a long, casual draw on it. The .450 double lay across his lap. He appeared totally unmoved by the recent action.

"Tsuro, were you ready to shoot this elephant?" I asked.

He glanced up at me, eyes narrowed at the sky's glare, then looked down at the elephant, slowly exhaling a cloud of smoke.

"No Bwana," he replied.

"Why not? It was close, not so?"

"Yah, Bwana. And when an elephant is so close, even you cannot miss it!" Yes, Willie also chuckled at that wisecrack.

In The Mud; In The Rain;
In The Drink; In The Corridor

Traditionally, the hunting season in Southern Rhodesia ran from May to October (generally the dry months), with May to August being the cool winter period and the other two months roughly equating to spring, much warmer but still dry. The main reason given for having this season was to prevent the shooting of game during the 'breeding period', a rather loose definition when one considers the various times of year that the species will mate and their differing gestation periods, thus dropping their young at widely varying times of the year. On a more practical note, most hunters would not have tried to penetrate the remote, big game areas during the 'closed season' due to the rains and higher temperatures. Roads of bottomless mud, swollen rivers, washed-away causeways, risky hunting in dense, green thickets plus the impossibility of drying meat and trophies all conspired against a successful hunt by Mr. Citizen Hunter.

As an honorary officer I had frequently hunted elephant on control during the rains; crop-raiding was in full swing from January to May, usually by bulls, which suited my quest for good ivory. Now as ranger, I lived for weeks at a stretch in the tsetse corridors throughout the wet months, using a small canvas tent with a flysheet for myself, food and kit, while the two Africans shared a slightly larger tent. During the later stages of the extension campaign we sometimes used the pole-and-thatch structures at the deserted tsetse camps, putting tarpaulins over the roofs of the best huts as they were not rain-proof, giving us cooler and far roomier accommodation.

Being cooped up in a tiny tent during prolonged wet spells was not my idea of fun, particularly when the convergence zone brought non-stop rain

for two or three days; clothing stayed damp, water seeped under my bed and the inactivity drove me mad. One can only read a paperback once, then wear out the rifle's barrel with a ramrod and patch half a dozen times a day, rearrange the food in the tin trunk ten times or cook up yet another cup of coffee. Writing my diary could use up a generous ten or fifteen seconds:

> 9th January.
> Rain all day. Stayed in camp. Sewed up hole in tent. Heard hyena calling.

> 10th January.
> Rain most of the night. Still drizzling. Too wet to move out. Caught small puff adder under the food trunk.
> PM: Walked along fence for an hour, then returned in heavy rain.

An interesting few days was spent accompanying a small expedition down to the Sabi/Lundi junction during the rains of 1967. Dr. Don Broadley, from the Umtali Museum in eastern Rhodesia and one of Africa's leading herpetologists, was accompanied by Tim Liversedge, a young, fair-haired, quiet man who was employed by the Smithsonian Institute to collect small mammals. Don was the epitome of a boffin, a true absent-minded professor who did not know nor care if there was any food to eat, drinks to drink or tentage and bedding to make into a home. However his knowledge of snakes, lizards, tortoises, frogs and any other cold-blooded reptilian creatures was phenomenal.

We would sneak around with torches at night, wading into muddy pools and reed beds in the Lundi, disregarding the possibility of disturbing crocodiles, hippos or elephants, and stalk a chirruping frog or gecko in thick, rain-soaked undergrowth, getting covered in spider webs and multitudes of creepy crawlies and biting insects. Don was in his element, snatching a terrapin here or a snake there, breaking into a real bout of excitement when he picked up the first Whyte's water snake to be found in Rhodesia. Don could also identify every single one of many frog calls, of which there was a continuous loud cacophony all night around camp. To add to the atmosphere of Tarzan's jungle, Pel's fishing owls living in the riverine forest occasionally emitted their unearthly, spine-tingling screams, while the seldom-seen Livingstone's suni could be approached with a spotlight to within yards in the thick understorey.

Tim Liversedge burnt a lot of shot-shell powder trying to knock bats out of the evening sky, but had more luck catching them with mist nets.

Apparently over fifty species of bats had been recorded in Rhodesia which surprised me. The most striking small creatures Tim collected were golden moles; common in the area but hard to trap. These exotic little jewels, a bare two or three inches in length, had extremely fine, silky fur of the deepest golden colour, and lived in their tunnels just under the surface of the earth, catching burrowing insects for food.

Don, oblivious to the niceties of the care and maintenance of Land Rovers, managed to burn out the clutch of his vehicle in deep mud, in pouring rain, in the middle of nowhere!

"Oh, dear," crooned the bespectacled Broadley. "Richard, I hear your middle name is Land Rover, so I'm sure you can do something. I must just check on that swamp for some Xenopus."

Do something! I shook my head and grumbled to Tsuro as we watched Don's figure receding down the track towards camp which fortunately was not far. 'Doing something' involved digging sloshy mud for an hour until we created a hole under the car large enough for me to lie down in and disconnect the propeller shafts, gearbox mountings, levers and linkages, and the bolts holding the bell-housing and engine together. Then the floor boards and seat mountings in the cab. By sundown I had the destroyed clutch plate for presentation to his reptilian highness.

"Oh...Yes...I see...Well...Yes...Well...Tim maybe you would be good enough to find another of those things for Richard to put in the car. You could probably get one in Chiredzi," Don suggested with the sweetest of tones. He sounds like a bloody black mamba telling a mouse, 'Now, this won't hurt, I promise,' I thought, watching him enjoying his Tsuro-cooked dinner. Chiredzi was a half-day of driving from where we were, on these 'roads', if one did not get seriously bogged down or held up at a flooded river.

Tim left early next morning, accompanied by his African assistant and Willie for scholarly conversation en route, returning by late afternoon with the new clutch plate. By mid-morning the following day I had the Land Rover assembled. No rain had fallen for the past day and a half, so we managed to extract the vehicle from it's mud wallow with the help of my own 'Landie' and a lot of spade work.

I soon decided that Don was likely to get into further trouble while single-mindedly pursuing the loves of his life, the nocturnal forays being particularly bothersome with the likelihood of elephants coming into the riverine forest, let alone a grouchy hippo or buffalo bull. So I carried my rifle everywhere, and instructed Tsuro and Willie to keep close, at the same time checking for any recent signs of big game and keeping their ears open.

Meanwhile I trailed right behind Don, which suited me anyway as I was fascinated by his knowledge of the subject. I don't think he even noticed the .458 over my shoulder; probably thought it was my pet airgun.

After seeing Don and Tim off safely back to civilization, my two comrades and I returned to the soggy roads and green, dripping forests of the tsetse corridor. Elephants were taking full advantage of the abundant food and water, probably also keen to get away temporarily from the even more saturated lower areas covering much of the block of country between the Sabi and Lundi rivers. I had plenty of work trying to persuade them to keep out of this most desirable tract of their home territory, and I cursed, not for the first nor the last time, the tsetse department's policies. Not to be confused with the tsetse field officers who were just carrying out orders, and with whom I was on very good terms.

Taking the tsetse fly out of Africa's wilderness generally means humans and domestic livestock will invade and destroy those environments thus rendered defenceless. Did not Negley Farson have a point when he asserted in his *Last Chance in Africa* (1949):

> "... the tsetse-fly, as it happens, if kept within bounds, is really a friend to the African : it prevents just such large areas from being opened : vital areas of bushland, which hold the rains that replenish the water table, prevent floods, hold erosion at bay etc. It is an obsolete idea to consider the tsetse-fly as Public Enemy No. 1. The deserts are already marching south in Africa..."

Fortunately, with Gonarezhou on the drawing board to be declared a National Park, the tsetse control exercise fell within Farson's 'kept within bounds' aspirations and the area would not be 'opened' i.e. to human settlement. However, the same cannot be said of the vast areas along the Zambezi Escarpment.

My elephants were strongly opposed to being subjected to violations of their rights, and gave no quarter. They received plenty of forgiveness, of which they were unaware; never to know that, had I wished, hundreds more *could* have been shot. There was no point in maximum killing, not at that particular time, and if they backed off and ran, I was happy to see them go even if it meant another confrontation tomorrow, next week or next month. Many times though, the elephants would be so determined to see *me* back off and run, or better still, stand and be ironed out, that several had to be shot before the herd realised that they were not winning. Naturally, I do not

recall ever feeling hesitant or reluctant about defensive shooting when under assault by a bunch of belligerent cows in the impenetrable stands of ironwoods during the wet season. It was a choice between the quick and the dead. The former was preferable.

After one such incident we were checking the several bodies strewn around in the undergrowth when a small grunt came from Willie, a few yards away from me but invisible in the greenery. A small grunt from Willie was, of course, something requiring serious attention. The remarkable telepathy and vocal shorthand the three of us had developed over hundreds of hunting days in the world of dangerous game required minimal audible response.

"Huh?" I grunted back, knowing he was seeing something but had yet to fully collate, analyse and evaluate all the evidence at hand, which could take Willie some seconds. Never rush Willie, and Willie never erred.

"*Ropa*," Willie's murmur told it all. 'Ror-pah' means blood. Of course there was blood; bloody stuff everywhere, but I knew then as Willie knew, that a blood trail of a wounded animal was leading away from the scene and that we must track this elephant immediately and without respite, till we found it. A short, sharp whistle brought Tsuro alongside, and for the hundredth time I enjoyed and marvelled at the way my guys silently threaded their way after the elephants, the difference this time being the necessity of keeping on the track of the wounded one in case it split from the rest, or stopped if badly hurt. It is necessary to avoid walking into badly hurt elephants standing in dense bush and my job was to guard against this possibility.

After a few hundred yards the herd had slowed from stampede pace, thereafter walking fast downwind for a long time, taking us to mid-afternoon on the spoor before they swung towards the south and crossed the cut-line of the proposed fence back into the game reserve. The blood had ceased after the first half-hour, and my guess was that the animal had a flesh wound from a bullet passing through from a side brain shot on another elephant. It would have been hit high up; maybe the neck, top of shoulder or somewhere on the rump, from where the blood had run down the body, wiping off on the vegetation at different heights, and not in large amounts.

Heavy, thundery clouds had built up during the afternoon. Now the evening sun, slipping under the western barrier of cumulus giants, lit the green world with shafts of gold, the magic effect heightened by towering backdrops of black cloud to the east.

Fortunately, we caught up with the elephant herd just when the first great, splashing drops of rain landed around us, as within a short time, the wetness of the elephant's hides would have made identifying the wounded

one's blood stains impossible. We quickly circled about the feeding animals, twelve in number, until Tsuro spotted the dark streak down the hip of a big cow. I ran up to her and dropped her with a brain shot from behind the ear, then stood next to a mopane tree while the remainder rushed off without any trouble. The first bullet had pierced the rump between hip and tail but below the spine; certainly not a bad wound to all appearances, but I was relieved to have settled the matter. And the rain poured down. The spine-tingling slaps of close lightning and huge rolls of deafening thunder with the darkness closing in fast, could have made Wagner's most tempestuous opera turn the gods into realities!

Three drowned mice, see how they shiver, huddled between the outstretched giant's legs and bulging body, the great beast they had hunted down relentlessly now, unknowingly, exacting a little retribution. In between the heaviest downpours at around eight o'clock, we managed to eat our biscuits and biltong and have a cigarette. The three little glowing-red orbs looked like oversized tipsy fireflies in the solid darkness, cruising up and down slowly, occasionally stopping at the peak of their dull movements to shine brightly for a second before slipping down again to rest near the ground. A flash of lightning showed up a miniature nuclear-mushroom of smoke hovering above the head of one of us.

More warm, steady rain followed but the sky broke up at midnight and the stars peeped at us through the gaps, encouraging us to stand up, with some creaking of joints and sloshing of shoes, to stroll around and get the circulation going. Frogs and insects were chorusing from puddles and bushes, but apart from the loud dripping of water off the big trees into the pools all about and an occasional grumble of gas inside the elephant, the still, refreshed air was calm and peaceful. Nothing was dry except my matches, cigarettes and ash bag in their plastic wrappings, and in the darkness we could not see any place from which we might pick some dryish grass or twigs to concoct a fire. We needed a fire. A long, tiring day's hunt, little food and hours of sitting in the rain getting colder as the night air dropped in temperature had knocked the stuffing out of us. If we could dry out our clothing and warm up, we would at least try to sleep a little.

"Willie, Tsuro. Feel around the elephant, where the head and ear might have dry grass underneath, and along the undersides of the legs and trunk. Maybe if there is a fallen tree with dry twigs or bark, we can try to make a fire. Pull some hairs from the tail also."

The ash bag, without its inert contents, and the plastic bag it was in, part of my cigarette carton and the spare carton of .458 ammunition (without its contents) which was still dry in the little canvas food bag, was our kindling.

Shupo and Tsuro in the ironwoods

Tsuro, Shupo and thirteen corridor elephant (Refer to Page 182)

Sabi river in flood

Major Desfountain collecting John Condy's buffalo

The fire-lighting ceremony, taken somewhat seriously as we would have one chance only, was successful. Anyone observing the scene would have wondered if we were performing brain surgery or, on closer examination, preparing to roast ants for the Lilliputians. The elephant tail hairs just melted and were not much help. However, in due course we had a substantial fire burning and dozed on and off for the remaining few hours before dawn. After a final warm up, we headed south to find a track we suspected was not too distant, hoping the tsetse fellows would retrieve the meat of the elephant if it was accessible to them. We did locate the bush road within a mile, marked the spot, then turned west to the corridor.

By late morning we had collected the Land Rover, visited the tsetse fencing gang's camp to give directions to the first group of carcasses and the single cow, and returned to our camp for a big lunch and some sleep. A Land Rover rudely interrupted our siesta by rushing into camp at three o'clock, very nearly receiving a .458 bullet between the headlights. It was Claud Leroy, one of the tsetse department staff and a good friend, particularly as being a Frenchman he enjoyed cooking and hosted many a fine dinner at Chipinda Pools. Claud's news was to the effect that a few elephants had broken into the North-east/South-west corridor somewhere towards the Guluene fence, south of the Lundi river, and that everyone was panicking in case they continued west through the second fence into the tribal area. Both the tsetse department and the District Commissioner wanted them dead, if not yesterday, then the day before!

"Look here, Claud," I told him. "Being French gives you no excuse to get overexcited. Sit down, stop chattering and waving your arms around and have some coffee. Now, keep it under your hat, but I was out all night with a female and didn't sleep a wink; not till this afternoon anyway. And furthermore, I cannot possibly get down there before nightfall, so here's the plan. After coffee you can go back to your camp, I'll pack up here, get home to Chipinda this evening and be into the corridor by sunrise. I'll see your boss, Dave, tonight and tell him you passed on the message."

Dave Madgen, a bachelor somewhat older than me, was only too happy to have company; we always had endless topics to discuss over dinner and inexhaustible wine. This time I had to excuse myself earlier than normal to catch up on sleep before my early morning departure. Slightly inebriated, I was weaving my way along the path through the bushes and trees between Dave's house and mine, a few hundred yards distance which I knew blindfolded. Strange then, when a particularly solid-looking bush blocked my route where no bush had been before. In the dark it appeared to be moving slightly from side to side, a mere three or four paces ahead, when suddenly

the scent hit me with certainty. Hippo! It was obviously strolling slowly in the same direction and luckily had neither smelt nor heard me. Stopping abruptly, I turned back for a few yards and halted next to a big tree, but shortly decided to circumvent the remainder of the path home by walking on the road which was not far away. On reaching the track, I could make out a large hippo shape standing on the light-coloured surface of the sandy road, so I called out and whistled, at which the big shadow trotted away into the scrub mopane bushes.

Having just passed the spot where the hippo had been, I was confronted by another standing across the track, facing the opposite direction to the first. Same one, I thought to myself, just going back to the river after my disturbing him. A faint crunching sound came from behind, giving me a start. Turning to find a hippo standing on the road hardly ten yards away, I felt heavily out-manoeuvred and about to be put under serious pressure. Darting into the bush I stood near a tree and shouted to all hippos, near and far, to get out of the damn way. I was tired and wanted to get to bed. Just at that moment, while I drew breath to start another tirade at my fat friends, a squeaking bicycle drew up on the road and a voice asked, "Good evening, Sah. Are you okay, Sah?"

Stepping back onto the track, I peered at the figure in the dark and recognised Shupo, one of the game scouts.

"Good evening, Shupo. Did you see the hippo just there?" I asked.

"No, Sah. I came from the tsetse people's compound but saw no hippo."

"Okay. But there is one ahead. He was on the road over there, just before you arrived. Let's go together," I suggested, hoping Shupo would lead the way.

"Yes, Sah. But I did not see the hippo ahead either. I could see you on the road. You stopped, then ran into the bush, and I was thinking what you were doing, Sah. Then I heard you shouting but not so angry in your voice."

"Okay, okay. Let us go home now. I have to rise early tomorrow," I cut Shupo short.

"Yes, Sah. Tsuro told me you did not sleep yesterday, then you went to Baas Madgen's house for drinking this afternoon. He says when you drink with that baas, you come home like a crab, walking sideways. Tsuro is worrying for you to hunt elephants after you go to Mistah Dave for long time tonight."

"Shupo, understand this," I admonished him. "When an African drinks too much *doro*, he is useless for work the next day. But a European will still do his job in the morning."

We waffled on while we strolled back, seeing and hearing no more hippos

at all. My dog, Bvekenya, gave me a withering look as I belatedly dished up his dinner. To make amends, I promised him he could come on the next camping trip. He had just recovered from a bout of tsetse-borne trypanosomiasis (often known as 'nagana') that I had cured with the drug Berenil, which unfortunately had harsh side-effects when used on dogs.

The Heuglin's robins joined the earliest Natal francolins in great voice to arouse me long before sunrise, and I heard Tsuro and Willie talking in low tones outside the kitchen hut.

"Coffee, Tsuro," I called out while dressing. He shortly came in with bread and fried eggs plus the coffee pot, announcing that I must eat breakfast today after running away from hippos all night. Obviously Shupo had spoken to him.

"Yah, Tsuro. The hippos made some road-blocks last night."

"Bwana, those hippos were inside the bottles you were drinking with Bwana Dave. His cook says there were many empty ones when he left the house last night."

"Put food in the box, enough for three days, and for Bvekenya also. Have you and Willie put your blankets and pots in the Land Rover?" Tsuro nodded, a sneaky smile on his face. The reason for this was soon apparent. Shupo was standing at the car, his kit already loaded, and he stood smartly to attention when I approached.

"Good morning, Shupo. Now you see I tell you the truth," I laughed as I helped load kit and rifles onto the vehicle. I was quite happy to have him along to stay in camp with Bvekenya, but he could also come hunting if Willie or Tsuro wanted to stay in camp. He was an excellent tracker and had hunted with me on several occasions when either of the others took a few days off work or felt unwell.

We dropped our camping gear with Willie and Bvekenya at a pool where our track crossed a stream, and continued up the game fence, at last finding fresh tracks of at least a dozen elephants. More than the 'few' I had been told about.

Although the herd had been around the area for a couple of days already, we had no particular problem keeping on the most recent spoor, only a few hours old and well-defined through the green grass and damp earth. Our problem was the wind, on which the herd picked up our scent before we knew they were that close ahead. They had run off for a short way then marched towards some low, stony hills I could see not too far away. We speeded up and caught sight of them moving through mopane woodland, almost at the edge of some thick jesse at the base of the high ground. We covered the couple of hundred yards separating us at the run, and I quickly

assessed the plan of attack. I had identified the lead cow and another big female with no tusks as being the key animals. The tuskless one would almost certainly charge when she discovered our presence, and this would be to my advantage. There was a bull present which I knew would take off as soon as the shooting started, leaving the cows to deal with me.

The 'swoop assault' was ideal for this situation, particularly as the herd would disappear into the dense stuff within the next minute or two and I would lose the initiative. Dodging rapidly between bushes and trees, I penetrated the herd which had spread out a little and shot the matriarch from a few paces then ran up the head onto the body. The tuskless cow rushed in as expected but I had time to shoot before her trunk reached me. I could not have stepped back without falling over backwards off the elephant's body! Out of the corner of my eye I saw the bull going off at full speed, just as predicted. I put down the remainder of the herd, the worst part being dealing with the odd calf (Often I would tell Tsuro to attend to this unpleasant job with his .450). Of the thirteen bodies, ten were touching one another. The photograph shows, from the right, two bodies one behind the other, then the lead cow's big frame from where I did the shooting with Shupo leaning against the tuskless cow and Tsuro in front of another cow. Behind those two elephants are two others and the remaining three are off the left of the picture. The grouping would not have been possible once they entered the jesse thicket right behind.

Returning to our little camp, we cooked lunch and I had a refreshing swim in the stream, washing away the last mental cobwebs left over from the previous night's attack of 'malcoholaria'. I was about to drive all the way back to Chipinda to call on Dave to send a gang to collect the meat when he drove into camp. While he returned to the station to send down people and a truck, we spent the afternoon cutting a track through to the elephants. The tsetse gang could not use everything, so word was sent to the villagers a couple of miles west of the corridor fence to come and help themselves.

Nobody had yet come up with an explanation about where or how these elephants had got into the corridor undetected. Tired as I was that night, I was not going to bother about the matter until morning when we would drive through the corridor and check for ourselves.

Hyenas woke me before dawn with their soulful whooping; a call I love to hear. So much part of Africa. Bvekenya sensed I was awake and gave a couple of tail whacks on the canvas ground sheet. He then passed a mighty elephant-meat-generated wind and I had to dash out of the tent and stand in the fresh air. Not far away, an elephant trumpeted. It took two seconds to penetrate – an elephant trumpeted! What the hell is going on here? The

game reserve was miles away across the corridor, and apart from the one bull which would have kept running right out of the district, all the others were dead. More mystery, at least until sunrise.

I woke the others early so that we could investigate in the direction from which the trumpeting had come, before the tsetse department vehicles started moving through the area. We drove a mile or two on a track south then walked towards a waterhole we knew of in mopane country. I smelt the elephants well before we found their tracks, which we discovered were heading away from the water. The herd was moving slowly, feeding at leisure on browse, green grass and occasional roots dug up by their big feet and trunks. We had no idea where this herd, estimated at a dozen or so, had come from or how long they had been living in the corridor. The tsetse fence guards could easily have assumed the elephants they had already reported were one and the same as those we had dealt with the previous day, when in fact there were two separate lots several miles apart. I knew the tsetse department guys were going to be shocked to hear of this second herd in their 'game-free' corridor.

Once we had caught up with the elephants we watched from a distance, counting fourteen animals, coincidentally the same number as yesterday's herd but without a mature bull in attendance nor any tuskless females. I was most reluctant to be heavy-handed with yet another group, but was aware of two potential problems if I simply tried to frighten them out of the corridor. Firstly, it may not work and I would end up spending days chasing them all over the place, particularly if they broke the cattle fence and went off deep into the tribal area. Secondly, the Tsetse Head Office, if they got to hear about me deciding which elephants should or should not be eliminated from *their* corridor, would go bananas and ministerial memos would be flying fast around Salisbury, and I would *hate* to be transferred away for 'dereliction of duty'!

The herd was still spread out, and I needed them grouped together without having to wait a couple of hours for them to gather in a shady place when the sun's heat and full stomachs led them to siesta time. I waited till the matriarch and three other big cows were reasonably close together, then walked up to them, being careful the wind did not carry my scent to any of the herd as the smell of a white man might have panicked them to run. Tsuro and Willie were right with me. The first cow to spot us raised her head, ears right out in a menacing fashion, immediately transmitting the alarm signal to her friends, while I purposely moved sideways to show up better.

At about twenty-five or thirty yards, the elephants felt threatened and after a short spell of shaking their heads, flapping their ears and a quick

blast of trumpeting, all four led by the long-tusked matriarch, came at us with heads down, flattening shrubs and small trees like bulldozers. The lead cow dropped dead to the brain shot, then I held my fire as the other three pulled up around her, screaming and growling but momentarily more concerned with her being down than with us. The other elephants came rushing in to join the angry confusion, which gave me the opportunity to quickly pick off each mature animal, thus systematically reducing the possibility of one elephant taking the initiative to lead the remainder to escape. The Mannlicher was as fast, smooth and reliable as ever in the heat of the moment, putting down all fourteen individuals without mishap.

We were only half an hour's drive from the nearest villages outside the corridor, so we went directly there to pass the word around the area, at the same time collecting a couple of men to drop off near the elephants. They could then direct the hordes to the spot. We then packed up camp and headed home to Chipinda for a break from living and working in the rain and dampness; looking forward to dry clothes, dry beds and a good night's sleep.

Just one good night at home! Tim Braybrooke at Mabala-uta radioed to ask me to come down to his area as soon as possible to deal with crop-raiding elephant bulls all over the place between the Limpopo river and the Nuanetsi. In addition to this, the D.C. was constructing a new game fence parallel to the Nuanetsi river where it entered Mozambique, to help keep elephants out of Sengwe Tribal Area. I had to harass any herds found west of this proposed line, rather as I was already doing in the Extension corridor in my own area.

"Come prepared to spend up to a fortnight in the district," Tim advised.

"No problem, Tim. I'll call in on my way down to the Limpopo and collect two hundred rounds of .458 off you. I'm short of the stuff up here and you can ask Bruce Austen to send you more. And please ask Bruce to tell Tsetse Department Head Office that I'll not be working in their corridors for a week or two. I will advise the local guys. They don't need me at the moment as things are quite well in hand. See you tomorrow." I switched off the set. Bvekenya sat watching me from the office door.

"Yes. You can come," I told him. "There are no dangerous tsetse flies in that part of the world. Just elephants. Let's go then."

The Vet Gets His Virus

The months when crop-raiding elephants were most active really put me in a squeeze trying to cover the complaints coming in from a huge area via the D.C.s from Nuanetsi and Chiredzi to Bruce Austen based at Zimbabwe Ruins, near Fort Victoria, the provincial capital. Bruce would then radio Mabala-uta or Chipinda Pools with the information.

On top of this control work, I was expected to keep up my operation in the Extension corridor, although there was no day-to-day urgency to be there while the new game fence was being erected. Some of the urgent jobs were to eliminate buffalo in the North Lundi corridor; elephants breaking fences into the Guluene corridor; lion killing donkeys in the Chikombedzi area; crocodile eating people on the Sabi river; and Ray Sparrow losing 18 calves to hyenas.

We had just returned to Chipinda after another week in the deep south of Sengwe Tribal Area, hunting big bull elephants around the Bubi and Limpopo rivers and shooting a pair of lionesses from a blind overlooking an ox they had killed next to a pool in the river. The locals had chased them off before they started feeding, then called me and I was unbelievably lucky to be in position in time because they returned before dark. I shot them both with the soft nose .458, one of the rare occasions I have used these rounds.

Back home, I really looked forward to a quiet weekend of catching up on odd jobs, servicing the vehicles, pumps, weapons and so on. Unfortunately, my girlfriend could not come down at short notice. We had not seen each other for months as I could never promise to be at Chipinda far enough in advance for her to take time off. Well, I would visit Claud Leroy or the Callow family over the river for some evening socialising.

It was a hot, lazy Saturday afternoon and I was about to take a cold shower when a Land Rover turned up behind my tin shack. The driver came rambling down to the house full of smiles and a strong hand shook mine enthusiastically. It was big, affable Dr. John Condy from the Research section of the Department of Veterinary Services.

I had met John a few times previously, and knew his casual manner and sense of humour belied a sharp intelligence and determination to pursue his professional goals. I had a nagging feeling that something was up; what on earth was John doing here anyway? He had achieved world-wide recognition for his work on Foot and Mouth Disease (F.M.D.) in cattle and buffalo, and had some tame buffalo and wildebeest in kraals at Hippo Valley Estates, near Chiredzi. Just a social visit, I decided.

We settled down with cold beers and traded news for a while, then John asked if I would come over to Hippo Valley the following day. Of course, I had nothing planned for Sunday.

"Sure, John. I'd like to see your buffalo and wildebeest. See how your domestication of them is going and hear more of your future plans."

"Yes, but I need some buffalo shot so I can take saliva, tongue and throat scrapings for F.M.D. tests," John continued.

"No problem," I said unsuspectingly. "Are they in pens or a small paddock? How many do you want killed?"

John took a long sip of beer and in the smoothest of voices explained that no, the buffalo were not penned up like cattle.

"There are some small herds of wild buffalo on the cattle section of Hippo Valley Estates and I have arranged to take ten animals for the F.M.D. samples. The Estate guys will be there to take over the carcasses for their labour force."

"Hold it, John," I exclaimed. "How the hell am I going to do this? I hope you have organised a tribe of hunters to do your little rabbit shoot. How else do you think you'll get ten buffalo from a random assortment of small groups all in one day?"

A huge grin split the handsome face. "Not in a day actually, Richard. You have to shoot them tomorrow afternoon between two o'clock and five-thirty. I must then get the specimens onto the evening plane from Buffalo Range airport to Salisbury to catch the overnight flight to London, so they will arrive fresh at Pirbright Virus Research Institute on Monday morning. The guys there are expecting the samples. They have unbelievable security arrangements because of the fear of the viruses escaping. Not even atom bombs are protected so securely!"

"Stuff your bloody security for your bloody viruses, Condy," I spluttered.

"You're mad! You make these commitments, plus international security fit for the Crown Jewels, then expect me to provide the goods like a bloody butcher's shop. If we see any buffalo, one or two shots will be your lot, end of story. And just where do we start looking for the animals over those thousands of acres? Forget it, John. Get a gang of *magotchas* with their .303s."

Twinkling eyes and a wicked smile told me my protests were useless. "See you for lunch at the Estate Visitors' Lodge tomorrow. I must get back now. Thanks for the beer." He waved cheerily as he drove off. I wandered up to the staff compound to warn Tsuro we would be going out the following day.

In the warm climates of Africa, the F.M.D. virus, although extremely contagious between cloven-hoofed animals, does not kill. The stricken animals have great difficulty chewing food and walking on tender feet, but normally recover in a few weeks. Only emaciated or sick individuals may die. However, in the cold and moist climates of Europe the virus becomes far more virulent, and any outbreak of the disease can only be contained by slaughtering all livestock within miles around, burying the carcasses, disinfecting all premises with chemicals and controlling movement of people and vehicles; all at a vast cost to the farmers and government. Not surprising that samples of live virus coming in to Pirbright Research Institute were treated as potential germ-warfare risks. Trust Condy to be playing around with dangerous things you cannot even see!

John's research involved trying to discover what triggered the outbreaks of the disease in cattle in Southern Rhodesia, and which wild animals could be carriers of the virus. Rhodesia wanted to export beef to Europe, but until the Europeans could be convinced that we had the disease under total control, they were not interested. John knew that buffalo harboured the virus, but why should it suddenly infect cattle after possibly several years of lying low? And to complicate matters further, there existed three different strains of F.M.D.: S.A.T. One, Two and Three! John wanted to know if the Hippo Valley buffalo were carriers of one or more strains, and if their systems developed antibodies to each type. Obviously there is a lot more to it all than I understood, and John deservedly received international recognition for finding many answers to the riddles of F.M.D.

Tsuro and I turned up at Hippo Valley at midday on Sunday to find John with Major Desfountain of the Estate management who would find me the buffalo, or so John assured me, and provide vehicles and labour to collect the carcasses. Well, I felt a bit more relaxed that somebody else had the responsibility of locating the buffalo – no finding, no shooting, no fault of mine! Major Des drove the Land Rover with John in the cab. Tsuro, a couple of cattle guards and I stood on the back, accompanied by the Mannlicher,

looking somewhat like a bunch of weekend biltong hunters. My mind wandered to the far-away boffins of Pirbright making arrangements for the arrival of Dangerous Substance 'X' and the various government ministries and departments liaising to allow 'X' fast passage through the loading and unloading procedures, customs, security, sniffer dogs and metal detectors, persistent porters, touting taxi drivers and whirlwind traffic out of Heathrow Airport. And what if 'X' was found *not* to be on the plane? I bruised a couple of ribs against the cab as Tsuro suddenly thumped the roof and Major Des jabbed the brakes. That woke me up. A buffalo was standing in a thicket surrounding an anthill about fifty yards away. I leapt off the back of the vehicle, rifle ready and approached the animal rapidly, wondering why it appeared semi-immobilised. The poor damn thing was tethered to a tree by a cable snare. I shot it and John took his samples of saliva, tongue scrapings and throat mucous.

Looking at his watch, John announced we still had three hours to collect the remaining nine.

"You'll be damn lucky to get any more after that shot," I reminded him. "Every buffalo on the ranch will have his head up in anticipation of trouble."

The Major seemed confident we would find one of the herds but even so, one shot, maybe two and that would be that. We cruised slowly through the bushveld, mowing down long grass and weaving amongst big trees and clumps of thicket. Within half an hour we spotted black shapes ahead, apparently not spooked by the sound of the car's engine. I checked the animals through binoculars; looked to be fifty to sixty bulls, cows and youngsters.

"Okay Des, Tsuro and I will jump off and you drive slowly obliquely to the left to keep their attention. The wind is left to right so we will go directly to them," I whispered through the window.

"Richard, don't shoot any juveniles," whispered John. "They may not have acquired the virus." I shook my head in despair. John Condy was pushing his luck.

The approach was easy through the long grass and clumps of bush and without further ado I shot three. Quickly reloading the .458 I ran up to the first buffalo and saw it was dying. Tsuro pointed out the second lying twenty yards away, heart-shot and dead. The third had followed the herd then stopped under a tree, facing us. We moved towards it, not wanting to fire a shot unnecessarily to scare the others. Seconds later it collapsed with a groan, so we ran on after the herd.

In spite of a diet of mostly meat, cigarettes and, in my case, an occasional bout of malignant poisoning of bottled liquids, we were

supremely fit and strong and soon caught up with the buffalo. They had halted, confused but on high alert. We approached carefully, using cover, to within fifty yards, but found open ground ahead, so I stood up next to a mopane tree and shot two more, both of which went down within yards, before we passed them by hot on the heels of the herd. Sprinting, dodging and leaping around and over obstacles, stopping instantly to shoot, we kept up with them until I was sure four more were down. The last one was a long way from the first so we started straight back, returning along the route of the stampeding herd.

Going through some tall thatching grass, we were suddenly charged by a buffalo cow at point-blank distance. It collapsed to the brain shot only a couple of barrel lengths from our feet. This was number eight and we had not checked it properly in our rush after the herd. Tsuro and I grinned at each other and moved on, meeting up after fifteen minutes with John and Major Des at number six. All was going well and John still had an hour to get his samples to the airfield. A gang of men with tractors and trailers were following, collecting the bodies; the Major's military strategy could not be faulted. It was a perfectly balmy lowveld evening, so Tsuro and I opted to walk the few miles back to the lodge rather than wait for the others. There was plenty of cold beer awaiting us.

We had a merry evening and fine dinner together. John was in good form, regaling the Major and I with stories of his years in the outback of Bechuanaland as a veterinary officer. After thanking me for putting in *two whole hours* of overtime on his behalf, he impudently added: "Can't think what you were fussing about, Richard. You must admit I made a good plan. I knew you wouldn't let me down."

"Thanks, John. Just don't forget the sleepless night worrying about how to lay out ten little piggies at a specific time. And the damage done to my hide by running through all those thorns and sticks. And your nice old cow trying to hug me with her horns."

John chuckled. "It's been a good weekend. We must get together again. We must make a plan."

John Condy and his plans! Years later we did indeed get together again: once to visit the Nata river and Makarikari Pan in Botswana, plus a couple of trips to the Chizarira Safari Area escarpment, and a cruise on Lake Kariba. It takes a good man to make a good plan.

Tsuro and Willie with record tusks

King Of Tuskers

This was a new experience. I had never dealt with a herd of university professors before, and have not done so since. A fine bunch of Afrikaans gentlemen from Potchefstroom University in South Africa, all five spoke good English and were keen and reasonably experienced hunters, at least with plains game. Tim Braybrooke came up from Mabala-uta to the camp site I had set up at Nyahungwe, a beautiful spot amongst giant Nyala trees on the south bank of the Lundi, to help with the guiding of these hunters.

South Africans are justifiably proud of their wines and never lose an opportunity to pull a cork. Even professors. Specially professors on a hunting safari. Being perfect hosts (unpaid) Tim and I could not possibly be churlish and turn down a glass of our guests' best. It was an extremely relaxed, happy time. The quintet shot assorted impala, kudu, duiker and several buffalo. They loved making biltong, helping in the kitchen preparing meals and uncorking wine bottles. Exactly how these guys came to be guests of the Southern Rhodesian government on a hunting trip in Gonarezhou State Land (not officially a National Park yet), I do not recall, but at the time it was not important. The recollection I have most vividly imprinted on my memory involved a buffalo hunt with Professor 'D'.

The Prof., Tsuro, Willie and I had been hot on the tracks of a herd of forty-odd buffalo half the morning, catching up with them in an expanse of scrubby mopane bush. The pair of us stalked them successfully, I pointed out a fine bull and D whacked it with his .375. Good shot. We waited a few minutes while the herd thundered away, before moving onto the scene carefully, Tsuro and I in front. I had checked D had reloaded and his rifle's

safety was on. On *safe*, that is.

We soon found plenty of blood, followed the trail and discovered the bull already dead nearby. Handshakes all round; fine trophy measuring nearly 42-inches across the spread and 14-inch wide bosses. Then Willie spoiled everything with a grunt. I had trained him too damn well. Twenty yards away he had found more blood following along the tracks of the herd. The .375 had indeed exited the first bull. Prof. D was most upset at apparently having wounded another animal, but I reassured him that it was accidental and that in the thick stuff one could not take all contingencies into consideration. Besides, we would find the buffalo and it would not be deducted from the party's allocation, I told him.

"Please follow at least five or ten yards behind me and Tsuro. Willie will be behind you. Keep your rifle on safe and do not fire at anything unless I tell you. Right, let's go," I instructed.

The wounded one soon split from the herd which was a good sign that it was hit hard, but the tension while sneaking through thickets and patches of head-high scrub mopane was extreme. I never knew if it might be standing behind the bushes we were just about to enter or just passing by, and I tried hard to put my faith in my intuition to once again warn me in time. It occurred to me suddenly that *this* was the warning. Why was I sure it was waiting for us instead of running on, or maybe already dead? I stopped Tsuro with a tiny hiss. He automatically dropped to one knee, peering intently through the bushes. I quickly glanced behind to see D and Willie had also stopped moving. I used my usual signal to indicate the buffalo was close, and held my hand up to them, a silent 'stay where you are'. I edged past Tsuro, glanced briefly at the hoof prints weaving through the nearby leafy bushes and eased off the .458's safety catch.

I smelt him first. It is difficult to describe the feeling of being close to an invisible but imminent attack from which, under the circumstances, one has about an even chance of successfully defending oneself. Wounded buffalo, once committed to vengeance, have to be killed or knocked down immediately. Failure to do so will mean a dead or smashed-up hunter. It is a heart-thumping, sweat-inducing, scary predicament.

I stopped, tightly wound as a spring, desperately looking and listening for any indication of the buffalo's location, before crossing an open space of a few paces width ahead of me. I stepped to the edge of the little clearing, backed up against a broken mopane stump and cleared my throat quietly. It worked and the buffalo crashed into the space between us, the bullet going in between the eyes of the raised head. A satisfyingly dead buffalo lay in front of me, with blood oozing from the first wound in the ribs behind the

left shoulder. Tsuro whistled and the other two appeared through the bushes. Professor D was looking tense but a half-smile of relief crept across his face. I turned back to the buffalo and, as I leant over to point at the .375's bullet hole in the hide, an almighty explosion detonated just above and behind my head.

After the past half-hour of intense concentration and nerve-racking stalking, I really did not need an unannounced accidental discharge of a .375 about three feet from my ear. Not sure if I was as dead as the bull and with shock turning my legs to jelly, I tipped over onto the animal's neck. Looking up, I saw D's chalk-white face contorted in horror. He thought he had shot me.

"Man, Richard. Are you okay? Man, I'm sorry. Gott, I yust don't know what happened," poor D stammered.

Getting up off the buffalo I propped my rifle against the body and taking D's rifle from his shaking hands I closed the bolt against the empty chamber, then lay it against the buffalo.

"I'm quite fine, D. Just got a hell of a fright but I get over these things eventually. Now, let's sit down and have a smoke then we'll have to get back to collect the Land Rover before it gets late. Lots of biltong work to do this evening."

That experience served me well when, years afterwards, I guided a broad spectrum of safari clients with an infinite mix of character and ability. Beware of the loaded weapon!

The Potchefstroom professors duly departed and I returned to the Extension corridor to find herds of elephant coming and going as if they owned the place, which of course they did. We had a great deal of conflict as I kept up the pressure, making life unpleasant for the great beasts. We hunted them incessantly for weeks at a stretch, coming into contact almost daily, sometimes without killing but more often with the necessity of shooting one or two. In some bad situations of self-defence against persistent aggression, I was not so forgiving.

While back at Chipinda for a couple of days break and the replenishment of supplies, Bruce Austen radioed with the news that another hunting safari was imminent; South Africans again but only two gentlemen this time. They were each to hunt a buffalo and an elephant bull, and Tim Braybrooke would be coming to assist again. Good. At the age of twenty-two and still fairly unworldly, I was not particularly at ease with elderly strangers and Tim was a good conversationalist.

Off I went down to the Nyahungwe camp site to ready things, with Tim and the two visitors arriving a couple of days later. We tossed a coin to

decide who would accompany whom while hunting. Tim would guide Pieter Henning and Victor Verster (pronounced Fir-stair) would have to put up with me, which I was delighted about when he quietly disclosed how much big game hunting he had done. Victor, I guessed, was around mid-sixty or older and Pieter was somewhat younger. Both were quieter, more serious characters than the academics but dedicated hunters, sporting fine English double rifles which had the patina of much use embedded in their wood and steel.

The first day out proved enormously exciting for Pieter, who shot an elephant carrying 73lbs and 55lbs of ivory, followed by a good buffalo bull. Tim was decidedly smug and feeling most relaxed, his work done. Even a little wink and nod, sort of "Take that, junior. Now you see how its done." Just great for 'junior's' confidence, but Victor's calm manner and reassuring demeanour soon restored my certitude. Anyhow, he was not the sort of person who could possibly feel competitive about his hunting buddy's good fortune in getting his fine trophies. That sort of daft attitude is for the inflated ego or the inferiority complex, which are probably psychotic cousins anyway. After all, what part did the human play in the growing of these tusks or the length of those horns? No, Victor was a true hunter.

We had checked out some cow elephant groups and tracks of buffalo herds on the first day, but decided to leave the buffalo hunting till later in case we disturbed the elephant bulls with gunfire. However, on the second day, we changed our minds when we came across the spoor of four buffalo bulls; one with enormous hoof prints. After two hours of difficult tracking, mostly through short but very dense clumps of dry grass, we found the bulls standing under a big shady pod mahogany tree. Victor had hunted plenty of buffalo, so I kept behind him as he planned the approach, chose the animal he wanted and shot it with his Rigby .470. It turned out not to be the one with exceptionally big hooves, but certainly carried the largest set of horns of the four, with a 44½-inch spread and long, tapering points curling up with powerful symmetry. Victor later had it registered in Rowland Ward's *Records of Big Game*.

From early morning on the third day we had worked on checking pans, roads and game trails for elephant bull spoor, and also stalked around the vicinity of two cow herds, but saw no mature males. Moving on by Land Rover to search in a different location, we met up with Tim and Pieter who had come looking for us. With much excitement they told us of three bulls they had seen not far from the Lundi, one of which showed a glimpse of big ivory as it wandered into the riverine forest. While the two old guys chatted in Afrikaans, Tim described the area to me, on the north side of the river

Pieter Henning and bull with 73/55lbs ivory

Victor Verster, Willie and Zhulamiti ivory

Ken Davey, Bob Cole and Tsuro, in Extension corridor

View of Lundi river, looking west from top of Chilojo cliffs

opposite the main section of the Chilojo cliffs. I knew those parts well and suspected that with the midday heat coming on, the elephants would not have progressed any great distance.

A few miles along the track I stopped the Land Rover and told my two trackers to check for the bull's spoor while Victor and I unpacked the rifles from their bags, loaded up, checked spare rounds, shook sand out of a shoe and chose the fullest water-bag.

"Pieter says the brief view he had of the big elephant's ivory was fantastic, although he only saw the right-hand tusk," Victor said quietly, with no trace of excitement in his voice.

"Yah, Victor, Tim said the same. Said it was the biggest tusk he had seen on a live elephant. You know Bulpin's book, *The Ivory Trail*, when Bvekenya Barnard reckons he hunted, but did not shoot, a bull with huge ivory known by the Shangaans as *Zhulamiti* (Taller than the Trees) at the end of his hunting career in this part of the world. Well, the tribespeople here still talk of *Zhulamiti*, but of course the bull of Bvekenya's day could not still be alive today, so I believe that any particularly big tusker with exceptional and recognisable ivories which takes up residence in this district is given the title. A sort of hereditary peerage in Shangaan traditional folklore. That old game scout with Tim, Sergeant Mac, is a Shangaan. I heard him say to Willie and Tsuro that the bull is *Zhulamiti*."

The trackers returned and reported finding the tracks of the three elephants, heading west along the jungle of the riverine forest.

"So, Victor. We now hunt the 'Legend of Gonarezhou'," I quipped. "I suggest we head parallel to the river but well out of the fringe of big trees. With the wind from the south and the elephants going west, we should stay on the north side of them and rely on hearing or seeing them. From time to time Tsuro will go and check that the tracks are heading along as we expect. His scent will probably not alarm them if by chance the wind changes, whereas our white man's smell will send them running. There are pools on this side of the river bed further along. Maybe they'll go there for a drink."

Victor nodded agreement to my suggestion. Although old enough to be my grandfather, he and I had formed a friendship based largely on our hunter's empathy. Over whisky and soda in the evenings, he had wheedled out of me enough of my past to be surprised at how much experience I had acquired, as I am sure at our first meeting he had wondered who would hold whose hand in a tight corner! Consequently, I respected his age and experience while he accepted my local knowledge and confidence with big game.

I briefly explained the plan to Tsuro and Willie, adding that we were not

to hurry, and in particular must not alarm any other game. We moved off, pausing now and again if one of us heard a sound or saw something move. A small group of nyala cows with youngsters saw us and disappeared into some dense bush, fortunately in the opposite direction to ours. Trumpeter hornbills flapped their heavy, undulating passage overhead, wailing like strangled babies. Little emerald-spotted doves lazily toot-tooted down the scales of their soporific song; a lovely call that always evokes for me a feeling of being alone in the wilds of Africa.

We had covered a mile or so when Tsuro stopped us with a hiss, his hand pointing to the edge of the forest ahead. A branch cracked and leaves shook on a tree less than a hundred yards away, a grey patch of hide moved and a huge shaft of ivory briefly materialised in the greenery.

Eyes wide, Victor turned to me, whispering "Did you see that?"

I nodded.

"That's him," Willie whispered, "Zhulamiti!"

Checking the wind with the ash bag, I led the way, hoping to find a gap in the forest where we could ambush the bull but mindful that the other two bulls could get in our way and ruin things. If they were youngsters they might be a bit cheeky.

Slipping smartly between trees and bushes we moved ahead of the spot where we had seen the bull feeding, to fortunately find an avenue through the forest leading towards the river bank. Magnificent spreading tamarind trees hung over the open space, with the dark green, dense foliage of Natal mahoganies forming a broken wall below. We waited. The swish of branches against hide turned our attention to a spot thirty yards away along the avenue, whereupon the great head carrying the long sweeps of ivory appeared.

The bull was old; very old. His sunken temples and slow, ponderous movements made him look tired. His body came into full view with the shuffling walk of the aged. Victor's .470 boomed once, then again. The bull momentarily shuddered, then turned away and hurried off into the undergrowth towards the river. Out of the corner of my eye, I saw Victor reload and check his safety catch.

The unmistakable thud of the elephant falling, accompanied by the sound of snapping twigs, was a great relief. I felt like sprinting through the bushes to make sure, but simply nodded and smiled at Victor then walked ahead, still wary of the two accomplices of the old bull. I had heard noises up at the pools and assumed it was them drinking but they still might come looking for their friend, although it was now unlikely. Victor's heart shots were faultless; the elephant was dead within fifty strides, and there was no

sight or sound of the younger bulls.

For a while we were speechless, overawed by the size of the tusks, my mental scale weighing steadily higher and higher. Turning to Victor, I shook his hand and could only say, "Incredible."

After a pause, he asked, "Well, Richard, do you think the long tusk is over a hundred pounds?"

I eyed Victor sideways, seeing the excitement in the old man's face and waited to answer slowly, "No, Victor." I gave him another few seconds. "But definitely over a hundred and twenty pounds," I added with a laugh at the look on his face. He smiled at the leg-pulling then asked how I had gauged the weight.

"Lots of practice, Victor."

"But you haven't seen ivory this size before, so how can you be so confident?" he asked.

"You are right, these are the biggest I've seen. But I have studied hard to be an elephant hunter from a very young age, not that it's many years in your time scale, but the ability to accurately assess ivory is a knack I have had for years. Anyway, I will go up to Chipinda tomorrow and fetch a scale to weigh them. Maybe I am way out, we'll see!"

We returned to camp with due jubilation, collected the others and returned to take photographs, measure the animal and start skinning and butchering. Tsuro set about the laborious job of removing the tusks with axe and knife, and by late afternoon he had them free with just a final layer of bone remaining from the sockets. We took them back to camp with a full load of meat on the vehicle and enjoyed an evening of relaxation and story-telling.

The following morning Tsuro carefully completed the work on the tusks while I drove to Chipinda Pools, returning with a spring scale which we quickly hung from a branch and hooked on a folded grain bag as a sling. Willie and Tsuro laid the 8-foot 6-inch long tusk in the loop while we watched the needle creep up to 132lbs. The shorter, right-hand 'working' tusk was 7-foot 1-inch long and weighed 107lbs. To the best of our combined knowledge, this was the heaviest pair of tusks on record taken by a hunter in Southern Rhodesia, and Victor had them entered in Rowland Ward's record book.

Inevitably there was some criticism when word got out about this event; mainly from some of the local anti-hunting folks, and of course, from a few envious hunters as well. Thirty-two years later, I wrote an article about the hunt for the Zimbabwe magazine *African Hunter*, which was probably the first account to be made generally public. Several acquaintances subsequently

censured me with comments like: "So *you* were the bastard who got that elephant shot" or "That elephant was a national treasure and should not have been killed." Okay, I take their point, but those people were not fully informed and really could have asked my opinion first on the rights or wrongs. I was there, after all!

The first point is that the government, including the National Parks head office, offered the hunt to these people in gratitude for invaluable services they had rendered the country, and with no strings attached. Secondly, I was the official guide and was doing my job with no mandate to obstruct the government's guest from shooting a particular animal. Thirdly, many large tuskers, as I personally knew, inhabited the south-eastern lowveld and Kruger National Park region, and this one certainly had acquired no public image or 'national treasure' status similar to Ahmed of Marsabit. Only many years later did the Kruger Park rangers begin publicising the individual giant tuskers living under their care.

Finally, and the only real issues that, to me, are of any real significance, were the elephant's age and it's value to another hunter, legal or otherwise. That elephant had not long to live out its natural span, and to die in the wilderness of Gonarezhou would almost certainly have meant those tusks lying and disintegrating in the sun and rain. Had the animal gone into neighbouring Mozambique, either a client of Safarilandia, Werner von Alvensleben's outfit, could have shot it, or a Portuguese official or African local could have poached it. Similarly, it could have been killed by white or black poachers on Rhodesian soil. So, King *Zhulamiti* the Sixth (or 10th, or 13th, take your pick) had served his role in fathering more potential big tuskers, had retired to see out his few remaining months, and *would* die. By one means or another. Fate decreed by the hand of Victor. Do I have any regrets? Yes, I would like to have inherited the tusks. Victor Verster has passed on to hunter's heaven; maybe he sits and watches *Zhulamiti* browsing the sweet, green leaves of everlasting abundance. But *what* has happened to those 239lbs of magnificent ivory?

TWENTY-EIGHT

Dark Deeds

T he fierce heat of the lowveld seemed to heighten the effects of the drought to a more severe degree than on the cooler Rhodesian highveld plateau, burning the life and nutrition out of the grass and foliage on which game and cattle depended. But water, or lack of it, was the major problem. Cattle were at an advantage; they could be moved to other parts of the ranch or to distant districts where water and food was available. Food could be brought to them and water could be piped across farms or supplied by boreholes.

For wild animals though, life could be brutal and short in the killer droughts. Elephants had the strength and the stamina to move long distances in their search for water, but often lacked the will to leave their home ranges to go far afield, or possibly they feared breaking through the game fences which they had learnt to respect. In 1992, hundreds of elephants died in Gonarezhou when an exceptionally severe drought struck and they were unable or unwilling to venture into areas where they may have survived, but would very likely have come into conflict with humans. Either tribespeople or cattle ranchers trying to protect their own resources of food and water would take exception to sharing anything with elephants.

On 26th January 1968, I noted in my diary that about fifty hippo and between thirty and fifty crocodiles were living in *one* pool near my house, the Lundi being reduced to just a few puddles mostly too shallow for these animals. Normally, after at least two to three months of the rainy season, the river should have been flowing well by the end of January. In March I received a S.O.S. from Bruce Austen to attend to elephants at a ranch in the Nuanetsi district. The desperate creatures were helping themselves to water

at the cattle troughs and at the same time breaking down fences and kraals continuously, resulting in chaos with the cattle herds all over the huge property.

Taking Tsuro and Willie, the .458, a .375 with a detachable 2x scope, spare battery and a 12-volt spotlight, I arrived late that afternoon at Umfula ranch, more than a hundred miles south-west of Chipinda, and promptly found the fresh tracks of eight elephants. We followed but gave up when the sun began to sneak behind the treetops. We arrived at the main centre of the disruptions in time to check out the surroundings. The fences of four paddocks met at a 'hub' where a circular drinking trough was situated. Nearby was a large, six feet high, brick reservoir and a plunge cattle dip for the eradication of ticks with its own kraal and raceway. The top layers of brickwork of the reservoir were breaking down from the pressure of elephants leaning against the wall while they reached for the water. The pole fences leading to the central water tank were also badly smashed up.

The elephants had mainly approached and departed on the south or east side of the hub, so we set up our simple little camp next to a baobab tree a couple of hundred yards north of the complex, ate an uncomplicated one-course dinner of curried bully-beef and rice, followed by strong coffee. As darkness fell, Tsuro and I returned to the walled plunge dip and settled in with rifles, battery and spotlight some thirty to forty yards from the drinking trough. Tsuro knew exactly how to operate the light after years of experience. He knew not to hold it behind me so as to cast shadows or reflect off the lens of the scope, nor to be in the way of the muzzle of the rifle by being too much in front. If we needed to move, he simply carried the battery on one shoulder and wielded the lamp with the other hand.

At around eight-thirty the sound of approaching elephants reached us. The night was absolutely dark with the sky mostly clouded over and, although we soon heard the sounds of splashing and blowing at the drinking trough, we could not make out any shapes. We stood up, I whispered to Tsuro to switch on as I raised the .375 ready to shoot, and was taken completely by surprise as the powerful beam lit up, but hardly penetrated, a great, thick cloud of billowing dust. It had not occurred to me that the fine dust of the kraal, pulverised by thousands of cattle's hooves, would be so stirred up by the milling of the frantically thirsty elephants!

Indistinct shapes moved around as the herd appeared to turn *en masse* away from the light, backsides towards us. I told Tsuro to pick up the battery and we quickly circled to the right until the beam disclosed a clearer view. The elephants had bunched together, tails to the light as if frightened of seeing it but not wanting to leave the water. They had obviously not picked

up our scent. I whispered to Tsuro and the light went out. The sudden blackness was extremely unnerving with the disturbed and unpredictable elephants hardly twenty-five yards away, but I managed not to panic for a count of five seconds, then whispered "Okay" to Tsuro. The little stratagem worked. The beam showed the herd shifting apart though the dust was also rising up again, but I quickly brain-shot a big cow which had turned broadside while the light was extinguished. Chaos ensued. The mayhem amongst the elephants was frightening; an almighty splash indicating that one had fallen into the tank while another charged into the dead animal, fell over onto the wooden fence, smashing the timbers and sending a yard-long piece flying towards us. The herd all seemed to be trumpeting and roaring at once, and with the dust cloud threatening to envelope us, we retreated back towards the haven of the dip-tank walls.

We were halfway there, the masonry walls just visible in the light beam ten yards away through the dust, when the walls suddenly moved! It was an elephant, confused by our light and the shadows of its own movements, turning this way and that. Firing twice for the heart, I was greatly relieved when it rushed off towards the main herd, allowing us to make a dash for safety in the dip's raceway. I was breathless with the nerve-racking events, and fumbled fresh rounds into the rifle while listening to the sounds of the panicking elephants departing. A muffled thump and gurgling noises raised my spirits greatly; the second cow was down.

We both lit cigarettes and smoked silently for several delicious minutes of peace, calm and relief, the shrill call of a disturbed plover sounding faintly ridiculous after the recent momentous upheaval. A tiny Scops owl trilled its short, measured calls in the distance, and once an elephant gave a short blast of anger, far away to the south. We walked about, finding the second elephant barely fifty yards beyond the hub.

Willie welcomed us with relief as he had no idea what had happened, having heard the uproar and caught occasional flashes of light. Suddenly, after a long day and much adrenalin-pumping over the past fifteen minutes, I was overcome by tiredness, flopping onto my stretcher exhausted.

Awake long before dawn I recaptured the night's events, thinking how shooting elephants at night in those conditions was venturing into a very foolhardy activity. As it was, the elephants never returned, justifying the effort but I was also keenly aware of the unfairness to the wild creatures. There was no malicious intent on their part. They were simply trying to survive and must have felt some kind of elephantine contentment when good, permanent water was located along with a great deal more food than they had in their homeland. Then a killer human appears and wrecks their

lives again. I had no useful answers to this type of problem, so consoled my conscience with the thought that they were temporary problems, rain would fall in due course, and that I had shot the minimum number and wounded none.

We made some makeshift repairs to the poles around the water trough as the cattle were beginning to arrive, and took some meat off one elephant for ourselves. I decided the ranch owner should keep the ivory of both cows as I saw no point in claiming the tusks for the government. I did not have time to chop them out and may not pass this way again for a long time.

On our journey to the ranch headquarters we found signs of five herds of elephants, which I reckoned totalled between fifty and eighty animals. The freshest tracks were new enough to warrant a follow-up, and we caught the herd of about a dozen after a couple of miles. However, as we made our approach up-wind, a cow and half-grown juvenile came from somewhere, straight at us, obviously also trying to catch up with the herd. I shot both, and hoped the escaping herd would pass on the alarm to other groups, to add to the events of last night. The herds appeared to be heading south for Nuanetsi ranch so could end up in the Buffalo Bend or Malipati area in due course.

After reporting to the rancher we departed for Chipinda Pools, arriving home in the evening, ready for a good night's sleep. However, Jim Pascall, the Senior Tsetse Officer who had recently replaced Dave Madgen, called round with a message and a bottle of whisky. Jim was a Scot; a small, fit man in his early fifties with a marvellous sense of humour, a love of classical music and Scotch, naturally. He stayed on for a leisurely supper in order to give us sufficient time to gently empty the bottle, and for him to deliver the message. Tinky Haslam, who had replaced Tim Braybrooke at Mabala-uta, had passed through Chipinda earlier in the day and asked Jim to tell me that crop-raiding elephants were dying to make my acquaintance down in the Nuanetsi district. I wondered why Tinky did not do the job himself, seeing that he lived in that area.

Jim and I waffled on many subjects deep into the night, and I awoke next morning struggling with a hangover and a conscience. The two were connected, but the former was the more powerful force so, as nobody knew I had returned from Umfula ranch, I would not turn on the station radio set thereby avoiding any lies about why it was important for me to stay in bed rather than drive to hell-and-gone to hunt elephants.

At midday, Tsuro called out that lunch was ready. I had already smelt the cooking meal and heard him loudly setting the tin table with cutlery, not so gently advising me that a world existed outside my semi-comatose cranium.

I got up and stood in the doorway, grinning foolishly at him.

"When are we leaving for Nuanetsi?" he asked with a straight face. I had told him the previous evening about the elephants destroying crops down there.

"After lunch. Two o'clock. We'll sleep at Mabala-uta tonight," I replied, suddenly feeling more human and ready to tuck into my lunch. Bvekenya wagged his tail, also happy that his boss had not died overnight. I would take him along on this trip. We would drive down through the North-east/South-west corridor and avoid the tsetse fly area.

Tinky Haslam had gone to Fort Victoria for a day or two, so we had an early night, rose at dawn and travelled south to the Limpopo river, stopping occasionally at villages to find out where the elephants were a problem. Eventually we made camp, having only gleaned vague information about three bulls in a remote area. I knew any complainants would find us promptly now that it was known we were in the district. Sure enough, a messenger arrived at sundown with news that three bulls had done much damage in some village plots far away to the north-west, apparently through some rugged territory which would be difficult to reach by Land Rover.

Tsuro, the local man and I started out before sunrise, leaving Willie to look after camp, vehicle and Bvekenya. We carried two water-bags, biltong, coffee and sugar, knowing the villagers would help us with food and a hut to sleep in. March is warm enough not to need blankets. Apart from the .458 and cartridge belt, I carried a cake of soap, cigarettes, matches and ash bag, travelling light and fast. Just as well, for it took five hours to reach the kraal of the headman. We sat down with him under a large marula tree in his yard while lengthy greetings took place and his wives brought an earthenware pot of *rapoko* beer with a drinking calabash each. The thick, bitter brew was a great reviver after our forced march and was most welcome as we listened to the tale of destruction by the elephants. They had apparently been in the area for ten days, visiting the crops on at least six nights but tending to move out if the villagers made enough noise with the beating of drums, tin cans and iron pipes.

At my request the headman led us to a kraal about half a mile away, roughly central to the various villages under his jurisdiction which had experienced visits by the bulls. We were given a hut each to sleep in, and offered some goat meat, pumpkin and sorghum *sadza* for lunch which we accepted gratefully. During the afternoon we toured the area to familiarise ourselves with the position of the other villages and croplands, and to view damage to the drought-stricken, sorry-looking plots of sorghum, millet, root crops and different types of pumpkins.

I was woken by drums at ten o'clock. The weather had cleared completely since our visit to Umfula ranch, and I stepped out of my hut to see a bright half-moon overhead. Calling to Tsuro, who was sharing a hut with the headman's son who was to be our guide, I put on shoes, ammunition belt and loaded the Mannlicher. The young man confirmed the drums indicated elephant presence, and said he knew the kraal about fifteen minutes walk away. The drums ceased according to our instructions that the people must not make so much noise that the bulls would depart before we had a chance to arrive at the scene.

In anticipation of close-up shooting of bull elephants in moonlight, I had opted for the .458 rather than the .375 with its scope. It suited me better for quick, both-eyes-open reflex shooting. Using a drop of mopane resin as glue, I had stuck a tiny triangle of white paper on the foresight which showed up quite well in the moonlight, but less so in the shadows of trees; a point which I mentally noted.

Slowing down as we approached the open areas of the untidy little fields, we could hear the elephants feeding. My throat became a little drier, my heart beat a little louder and my nerves tautened as I took the lead towards the downwind side of the plots; the fright I had had with the herd at Umfula just a few nights previously was still with me. Two big, moonlight-grey hulks appeared, close together, moving slowly through the sparse stalks. Indicating to Tsuro and the guide to stay put, I quickly moved up close to the bulls, keeping on the 'moonward' side for the best illumination. I waited, twenty paces from them until one turned side-on, which instantly collapsed to a brain shot. His friend rushed off, much to my relief, and I was about to fire another shot to frighten him a bit more when Tsuro shouted from behind, "*Hokoyo*, Bwana! (Watch out!)."

The third bull, who had not disclosed his position by sound or movement until now, came crashing out of the nearby bushes and through the field to my left, obviously following the other one. I dropped down on one knee, expecting him to pass by at full tilt and with no intention of shooting him, but he must have seen my quick movement. He promptly altered course, coming directly at me, and gave a short, frightening roar of anger. From my low position I was aiming at his huge head looming towards me, but with little chance of a successful brain shot at that acute angle and in the dark. With the blast of the .458 his right tusk disintegrated; the sight of pieces of white ivory flying into the night is still clear in my mind.

The bull's back legs collapsed, but with his head swinging and trunk flailing about, I had difficulty trying for another brain shot, even though we were only five or six yards apart by then. I fired into his chest twice as his

hindquarters rose up, then my last round into the shoulder as he turned to crash away past the huts into the mopane forest beyond. As I reloaded the Mannlicher, a grinning Tsuro arrived, followed by our nervous young guide.

"Why did you sit down like a pumpkin?" Tsuro asked. "It's better to stay standing so you look like a sorghum stalk."

"Stop talking rubbish, Tsuro. And why did you not come and tell me that elephant was waiting in the trees. You are so old you can't see or hear anymore," I retorted. The repartee relaxed my tenseness, and even our guide was now smiling. Some people began calling to each other from their huts and we told them not to come out until we discovered what had happened to the wounded animal.

Taking Tsuro with me, I walked to the edge of the open mopane forest along the path taken by the bull through the sorghum plants. Wetness brushed off a stalk onto my arm, which the light of a match showed up as being the elephant's blood. Dark, arterial blood; a good sign. With the shadows of big trees in the monotones of grey light it was difficult to make out shapes beyond thirty or forty yards, so we moved very slowly, listening hard and staring at shadows, treading like fairies so as not to give our position away by crushing a twig or leaves. I froze as Tsuro hissed next to me and pointed to our left. A huge heap was motionless amongst some trees, but we approached cautiously, still on adrenalin level three. We then saw the reason for us not hearing the bull fall earlier on. It had toppled over against a pair of big mopanes and slid quietly down onto its knees.

Next morning we examined the effect of my first shot at this elephant. After hitting the tusk close to the skull the bullet went into the head below the eye and stopped about a foot inside. Fortunately the impact had been sufficient to briefly stop the elephant and upset his balance. The tusk was shattered right up into the socket with shreds of the big nerve hanging out. This must have sent severe shock waves into his skull, causing the wild head shaking and thrashing of the trunk.

Tribespeople from far and wide arrived by the score and soon the familiar scene of jubilation, blood and guts was in full swing. The grateful headman insisted on three women accompanying us back to camp, to carry the melons and pumpkins which had been bestowed upon us. We reached camp that afternoon and Tsuro, who had been appraising the lasses, tried to convince one of them to stay over. He reckoned she should wash his clothes and cook some meals while he rested.

"Tsuro, you saw that huge Shangaan fellow carrying a long spear and big axe. That's her husband, you know," I told him with mock severity.

"All this elephant hunting is bad for your head," he complained as he

watched the women hurrying off to their distant homes.

On the six-hour drive back to Chipinda Pools the following day I thought about Tsuro's comment. Maybe he had a point. Yes, I decided that a change of environment would be a great idea. As a couple of friends, young police fellows from Vila Salazar, the tiny settlement where the rail line crossed the Southern Rhodesia/Mozambique border, were going to Europe, I would join up with them in London. Tsuro could go back to the farm at Rusape for a few weeks, Willie to his local village and Bvekenya would stay with the Callows at Chipinda. A *good plan*, as Dr. John Condy would have put it. Only the plan was almost spiked by an unseen enemy.

Defying Death in Darkest Europe

Something was wrong. Probably a bout of 'flu, I thought; aches, sweats, passing headaches, but all pushed into the background with the excitement of shortly leaving for Europe. I drove down to Twiza, a two-tin-huts-and-watertank railway siding in Gonarezhou where I boarded a passing train going to Lourenço Marques on the coast of Mozambique. The sole resident of Twiza (meaning giraffe), an elderly African employed by the Rhodesian Railways, was happy to take care of my Land Rover; that scum of the sewage system, the car thief, did not exist in or around Twiza town.

Feeling a whole lot worse on the overnight train journey to Lourenço Marques, I nevertheless managed to board the plane and after a nightmarish flight with fevers, searing headaches and rushing to the toilet, I landed at Basle in Switzerland. I staggered onto a train, reduced to a total wreck, not really enjoying my great holiday at all. I had intended to wend my way through Germany, Holland and Belgium *en route* to London, stopping by as many cities' red-light districts as possible to trade good Rhodesian pounds for feminine favours. What a sad failure I turned out; not one girl had the pleasure, nor the money! After a few hours on the train, I was struck by the horror of being found dead in a Swiss railway carriage. The Swiss would hate that. Probably think I was a heroin addict or an alcoholic. Very messy. No, I would rather die on solid ground, so when the train stopped I dragged my body and suitcase out of the carriage door and promptly collapsed unconscious on the station platform.

As I reeked of neither drugs nor alcohol, some kind soul took pity on the corpse-to-be crumpled on the concrete. I regained consciousness in an ambulance speeding through a city. What city? It turned out this was

Heidelberg in Germany. Later, I came around again in cool, white sheets in a small, cool, white room in the Isolation Ward at Heidelberg University Hospital. I hazily noticed a bag of saline liquid and another of blood hanging above me with little tubes coming down to my arms.

For three days I lived in hell. They did unspeakable things to me with pipes like we use for irrigating tobacco at home, trying to find out what caused the severe intestinal bleeding. I also urinated blood and vomited blood. I cried sometimes, but the tears were only salty. Medical students came visiting with their professors, prodding my distended liver and spleen, gabbling in low tones of German while I swore at them in pain-filled English. They nodded in German, smiled in German and filed out of the door, leaving me to carry on dying. Blood loss was well ahead of the replacement rate from the plastic bags hanging overhead. They also took blood samples by the dozen, particularly during the bone-wrenching fevers and shivers, but only on the fourth day did the verdict come: "Vee see zat you haf zee malaria." Pills were brought, the first solid objects I had eaten for days, and I managed a smile for my nurse, Maria. I would live.

Maria was entirely responsible for my hanging on when I felt like pulling the pipes out and sinking into history. Pretty, brown-eyed, black-haired, cream-complexioned Maria was my saviour, tending me with strong but gentle hands, always smiling and amusing me with her lovable broken English. With a thermometer in my mouth, I would stare up at her, holding her hand, inhaling her womanly fragrance almost swamped by the chemical aromas of hospitals but not quite, just as the starched uniform could not swamp the delicious curves of the girl beneath. When the thermometer was removed, with my fantasies at fever pitch, I would beseech her to get into my bed. A cheeky, sexy giggle would be the response while she stared at the tiny numbers on the glass tube and wrote on the chart. Of course, I was totally impotent with the illness; doubt I had enough of the red stuff in my veins to feed even a baby mosquito. My weight had dropped from 160lbs to 130lbs in ten days, so it took a fair while before things began to perk up again. But during the most desperate moments of that time in hospital, alone and lonely, it was Maria's presence that gave me the spark to keep breathing and hoping.

My recovery was rapid, and a few days after beginning the medicine I was staggering around on wobbly legs, looking for my clothes and suitcase and telling the doctors and nurses I wanted to leave. I could hardly believe how weak I had become, but it seemed that with every hour I felt a little stronger, and more determined to get out of hospital. The staff were horrified and refused to allow me to be discharged, and I heard Maria being told things in

the corridor but she came in to see me without handcuffs or chains, just her disarming smile and a plea to behave myself. She did not know I had found the cupboard containing my possessions.

I left a note for Maria, apologising for running away, thanking her for saving my life and wishing her well in the future. I felt a surge of emotion at the thought that I would never see her again. I sneaked out of the hospital before any staff had arrived at reception, hailed a taxi and was soon on a train across the Continent, bound for London.

I now knew how Samson felt when his locks of hair were cut off. I was so weak that I was unable to carry my little suitcase more than thirty or forty paces before sitting down on it for a rest. I looked like a scarecrow with my clothes hanging, oversized and baggy, my belt tightened up six inches shorter than normal to prevent my trousers falling down. But my spirits were up and I began eating like mad, with an insatiable appetite which cost a lot of money!

My two policeman friends, both named Tony, from Vila Salazar in Gonarezhou, were lodging in the basement of a flat in the Earls Court area, the residential centre for all colonial youth visiting London. Two or three girls were sharing, but room was made for me to sleep there, at least for a few days while I found my bearings and alternative lodgings. The two Tony's were working at various odd jobs, having resigned from their positions in Rhodesia with the intention of 'seeing the world'.

I soon moved into a small room at a bed and breakfast establishment in the same area and, with my health and strength fast recovering, began enjoying London life. I was lucky to have been raised in a home where classical and operatic music records were played just as often as those of the 'Crooners', the Blues, Elvis and the rest. I now had my first taste of live opera and symphonic performances which opened up my music world into a new dimension. I visited Rigby's, Holland & Holland and several less famous establishments of interest to hunters. A highlight was finding my way into the basement of the British Museum of Natural History to admire, touch and meditate upon the 'world record' elephant tusks. They lay across two wooden planks on the floor of a dark corridor, hidden away, unseen and unwanted. I found a light switch which lit up the passageway, squatted down and ran my hands over the huge yellow curves, lost in reverie for several minutes. To an elephant hunter, they are simply astounding, weighing 226lbs and 214lbs.

After some weeks I got itchy feet and decided to head back to the mainland. I asked Tony St. Clair, one of my police pals, to come along. Tony was broke, but with my promise to pay his train fares and buy food, plus an

aside that I was heading for Pamplona in Spain for the Festival of San Fermin, better known as 'The Running of The Bulls', he jumped at the suggestion. We left the following morning.

Budgeting constraints dictated that corners should be cut where possible, so having crossed the Channel, we bought tickets in Calais for the slow train to Paris, but paid only enough to make the next stop. We successfully passed many stops until, about forty miles out of Paris, the inspector discovered our little ruse. We sweetly oohed and aahed, professing no knowledge of French (which I had learnt at school) and he spoke no English. Tony and I only communicated in *Chilapalapa*, the lingua franca of our country. At the next stop, Monsieur Inspector came to our compartment and indicated the door! We jumped off the train only to find ourselves in a place one star up from Twiza siding in Gonarezhou. No trains came by, or rather, no slow trains stopped, though several sped past. We slept on the ground next to the platform and it drizzled during the night. A cold, damp, uncomfortable night was the price of a free ride! But we laughed a lot.

After Paris, which was too expensive for more than a couple of days, came Barcelona, Tarragona, Zaragoza and Pamplona. This was more like it. Big country, harsh country, friendly folks and cheap living costs. Pamplona was gearing up for the festival in honour of the town's patron saint, San Fermin. Floats were being prepared, wine shipped in by the tanker-load, shop fronts groaned under the weight of hanging hams and smoked beef, onions, garlic and trays of fruit, while visitors arrived to double the town's population almost overnight.

We opted to sleep on the grass in amongst the trees of the park, along with many other youngsters of assorted nationalities, which would result in us having more money to spend on the essential beverage, *vino tinto*. The cheap red wine came in various containers, the easiest and safest being the 'wine-skin', a kidney-shaped bag with a strap to hang over the shoulder and a spout at one end. One could feel very underdressed if seen without it.

We wandered through the streets, seeing workmen preparing movable wooden barriers which would be used to close off intersections when the herd of Spanish bulls was let loose daily for a mad gallop through town. The bullring, Plaza de Toros, was the venue every afternoon for a huge crowd to roar and cheer as seven bulls were fought and killed by the country's top picadors, toreadors and matadors. I saw forty-two bulls killed in the six afternoons. Sunday is of course a holy day – no violence.

To run through the streets with the bulls careering wildly along behind you was, I thought, really no more than a lot of fun and an act of bravado,

Six of the ten shot in dense jesse - Tsuro and I had a 'perfect duet' with first shots

Zambezi bull with unusually slim tusks

Sapi hunting area, Zambezi - Author, Zack Miller, Peter le Roux, Fritz Meyer

Fritz Meyer in Sapi hunting area, Zambezi

possibly to impress a dark-eyed damsel with a red carnation in her hair, watching from her balcony. I soon learnt that people actually got hurt! My girlfriend, an Australian sheila named Alison, whom I had picked up and fallen for in Barcelona, dared me to run the course. She had not threatened to divorce my sleeping bag for that of another man, so I could not understand why she demanded this potentially suicidal mission. Of course, I ran. Well ahead of the dense mob who were just ahead of the bulls, and going some distance before scrambling over a barrier, once out of sight of the eagle-eyed Alison. Later I heard two fellows were hospitalised after some horn and hoof damage. Another day, one was run down and killed.

By Saturday, the final day of grand celebrations, I was probably a little lust-struck. Blood-lust from bullfights, wine-lust from *el-tinto*, Alison-lust. So, to reduce the symptoms, I ran with the bulls; right with them for quite a long way until some fool ahead fell, causing a pile-up of runners in front of me. In a flash I glanced round at the oncoming bulls, a fatal loss of split seconds, and leapt sideways on top of several prone, thrashing bodies. A blow to my thigh helped propel me against a wall where I collapsed flat on my face, hearing the bulls thunder past. A couple of groans indicated someone was hurt, but apparently he only had a couple of cracked ribs. Miraculously, nobody was seriously damaged.

"Why are you limping, lover?" asked Alison later.

"Hell, Ali! Didn't you see the action? Nearly had a horn in the whatsits," I exclaimed, flopping down on the grass, rubbing the bruised muscles.

"No, I don't believe it! What a fantastic headline that would have made for the newspapers: "Bull bags boy's balls." You could try an encore in the ring this afternoon, you know."

"If I didn't love you, Alison, I would put you on short rations for those crude, cruel, words. Bloody Whorestralians have rocks in their hearts as well as their heads," I told her.

We moved on to the coastal resort of San Sebastian for a beach holiday, necessary for full recovery from the perils of Pamplona. Budgetary measures meant booking a double room in a small *pension* for Alison and Tony's companion, June, then us guys would sneak in late at night and share the place. One night loud knocks on the door and gruff voices sounded like trouble. I prodded Alison and told her to see who it was. It was policemen, that's who! They shone torches in Tony's and my faces and made rude Spanish noises which meant 'get the hell out of here'.

"Si, si, Senhor," we hurriedly replied, reaching for our clothes.

Tony and I found a park corner for the rest of the night, then counted our money next morning. There was enough for a few more days holiday, for

train fares to London and Basle for Tony and myself respectively and not much else. I was due to return to my elephants shortly anyway, and tried very hard to convince Alison to come back with me. Being married to an elephant hunter was as secure and blissful as a lass could wish, I assured her, but she smiled sweetly, kissed me and let me down ever so gently.

Chipinda Pools was still there on my return: Bvekenya very pleased to welcome me back; Willie fat, shiny and smiling; Tsuro with a wife, Janet, whom he had brought back from the farm. He had also had a bad bout of malaria! Later I heard from my sister who had visited me shortly before I went to Europe that she also went down with the disease.

Heidelberg University Hospital sent me a huge bill for doing their best to turn me into a sad statistic. I wrote back with the utmost respect, pointing out that I did not have the money, and I felt that my services as an object of unusual medical interest to their students amply covered their costs. Furthermore, I felt they had failed seriously in an excessively slow diagnosis of a straightforward case of malaria. And finally, I told them that had it not been for Maria, I would be dead and they would not have been paid anyway.

THIRTY

Brass On The Anthills

The major change in the world of Chipinda Pools was the completion of the Extension corridor fence during my absence on holiday, meaning that the tsetse department wanted all elephant and buffalo eliminated inside the corridor. It was going to be interesting to see how effective my previous work had been in keeping the animals out of the area, so I packed my gear into the Land Rover along with Tsuro and Willie for a few days of reconnaissance.

We drove over most of the tracks, walked most of the streams, visited pans and both the Sabi and Lundi rivers at the ends of the corridor. I was surprised and a bit disheartened to find signs of elephant all over the place, but had no idea at all if a few herds were moving around a lot, making it look as if there were more than was actually the case. Bruce Austen was quite adamant: kill all elephant and buffalo as soon as possible. I certainly concurred with him that there would be no serious depletion of the Gonarezhou population by this action, and the tsetse department agreed that the tribespeople from the areas west of the corridor could come to collect as much meat as possible.

Before I started on the corridor job I had a call from the South African Chief of Spraying Operations, Alex Kritzinger, who asked if I would come down to the Sabi/Lundi junction area and see what could be done about the occasional aggressive elephants putting the fear of the devil into the Africans working in the spraying teams. Alex was a quiet-spoken, calm sort of character, not at all keen on having elephants shot, but naturally concerned about the possibility of his gangs going on strike if they were frightened of walking through the bush with their knapsack spray tanks.

I spent two days traipsing around with different groups of sprayers but there were no incidents, which supported my advice to them when I had arrived: "Make a noise. Talk. Call out to each other. The elephants will hear you and move on before you are close enough to make them feel threatened. Elephants generally dislike the human voice." The men had thought that by moving around silently they would be safe, and if they made a sound the elephants would attack them. There were no more bad frights for the rest of the spraying season.

A couple of teams of *magotchas* with their tsetse field officer supervisors were operating in the Extension, spending twenty-five days in the bush hunting down kudu, bushbuck, warthog and bush pig, then taking five or six days off back at base. Their presence was useful to me as the hunters would cover a large area daily and by reporting sign of elephants to their supervisor, that information reached me quickly enough to be useful. A typical example was an occasion when Claud Leroy arrived at my camp at four o'clock one afternoon, an hour after my trackers and I had returned from shooting three buffalo bulls which had tried to force their way through the fence during the previous night.

"My fellows heard elephants breaking trees near the Masasanya river a couple of hours ago. Somewhere around here," said Claud, waving a finger over the map spread out on his Land Rover's bonnet. "Probably the same three or four bulls whose spoor was seen yesterday."

The area was a quick half-hour drive away along the fence. We left the vehicle and walked westwards for a couple of miles down into the valley. We soon picked up fresh tracks going up the dry river bed, eventually hearing rumbles of jumbo language ahead where the rocky valley narrowed. Keeping to the left side, we came across a sight that sent a tingle of shivers down my spine. Talk about *deja-vu*! The scene of several years previously, when I shot nine bulls out of a group of fifteen of which eleven were drinking from a pool in a rocky enclosure, was almost exactly repeated, only this was hundreds of miles south. Fourteen bull elephants were clustered around a pool in a rocky enclosure with a narrow entrance and a little sandy beach! Even the flat areas of surrounding granite were similar.

The three of us stood watching, and I wondered what passed through the minds of Willie and Tsuro. Did Tsuro recall the scene in the Zambezi Valley? I turned my thoughts to the job I had to do. There appeared to be four animals with ivory of 40 to 50lbs, though it was difficult to see what was what in the scrum of great bodies. To hell with the tsetse department. I was not going to kill those. I rather hoped they would break out of the corridor if frightened enough. I also did not want to kill any right in the pool because

the whole stream would be polluted once the rains started in a few weeks time.

Telling Willie to go upwind of the pool, but to keep behind a rock in case of bullets coming his way, Tsuro and I took up a position where I could cover every eventuality. The elephants got Willie's scent but were not really alarmed; once again I put this down to them not being afraid of Africans. I shouted "Nzou" then lobbed a fist-sized stone onto the slab of rock above their backs which seemed to gain their attention, and they began pushing their way out of the confined space up the slope and through the four-yard-wide gap in the boulders. The first shot was the start of the uproar proper, and for the next thirty seconds I kept shooting, letting the three carrying nice ivories go by accompanied by one smaller bull. Tsuro finished off one which was only stunned and had begun to rise. Its left tusk had been smashed off when it first dropped against a protruding boulder while two others had broken their ivory for the same reason.

Claud Leroy later told me a small group of bulls had forced their way out of the fence not far from his camp, and these I took to be the four from that encounter. I never discovered how, where or when a herd of fourteen bulls had found their way into the corridor, but of course they may have previously been in small scattered groups which had slowly amalgamated. I just hoped there were not many bulls left in the corridor.

On one of my brief visits to Chipinda, Bruce Austen radioed the news that two honorary officers would like to come down to assist me for a few days. Bob Cole, a lawyer from Bulawayo, and my good friend Ken Davey, the doctor from my home town Rusape, were old hunting buddies; both had plenty of big game experience, so I looked forward to their company.

Ken and Bob spent six days with me during which we accounted for twenty-plus elephants, but unfortunately on the day when I had to attend a court case in Chiredzi, the hunters wounded two animals in addition to killing five. We later shot one of the two. The evenings in camp with these two guys were memorable indeed, with the jokes, repartee and teasing between the pair keeping me in stitches. We also had deep discussions of a philosophical nature on Africa, politics, hunting in general and elephants in particular. I was really sorry to say goodbye to these fine gentlemen after such a fleeting visit.

Taking a break from continuous hunting, I decided to go on a trip around the lower Lundi river, the Chilojo cliffs and Tamboharta pan, not having seen that part of my area since hunting with the South African parties. It was the end of the dry season, very hot, with game concentrated along the Lundi where there were always permanent pools. Late one afternoon I sat with

Tsuro and Willie on a ridge protruding from the base of the Chilojo escarpment near Nyahungwe crossing point, watching buffalo plod wearily below us to water. The column of black beasts took nearly half an hour to pass by; I estimated between three and four thousand head, an accumulation of many groups forced by the shortage of food and water to congregate in the few remaining sections of territory able to sustain them.

Later, we camped miles downstream at Chitove, another crossing point used by vehicles, and took a walk into the undulating, mopane-covered country south of the river. There was sign of many elephants having been around recently, but we were completely surprised when we topped some high ground giving us a view for up to a mile all around. Half or more of that view was covered in elephants. Many hundreds. Grey bodies of all sizes moved slowly, randomly, in every direction through the scrub mopane and groves of bigger trees, appearing and disappearing as they crossed small ravines and hillocks. Incredibly there was very little noise from the assembled masses. No trumpeting nor growls of annoyance, just the slap of fanning ears or an occasional crack of a branch being broken off a tree. The whole scene had an almost religious air about it, the peace and quiet being absolutely eerie, making me feel I was an intruder at this elephantine Mecca.

We watched from our vantage point for a long time until the setting sun hinted that we should leave lest we become entangled with elephants in the dark. Relaxed in the warm evening breeze blowing along the river, we discussed the extraordinary event. Tsuro thought it was simply the result of animals concentrating on dwindling water supplies. Willie, however, told of Shangaan folklore which held that the elephants congregated thus from time to time, but with unpredictable intervals varying by several years, and not always in the same area.

"Do your people know the purpose of this gathering of many elephants? Some herds must come from distant areas and do not even know of these meeting places," I prompted Willie who had lapsed into a thoughtful silence. More seconds of silence. Give Willie time.

"Baas, we see the herds of cow elephants are sometimes ten or twenty, maybe thirty in number. We do not find sixty or a hundred living together all the time. Herds like that would break too many trees, eat too much food and drink too much water in their areas. So, in some years the elephants meet together for two or three days, mix up the herds like we saw today and then the old cows take away a new group, but a bit smaller than the old group, and return to their homelands."

"Yes, I understand. But Willie, how do the elephants know when it is time

to mix the herds, and where the meeting place is to be?"

Willie poked at the embers of our little fire with a dry stick and a small flame lit up his smiling face.

"We don't know how they decide the time, but when they do, they pass the message in their own language from herd to herd, and by the bulls which travel far across the elephants' country. These are the stories we hear from the old Shangaans."

I told my two friends how, in the book *The Ivory Trail*, Bvekenya Barnard describes a big gathering of elephants not far from where we were, about thirty miles east into Mozambique. Willie nodded sagely. What I was not able to tell them was the other experience of the 'gathering of the clans' which I had witnessed three years after this occasion, when I was living a different existence. I took my newly-wed wife, Brita, on a trip into Gonarezhou, and was amazed to be able to show her the rare sight of hundreds upon hundreds of elephants, south of Chitove Pools, barely two miles from the point I had stood on with Tsuro and Willie!

Devastating news greeted me when we returned to Chipinda Pools. My beloved Labrador, Bvekenya, was seriously ill with trypanosomiasis; his third infection in three years. My gardener had called in Jim Pascall to treat him but this time the Berenil injections could not save him. Bvekenya died the night we came home, a comatose wreck lying on the floor with his head resting on my lap. I was grief-stricken and blamed myself for taking him on trips into the corridors, even though we hardly ever saw tsetses due to the lack of game. Tsuro buried him next morning, then we left immediately for hunting in the Extension. I could not bear to stay in the little tin cottage without my pal.

The herds of elephant still residing in the corridor were now destroyed systematically, using all my experience and skills to the full, as any that escaped the kill meant another day's hunting at least, and possibly several days. In open grassland or light forest I welcomed an aggressive attitude by the older cows; two or three frontal brain shots at the leaders would cause the remainder to mill around directionless, and fast footwork coupled with quick shooting would take care of the herd.

It was quite different in the middle of msimbiti thickets and patches of jesse-type bush. There were often convenient termite mounds (anthills in local parlance) to gain an advantage in visibility and an element of safety. Dozens of anthills in that corridor were sprinkled with empty .458 brass on their summits! Many were bare or grass-covered with maybe a couple of shrubs or a tree growing on them, but some were buried deep under thick jesse and creepers. We would sneak through impossible stuff, find a low

mound maybe five or ten yards in diameter and a few feet high in the centre, but so densely vegetated that we were worse off for visibility.

It was on one such occasion that Tsuro, using the .450, and I had a perfect duet, each firing a shot so exactly simultaneously that Willie, a few paces behind, saw two elephants collapse side by side but with apparently only one shot fired!

We had no idea how many elephants were in the thicket, their spoor being concentrated on a few paths weaving through the overhanging bushes, but my feeling was between ten and fifteen. They were feeding but quite invisible, the wind was good but the deeper we penetrated the dense stuff, the more the air eddied about us. Bent double, we eased our way up the slope of a small anthill but it had no open areas on it. Leaves ahead and above us shook as an elephant pulled at a small tree a few feet in front. As I rose to a standing position, rifle ready, Tsuro came to my left and also stood up. There were actually two elephants before us, the one nearest to me being tuskless, wide-awake and instantly on the attack, accompanied by her companion at her side. There was no charging through the thicket, simply because we were within a trunk's length already; just a squeal and a big head a yard beyond the rifle's muzzle.

Everything happened in a second – looking the big cow in the eye, the scream of anger, the boom of the .458, the smashing of vegetation as the two bodies collapsed. I only partly registered that Tsuro had fired and flattened the other cow as I reloaded while quickly pushing my way past the dead elephants to try for the others behind them. Fortunately they were coming to see why the leaders had a fight on the go, or because there was no other senior cow to lead them away, and I put the remaining eight animals down. Hearing no other elephants crashing through the jesse, I assumed this was the complete herd and had this confirmed by Tsuro and Willie.

We sat down on the spot from which we had fired the first pair of shots and discussed the hunt over a cigarette. I thanked Tsuro for his quick, straight shooting to which he replied, "I wasn't worried about you, I was worried about *me*! But with this 'two-pipe' (double rifle) I would have shot your elephant also if you had been too slow."

After giving the subject some thought, I decided that this occasion was the *only* one where, had I been on my own, a double-barrel might have served me better than my Mannlicher. And I specifically say the Mannlicher-Schönauer, not any other large bore bolt-action rifle. A left and a right from a double rifle, *aiming to hit* two separate targets, even if those two targets are for example, the same charging buffalo's head at eight yards and again at six

yards, are measurably faster than the same two shots from a magazine-fed single barrel. Unequivocally faster. But a second shot from the quick-silver-smooth Mannlicher-Schönauer action with the short .458 round can be amply quick enough for the aforementioned charging buffalo. If those hunters who, having fired both barrels of their doubles and had still been savaged by the animal, were to be perfectly honest, I suspect they would admit to using the first shot too hastily *because* they felt confident with the instantly available second barrel. In any event, that second shot is frequently not quite as easy to pull off as one imagines, when one is *aiming to kill*. For many, including myself, the single barrel means one chance so place the bullet first time. With practice this can be done very fast with a well-fitted magazine rifle, notwithstanding the double's advantage of shortness and 'pointability'.

"Good double rifles are less prone to mechanical failure than bolt-actions" is of course a statement of fact. However, until someone statistically proves that mechanical failure accounts for more deaths or damage by big game on the users of single barrel rifles than doubles, this is misleading. Rare failures by cartridge misfire, often due to poor bullet construction and mostly operator error, are the real causes of maulings and apply to any weapon.

In fact, the human component is the critical variant often overlooked in this debate. The hunter who has the utmost faith in, and skill with, a double rifle will perform well with practice and confidence. The same person, if only accustomed to bolt-action big bores, given the same amount of practice, will be equally as deadly with his chosen weapon. I suggest it's the man, not the machine, that is important for survival.

Anyway, how is it that tennis players, golfers and cricketers, using utterly simple weapons with no moving parts, make all that money?

My *gaboon vipers: "… a stroll on the lawn."*

THIRTY-ONE

The Snake-Snatcher

Over the past year or so I had taken an interest in the variety of snakes found in the widely differing habitats of my district. Two friends working on the Hippo Valley Estates, Barry Washington and Basil 'Mac' McMenamin had a hobby going consisting of a couple of brick snake-pits and an outbuilding at Barry's plot where certain special snakes were housed in individual containers. White rats were bred to feed the snakes and basic equipment was kept for venom extraction and crystallisation. Barry and Mac had begun exporting desiccated venoms to the South African Institute for Medical Research near Johannesburg, where antivenom was manufactured for treating snake bites.

The species of commercial value to my friends were puff adder, Egyptian cobra, spitting cobra and black mamba, all common in the lowveld, plus gaboon viper which they obtained from an acquaintance living in the low-lying evergreen forests of the eastern border area of Rhodesia. Having learnt the techniques of catching and handling the four local species, I collected any that came my way and delivered them to my friends on my shopping-cum-boozing trips to Chiredzi town and Hippo Valley Club, a 'White Mischief' establishment of some repute in those times.

A series of events, silly old fate at work again, began to unfold and gently propelled me from one life into another, the transition accompanied by plenty of heart-searching and regret, tempered by youthful enthusiasm for an uncertain but carefree future and a totally irresponsible attitude to life in general.

Not so slowly but very surely, I hunted down all the remaining elephants in the Extension corridor, occasionally breaking off to do control work on

crop-raiders in the southern tribal areas or to cull a couple of elephants for a rancher. The hunting of elephant rather suddenly dwindled to nearly zero. A new ranger, John Osborne, had arrived to replace the long-gone Derek Tomlinson, and there was an awful lot of not-very-much for two rangers to occupy themselves with. The final straw showed up in the form of a major shuffle of rangers and other National Parks staff. My name was on the list of those to be transferred to some mini park where I would mend broken toilets, parade game scouts each morning to see if their brass buttons were shining and tell a couple of hundred tourists every weekend not to drop their litter! My letter of resignation from the Department of National Parks and Wildlife Management was on the very next game scout's bicycle heading for civilization.

Over a few beers at Hippo Valley Club, I told Mac and Barry of my decision to leave the department, how dejected I was at this major turn of events causing me to leave my beloved Gonarezhou, and that I knew it was partly my fault for not being prepared to accept authority, bosses, seniors or orders from anyone. In short, there was no chance of me ever knuckling down to become a civil servant. Wrong temperament entirely.

"So what are your plans?" Barry asked.

"Well, in the government service one has to work a three-month notice period, so I'm going to Zimbabwe Ruins Park for that time, then I'll look around," I explained.

Barry and Mac looked at each other and nodded. Mac spoke up: "Our snake venom business has grown quite well but is becoming too time consuming for us to pay it sufficient attention, and neither of us can afford to give up our jobs with the company. Why don't you join us and run the show. If you can keep expanding the production there should be a fair bit of cash in it for you."

"Yes, I'm interested," I replied, "so tomorrow let's have a look at just what you guys have been up to, what the sales of venom bring in, and what finances are involved. If it looks promising and we agree, I'll only come in as a partner. My present job is the last time I will work under anyone and I can put a bit of cash in for my share."

We duly agreed on the deal and I went off to complete my three months remaining in the department at the Zimbabwe Ruins National Park. This small area contained the famed ruins of historical interest and a number of attractive self-catering lodges, plus a block of offices and staff housing. Being resident for such a short period, I took over a double-roomed tourist lodge where Tsuro 'kept house' and cooked for me. Unfortunately, the Zimbabwe Ruins Hotel was only a few hundred yards from the National Park

establishment; this fact being the cause of my undoing on many a night.

The hotel business was owned by one Tony Davey, whose most attractive wife, Yvonne, worked as secretary for Bruce Austen. An ex-policeman, a bachelor named Brian Street, was employed as manager at the hotel. Brian and I hatched a mutually beneficial scheme designed to waylay lady tourists whom we fancied. Should a couple of girls arrive at the hotel reception to book a room, Brian would apologise, saying the hotel was fully booked and suggesting they try for a lodge down in the park. As they left to drive down the hill to my offices, Brian would phone to tell me to be prepared. I would tell the game scouts on duty at our reception office to advise the next arrivals that the lodges were all occupied, but to speak to the ranger who might be able to help.

I would listen to the groans of dismay as the visitors were told, most apologetically, that there was no available accommodation. Next, they would be ushered into my office whereupon I would offer them the unoccupied room in my lodge, naturally free of charge. Having settled them in, I would offer them dinner at the hotel, at which Brian would join us. It was a *good* plan!

The majority of my evenings were spent at the hotel bar counter; the voluminous intake of alcohol not doing my malaria-damaged liver any favours at all, having already lost some of its ability to fight off monumental hangovers. My days included repairing plumbing, seeing the game scouts had shining brass buttons and asking tourists not to drop litter – exactly as I had feared.

When Tony Davey discovered that I was about to make a new career as a snake-snatcher he was absolutely aghast. He had a blinding phobia towards the reptiles and could barely discuss the subject. With eyes closed and grey moustache bristling he would shout, "You're bloody mad, Harland. Now shut up. Talk about something else!" So one evening I took along a four-foot olive grass snake around my waist inside my shirt, and sat at the bar chatting with Brian and Roland Russell, the other ranger. When Tony turned up, Roland asked him casually if he would object to my bringing a little pet snake into the bar.

Fixing me with a murderous stare, Tony loudly threatened: "Don't ever try it, Harland. I'll bloody well kill you if you ever do that." A few strangers sitting around a table looked on in interest at this outburst, rather as if they expected a gunfight in the saloon.

Slightly warming to the occasion with half a dozen brandies in me, I rose off my bar stool and hitched up my trousers waistband, resulting in a certain amount of writhing under my shirt and the snake's head popping up behind

my neck. Well, amidst my and Roland's uproarious mirth, poor Tony became apoplectic, backing off down the length of the counter, face contorted and red, screaming all sorts of unpleasant things. The other customers drew back out of the line of fire should bullets fly. Fortunately Tony did not have a gun on him! I knew all along he would not attack me physically; the snake was pure armour-plate defence. However, before Tony could bring on a heart attack, I shouted an apology and left. Next day I asked for forgiveness which he was man enough to grant and we remained on good terms.

The fun and games, grog and girls were all part of a brief brush with civilization which, apart from the weeks in Europe, I had avoided for several years and probably developed a few idiosyncrasies along the way. Letting off steam was good for body and soul, but certainly not my idea of how this particular little human wished to exist for long. I was quite happy to pack my belongings and get back into the heat and familiar ambience of the lowveld. Mac McMenamin was manager of one sugar cane section on Hippo Valley Estates situated near the north boundary, and he had arranged with the neighbouring rancher that I could live on an isolated corner where the main water canal feeding the estate crossed from the ranch onto Hippo Valley land. I had acquired a large pile of corrugated iron roofing sheets and some timber, Mac provided sand and cement, and we soon had a tin shanty erected complete with kitchen, bathroom, bedroom and living area, doors and windows and cement floors. The walls and roof were all corrugated metal, hot as hell in summer and noisy in heavy rain. Second-hand furniture and fittings soon turned 'The Shack' as it became known, into a comfortable dwelling, secreted away in mopane forest far from sight and sound of humanity.

Barry and Mac had an excellent intelligence network through the many section managers who in turn had briefed their respective teams of workers, so anyone who saw a snake up a tree, go down a hole, hide in a pile of sugar cane stalks or wherever, would get word to one of us. With many thousands of people working over the vast cane fields, calls to catch snakes could number between two and a dozen per day. We paid the informant a reward based on the species and length of the snake, if caught, with the venomous types attracting the highest payment.

This system kept up the Africans' interest to report sightings, as they have a great fear of snakes and would rather run as fast and as far as possible when a *nyoka* is seen. Over a few weeks we would build up a big number of non-commercial species which I would then cart off and release in the wild a few miles away from the Estate. These were mainly house snakes, olive grass snakes, boomslangs, striped sand snakes, vine snakes,

pythons and half a dozen lesser species.

Puff adders up to two and a half feet, Mozambique spitting cobras going up to five feet, Egyptian cobras reaching eight feet and black mambas to twelve feet in length, were all reasonably common, but mambas being very alert, shy and fast moving, were the least frequently seen of the commercial snakes. Each species required different techniques for capture, subduing and transferring into a bag for transporting back to base, the puff adders being the simplest to catch. Big Egyptian cobras are very muscular, strong snakes and with the head and neck being the same girth, can be most difficult to hold onto for any length of time as they pull backwards in one's hand. However, they are not particularly aggressive and have a slow strike.

The 'spitter' is a different creature, ever more ready to take a stand and fire off jets of venom at one's eyes. However, they generally settled down well in captivity and would stop wasting their valuable product in self-defence. I had only one bad shot by a spitting cobra, a big fellow which had embedded itself amongst roots and holes at the base of a large tree. I had hold of its tail and could see parts of the body in amongst the woodwork, but could not find the head. Whilst kneeling down and peering under and around the roots, he stuck his head out from somewhere and gave me both barrels from less than two feet. As his lips parted I closed my eyes and felt the venom hit my cheeks below my glasses. As I opened my eyes the second squirt hit and splashed up under the spectacles into my eyes. I always carried a small bucket and a couple of gallons of water in the car, and within ten or fifteen seconds had my face in the water, eyes blinking rapidly to rinse out the poison. That saved my eyes from lasting damage. I could barely keep them open to drive home where I spent three days in the bedroom with the curtains closed, living in exquisite hell for the first night. It felt like a mixture of sand and sulphuric acid.

Mac, always the humorist, asked if the snake was in a bag still in the car when he visited the next morning.

"Go to hell, I'm not in the mood for stupid jokes," I groaned.

"So apart from wasting the valuable venom, you then let the thing escape. How are we going to make any profits? And we can't have you lying around like this all the time when there are snakes out there waiting to be caught."

Milking day was Monday. Working through the two large snake-pits, I would start with puff adders and after gently massaging the poison glands and pushing the venom down the long hollow fangs into a glass beaker, I would drop the snake into a large bin. Once finished with the adders, the bin would be tipped up to release them back into the pit, and I would go on

to the cobras. The venom of each species was of course kept separate, and a plastic membrane stretched over the mouth of the receptacle kept saliva and foreign objects like sand out. The jars were put into a laboratory desiccator with silica gel as the drying agent, becoming quite dehydrated in twenty-four hours. Puff adder and gaboon viper venom dries into dark, mustardy-yellow flakes, the cobra's becomes clear, pale yellow crystals, and mamba venom is colourless and resembles sugar when dry.

Gaboons were definitely my favourites. Wonderful colours and patterns, delightfully laid-back dispositions and huge volumes of venom made these great, fat, lazy fellows a pleasure to own. They ate their mice dutifully at meal times, the inch-plus long fangs dispatching the prey in seconds, then they curled up in a corner of their individual quarters to await the next session of venom extraction, followed by a stroll on the lawn and dinner.

Black mambas, on the other hand, were very difficult creatures to catch in the wild, keep in captivity and handle while extracting the poison. Snakes of around six or seven feet were slightly easier to control once the head was firmly held in one hand, but the big ones of ten feet or so would twist and writhe around so violently that they could dislocate the thin neck just behind the head. Normally, two of us would do the operation together to keep the yards of body getting out of control. The actual manoeuvring of the fingers to grip the head and the releasing of the snake after handling were the moments of particular danger; a bite, or even a scratch by a fang, could be a terminal event, so powerful is the neurotoxic venom. Still, like our professional golfer or tennis player taking a risky shot when pushed, I did it for money. Mamba venom was quite rare and very costly.

I would drive to Johannesburg bimonthly with the goods to personally hand them over at the Institute of Medical Research, a huge complex of buildings including stables for around one hundred and forty horses, used for the production of many types of vaccines for human use.

Nearly half the horses were occupied with manufacturing snake-bite serums, a lengthy process of bringing up the horse's antibodies to a high level of immunity over many weeks, then bleeding off several gallons of blood, reducing it to the clear serum content which contained the antibodies, followed by sterilisation and drying. The resultant cake was then reconstituted with sterile water and packed in glass phials for use. Meanwhile, the horse had a rest period of a couple of months before its next cycle of venom injections. To avoid trauma from the toxins, the injections contained a colloidal substance which allowed very gradual release of the venom molecules into the blood stream.

There were many lighter moments all in a day's work, such as the

At home on the Kwekwe ranch

Tsuro still cooking after twenty-five years

George, Tsuro's son, with bull in jesse

Dick Smith with 50¾ inch trophy, Chirisa

Dr Patrick Guinebertiere shortly before working on man shot in ambush

occasion when Tsuro went swimming, which really was not his favourite pastime. While standing on the edge of the concrete-lined canal with a width of five yards, working the hand pump which pushed water to the house tank, he observed a seven-foot Egyptian cobra floating past in the strong current. Tsuro was most adept at catching snakes and knew the it was worth several pounds of cash to him, so he rushed into the bush to find a branch with which to hook the big cobra out of the water. Running beside the canal he caught up with the snake being swept along and managed to stop the big reptile with the end of his piece of dead stick. As he lifted the heavy body out of the water, the branch snapped, Tsuro lost his balance and pitched head first into the rushing torrent next to the cobra. The two kept a wary eye on each other as they floated along for the next two hundred yards to where the canal divided. As the snake dropped over the dividing wall, Tsuro caught its tail and pulled himself onto the wall and out onto land, towing the cobra along until he found a stick with which to pin its head down and get a hold of it.

Barry Washington and I were chatting over a few beers at Hippo Valley Club one night when the discussion turned to venom. Barry insisted that night adder venom did not dry out completely but remained toffee-like, no matter how long it was left in the desiccator. He had no explanation and I did not believe him.

"Right," said Barry, downing the remains of his drink, "let's go and milk a couple of those snouted night adders in the laboratory and prove it to you." Impulsive sort of fellow was Barry.

It was quite late, we had consumed several beers, and I was probably not quite my usual cautious self. Dragging a foot-long, cigar-thick snouted adder out of its glass-fronted box, I laid it on the table and, mumbling to it, "Who's faster, snake, you or me?" I made a lightning strike with my hand at the head without first pinning it down. It looked so easy. The snake took a different view and, having drunk no beer, its strike was twice as fast as the aforesaid lightning. The fangs fastened neatly, deeply and determinedly into my little finger before I even touched the snake.

"There you go again. Wasting venom. Suppose I'd better do another one properly," came the unsympathetic comment from Barry.

Fortunately, night adders being small and not in the serious league of power poisons, the bite did not require antivenom. My inherent toxin resistance, plus a lot more beer when we returned to the pub, helped counteract the effects; plenty of pain, red and swollen fingers and hand, all began to subside after ten or twelve hours and two days later all signs had disappeared. The venom we put in the desiccator turned to a dark, toffee-

like substance which never dried out. Just as Barry had said. Cannot think why I had to reinvent the wheel!

During my time at Chipinda Pools, on one of my rare visits to Salisbury, I had met a girl who, much to my pleasant surprise, agreed to dine out with me on two or three consecutive evenings. I disappeared back into Gonarezhou to hunt elephants, reappearing on her doorstep six months later. Things progressed nicely. A very cuddly situation in fact. I drifted back into the backwoods, then managed to convince her that, whereas a game ranger was a reckless, footloose, no-good sort, this new-look keeper of reptiles was a truly solid citizen worthy of close attention. She really must visit The Shack down in the lovely lowveld, help with the garden and teach Tsuro some nouvelle cuisine. A long weekend date was set.

Heart beating a little faster, somewhere between facing an attack by cow elephants and catching a mamba, I met my girl off the clattering old DC3 aircraft at Buffalo Range airport and rushed her off to the humble, second-hand tin dwelling. Regrettably, I had recently tipped out a drum full of non-venomous and back-fanged snakes near the house, and a few striped sand snakes, vine snakes, boomslangs and grass snakes were lying around on the shrubs and cacti in the little garden. I introduced her ever so gently to them and she seemed to keep her nerve. However, half a dozen brown house snakes had sneaked into the house and were sunning themselves on window sills and chairs, and this was a bit much. I apologetically picked them all up and removed them to the sugar cane plantation a few hundred yards away.

I introduced her to lowveld life and the good-natured, hard-working types who had pioneered the huge sugar industry in the isolated world of Hippo Valley and Triangle Estates, most of which she hardly knew existed. In the evenings we chatted as those falling in love do, listened to classical music and opera, and overflowed with the excitement and wonder of discovering the million and one facts of each other's character, and the courses our lives had run thus far.

More weekend visits followed. Brita and I were married in December 1969 and I left the lowveld for the third and last time to return to the family farming business at Rusape.

THIRTY-TWO

Back To The Bush

It did not work out. Uncle Dick and my father, Nevill, had an amazing partnership which lasted over fifty years, but I could not fit in with the family business. Not with the continuous daily contact, the living cheek-by-jowl, the forced socialising. I found it difficult to fall in love with crop farming anyway. After a year Brita and I left for the Midlands district of Rhodesia where her parents lived on a cattle ranch near the town of Que Que; her father, Sonny Field, having retired from his position with the copper mine at Mufulira in Northern Rhodesia. The ranch was a legacy to Brita's mother, Rose, from her father, John Austen, who had acquired several farms in the area. Coincidentally, Bruce Austen's father, George, and Rose were brother and sister, thus Brita and Bruce were cousins.

Sonny Field had fought, aged eighteen, in the East Africa Campaign against troops of von Lettow-Vorbeck and was only a few miles distant at the time when Frederick Selous was killed. Sonny was later wounded and invalided back to South Africa. He also met the famed P.J. Pretorius who was a serious thorn in the Germans' side in the Tanganyika territory.

We set up house on the bank of a beautiful river, the Bembezaan, at the north end of the farm, with no electric power or telephone in the little dwelling we built, which was not dissimilar to The Shack at Hippo Valley. We also built a brick house for Tsuro and his family; he had progressed to being a talented cook under Brita's guidance.

For over two years I had not seen an elephant, buffalo, lion or leopard. Only the local kudu, warthog, duiker and steenbok on the ranch, or some introduced species of large antelope on friend's farms. But no big game and that was not good for my soul, so we rectified the omission with a trip to

Gonarezhou. Back to my piece of paradise where I was able to introduce Brita, who had spent most of her adult life in Salisbury and Europe, to another world. The highlight was seeing that vast number of elephants near Chitove, where Tsuro, Willie and I had witnessed the spectacle of the elephant gathering three years previously. Brita found the unspoilt wilderness, the beautiful riverine forests and limitless stretches of mopane as enthralling as the large and small game living there, and promptly became a 'mopane' person, permanently imprinted on the bushveld, much to my joy.

Enquiries came from friends and acquaintances needing assistance on hunting trips to the Zambezi Valley. We were only too pleased to help outfit and guide the hunters on these private safaris, particularly as there was no commercial value attached and the 'client' was not pushing himself to get every trophy, to seek a good return on a big investment, as is usually the case with the commercial safari.

Some of these folks were foreigners, with one of whom we guided on two trips probably being the most eccentric person I ever took into the bush. Zachary T. Miller hailed from Ponca City area in Oklahoma, and was the last in the line of the once-famous Miller family of The 101 Ranch. Zack had been raised in a world of vast agricultural projects, cattle trading on a massive scale,and the tail-end of the '101 Wild West Show'. In its heyday, the Show had travelled through Europe and the Americas; a great circus of horses, cattle, cowboys, cowgirls, sharpshooters and a host of other Wild West performers including American Indian tribesmen.

Zack related many tales of the 101 Ranch, but his most exotic stories revolved around himself, his exploits, the allegations surrounding his wife's death and various folk of Ponca City. He apparently had a collection of firearms numbering well over a hundred pieces, and always wore an enormous single-action .44 revolver on his belt. He would give away weapons like candy to anyone who was nice to him. Brita was given a .22 Magnum revolver and I still have a beautiful .458 custom-made Flaig with all the finest components such as a Douglas Premium barrel, Timney trigger and nicely engraved lion, buffalo and antelope on the steel work; a gift from Zack after a buffalo hunt.

A rhino once charged into a group of us walking through some fairly thick bush in the Zambezi Valley, and while the trackers, Brita and I rapidly climbed trees, Zack stood firm, .44 in hand, quite prepared to do battle with "that goddamn great big ol' rhino-sore-arse who cumma chargin' right at us. Ah wuz gonna just put him down wi' mah ol' navy here." Navy, in Zack's parlance, was a generic term for all handguns of any description.

Fortunately the rhino got the message and kept out of Zack's sight as it hurtled off huffing with annoyance.

Some Zambezi Valley trips were simply 'citizen hunts' whereby my friend and future safari business partner, Fritz Meyer and I took buffalo and elephant on ten-day private hunts. The valley was as wild and wonderful as ever, still free of the scourges of organised commercial poaching and commercial mass tourism. Brita and I also spent six months assisting wildlife artist Paul Bosman at his Malapati Lodge, south of Buffalo Bend on the Nuanetsi river, right in the heart of the wonderful countryside I knew so well. The job of being a Land Rover courier certainly failed to amuse me and Brita intensely disliked playing hostess to the visitors, but we loved the times when no clients were staying and besides we needed the money.

Back at home, Foot and Mouth Disease wreaked havoc on the ranch with a ban on all movement of cattle, and therefore no sales of livestock for at least six months. Worse still, the stricken dairy cows could barely walk to grazing areas and found difficulty in eating anything. Milk production dropped by seventy-five percent and we were on the brink of bankruptcy so we sold firewood to the local prison and gill-netted fish to sell to the motel in town. Bad times got worse when the bush war intensified between the Nkomo/Mugabe forces and the Rhodesian troops, which resulted in regular 'call-ups' for all civilian white males of suitable age. Like all farmer's wives, Brita ran the show at home while I was away.

We looked increasingly at supplementing our finances with commercial safari hunting, the only profession for which I had any qualifications other than farming, and in 1977 formed an alliance with two other outfitters, National Safaris and Peter Seymour-Smith's Iwaba Safaris. National Safaris, run by John and Douglas Dryden in Salisbury, already represented the big game concessions of Dan Landrey in the Matetsi area and Rupert van der Riet on Lake Kariba, plus some Midlands plains game operators. Iwaba had exceptional quantities and quality of a wide variety of plains game but no steady access to big game, so my concession in the Chirisa Safari Area was ideal with buffalo, elephant and lion being the only species on quota. I was more than happy with that, of course. Just my cup of tea so to speak.

Chipper Bazzy, 10, with great trophy

A Meander
Through Safari Land

Guiding folks who pay good money to come on safari can be immensely fulfiling, often a lot of fun and usually damn hard work with long hours. Rather like school teachers. Lots of vacation time in the rainy season too. But like every classroom where the teacher has a problem kid or two, occasionally a safari is difficult or unpleasant or nothing goes right for the client or guide, usually the fault of one or the other. In the odd case I experienced, the fault was probably of 'the other' – me, that is.

Being somewhat of a loner, rather antisocial and possessing a disappointingly high level of intolerance, the adage 'safaris (for the professional hunter) are ten percent hunting and ninety percent socialising' did not sit too well with me. Mostly I related well to my clients, or thought I did, and really enjoyed their company, even those who spoke little English and we struggled with communication. But I found difficulty with unreasonable, sulky or 'spoilt brat' clients, and was not prepared to be treated as a hotel porter or second-class valet. Wrong temperament, again.

Fortunately very few clients slotted themselves into my 'glad to see the last of' category. In any event the great guys, good sports, appreciative characters, sometimes accompanied by their wives or girlfriends, made the safari business a pleasurable pursuit. But, absolutely not the same as burying oneself in remote corners of original, pristine Africa, living on the elephant's trail, pretty well free and unfettered to surrender the spirit and body to the hunter's life.

It is nearly impossible to do that now so we go on safari instead. The visiting clients, the professionals guiding them and their respective organisations need to show real benefits to the country concerned. This can

be difficult in Africa where the individuals composing a government frequently exhibit the worst traits that the human race has managed to accumulate during its evolution. Luckily, there is usually someone around with whom one can eventually debate sensibly and who makes the correct decision. Unluckily, there are also operators, professional hunters and clients who hunt unethically, pay bribes or are just plain greedy and dishonest; all of which encourages the other side of the table to act equally dishonourably.

Chirisa Safari Area was virgin hunting territory, and the two seasons we had there were memorable for exceptional buffalo trophies and good lion, though ivory was disappointing. I concede I was spoilt after Gonarezhou standards, but in those two years I never saw tusks over fifty pounds. Conversely, the clients almost all took buffalo with a better than 40-inch spread, the largest measuring a fine 50¾-inches, shot by Dick Smith of Michigan, U.S.A. According to ageing by the wear on its teeth, this bull was fifteen years old.

My chief concern was not good hunting for the clients but rather their safety. Independence for Zimbabwe was still more than two years in the future and the bush war was everywhere. This made life a bit hazardous, particularly on our trips for provisioning which involved three hours driving on bush tracks via an outpost in the tribal area, Gokwe, then two hours on a rough dirt road to Que Que. On one occasion Brita and I drove unknowingly through an ambush position, only hearing the following day that ten or fifteen minutes after we passed a government vehicle going the other way was shot up by guerrillas. Closer to camp, another incident occurred and one police reservist was wounded. I had two French medical doctors on safari at the time, one of whom, Patrick Guinebertiere was in camp that day after shooting his lion. I was out with his friend when the wounded man was brought in to nearby Sengwa Research Station and the staff called on Patrick to patch up the fellow while they waited for a light aircraft to arrive and take him to hospital.

We provided a bit of protection around each tent with a low wall of sandbags and a slit trench dug nearby, and we all wore sidearms. Most American hunters also brought their own handguns which we encouraged. Those folks who came hunting in Southern Rhodesia during those difficult and risky times all deserved medals.

Meeting new clients is always an interesting moment. The plane lands or the vehicle arrives, one observes from a little way off as the visitors appear from within and one makes preliminary assessments not excluding, of course, an appraisal of any ladies in the party. Once, John Dryden's message

Bullet protection around our tent -
Chirisa

Brita with .450 Colt, Babette Conway
with sub-machine gun

Sydney Dyer and Bill Ellis

Alan Louw with Dr Karl-Heinz Bund - Chete

My original George Gibbs .505, built in 1927

Caroline Williams of Texas used my .458 Flaig

from Salisbury indicated to me that three hunters from the U.S.A. were coming, and I was surprised when the party turned up to find one of the three was a ten-year-old lad, accompanying his father, Chuck Bazzy, and a friend of Chuck's named Peter. Chuck had done plenty of big game hunting and was not intending to take anything himself on this occasion, simply wanting young 'Chipper' to shoot a buffalo bull and cow elephant. I thanked my good fortune to be in Chirisa for this hunt, where it should not be too tricky to find the animals without having to walk great distances. Then came the sting in the tail: father wanted to film son doing the shooting. Bit of a sleepless night on this one, particularly over finding a buffalo prepared to stand around like a bored film star while the director got the technicians into their correct positions, plus the director had to consider noise, movement and wind direction, and any of the star's friends who may upset the carefully set scene. And there would not be a second opportunity if the cameraman missed his cue – I had no spare buffalo on quota. I decided that the dress rehearsal must be on the elephant hunt where our concealment would be a lesser consideration.

Next morning we took up the fresh spoor of a herd of elephant and set off from the vehicle looking a bit like a medium-scale foot safari out on a week's hunting. Leading the way was Tsuro who carried Chipper's rifle and a tripod of sticks for Chipper to use as a rest, followed by my second tracker Damson, carrying a water-bag and axe. I came next, with Chuck and Chipper behind. Following them was a man with an enormous aluminium case containing the camera and accessories, then another carrying the tripod and Chuck's double .500 rifle. Lastly, tail-end-charlie carried a second water-bag and the lunch box. Ah yes, I forgot the game scout with his F.N. rifle tagging along.

Having caught up with the herd (of elephants, not humans) we moved into phase two: camera case opened and equipment set up on tripod; with Chipper's rifle checked and on safe, I take over this weapon, plus shooting sticks plus my .458 and ash bag; Chuck picks up his load. Tsuro shoulders the double rifle and stays close to Chuck. I tell the supporting cast to sit quiet and only take orders from the game scout. This was better. I could now concentrate on phase three. This involved making the approach up to the feeding elephants, trying to select a big cow reasonably accessible on our side of the herd, keeping an eye on the wind, whispering sweet nothings to my diminutive but amazingly calm client and, rather distractingly, turning around every few yards to see how Chuck was doing. I had no idea when he wanted to stop and set up for filming.

The closer we approached the chosen target, the more Chuck and I

signalled to each other; one or other of us would not quite be in the best position, sometimes made the tiniest bit more difficult by the fact that the leading lady had not read her script and would move at the wrong moment. Then the tripod of sticks had to be spread wider to lower the rifle to the correct height; then the safety catch checked to firing position; another glance backwards to see if Chuck was filming; get a thumbs up; oops, the elephant has moved again. Wait. Okay, you see that mark there ... Okay, give it a go. Bingo! Chipper gets his elephant. However, I soon started having recurring nightmares, despairing of finding some old buffalo bulls who would feel that standing watching two humans playing semaphore in the middle of the bush was sufficiently entertaining to keep them rooted to the spot in wonderment, waiting to get shot.

Diana, goddess of hunting, blessed Chipper Bazzy and I loved her for that. Our single rehearsal with the elephants had proved valuable practical experience on stage, but the greatest stroke of fortune was tracking and locating a magnificent buffalo all on his own, then ambushing him in a river bed with tall grass, followed by a perfect shot and almost no semaphore to speak of.

Some friendships formed on safari develop into long-lasting associations and we have such relationships still existing today from those Chirisa hunts. Herbert Scholl and his girlfriend 'Biggy' from Hamburg in Germany, are amongst our closest friends after five years of consecutive safaris, several other non-hunting visits and 'Kariba cruising'; and we equally enjoy their hospitality in Europe and the Bahamas. Two experienced hunters from America, Bill Ellis and Syd Dyer, were also among our first Chirisa clients whom we have visited at their homes and correspond with regularly. Sometimes one just 'clicks' with a certain character and this kind of friendship is the one of value, even if actual get-togethers are infrequent.

In 1979, a friend and fellow cattle rancher from Que Que area, Alan Lowe, was keen to do his apprenticeship on dangerous game to qualify for a full professional hunter licence, and approached me about the matter. I immediately agreed to him joining us in Chirisa for the season, and hopefully for the future as well.

Several years older than me, Alan was exactly the right type I needed as a partner. An excellent and experienced hunter on plains game, a great sense of humour, steady, reliable and superb with clients. He soon gained confidence with big game and was successful in obtaining his licence. The other aspect of Alan's character that really pleased me was that he never bragged, never embellished (a.k.a. bullshitting), and was never a big deal. He had the maturity, self-confidence and strength of character to be himself,

most definitely not requiring a pseudo-macho image to impress. Alan would not belong to the 'bare-foot, beard and torn-off shirtsleeves' brigade that occasionally pops out of the woodwork today!

In between safari seasons we still did stints of military call-up, and on one of these I happened to be visiting a farmhouse where I picked up a newspaper and for some reason glanced at the "Firearms for sale" advertisements. The words caught my eye instantly: "Gibbs .505 plus 140 cartridges. Tel: 1234...". Borrowing the farmer's phone, I called and with bated breath asked the person if the rifle was sold. No, not yet, was the reply.

"Please hold it for me. I will come to Salisbury either tomorrow or the next day, I promise," I told him.

I found Hugh Sutherns in his office awaiting me. He was District Commissioner for the rural areas outside Salisbury and, due to retire shortly, was disposing of the Gibbs rifle prior to emigrating to England. He had been D.C. in Gokwe and Kariba districts in the 1960s, using the .505 occasionally on elephant control, and in answer to my question about how he had acquired the weapon, the amazing reply was that he had bought it from a game ranger named Lofty Stokes. Amazing because this was the rifle I had coveted as a schoolboy when Lofty had visited our camp in the Zambezi valley seventeen years previously! Fate again?

The firm of George Gibbs, established 1830 in the English city of Bristol, had its premises and records therein largely destroyed by German bombs in 1941, but in personal communications with the Crudgington family who own the Gibbs company, I tried to trace some of my rifle's history. The first .505 calibre was produced in 1913 and Mark Crudgington believes that mine dates around 1927/28. He tells me that only around seventy have ever been built under the George Gibbs name, including those he has made in more recent times. This makes an original Bristol-produced .505 a relatively rare piece. I have traced back two former owners before Stokes, into the 1940s, but will never know the name of the first owner. The .505 proved to be as expected, a fine big game weapon noticeably outperforming the .458, with astounding penetration which is great for difficult shots on clients' wounded trophies arriving or departing at speed.

On 18th April 1980 Rhodesia changed its name to Zimbabwe, the bush war stopped and peace reigned. Alan Lowe and I took on the Chete Safari Area with some trepidation as we were not certain every single land mine had been dug out of the mostly abandoned tracks. A couple of years previously an operator, Adelino Serras Pires, had two Spanish clients hunting in Chete who were killed by a land mine.

We set up a tented camp on the rocky sides of an inlet a hundred yards off the shore of Kariba, overlooking Chete island which was close by but in Zambian territory. We had a couple of motor launches for hunting along the lake's edge and a landing strip a mile away on some flat ground. Flat ground is a rare sight in Chete as most of the area is full of small valleys and hills, and just plain rocky territory. Rhino were common, buffalo numbers were fair, elephant reasonably plentiful but lions a bit short on numbers.

Leopards however were in a class of their own and it was difficult to understand how so many co-existed, particularly as small game was not especially abundant. A colleague hunting for Rupert van der Riet, Charl Beukes, was camped with his clients a two-hour drive away from us, and we chanced to meet him on the track one morning halfway between our camps. We had just checked three baits, each of which had been fed on by leopards, while Charl announced that five of his baits had been eaten. To have *eight* different leopards on bait the same night was a fair indication of their density!

I had a particular spot not far from camp where a large flat boulder was overhung by a tree, making a perfect dining room table for leopards to consume their meal hanging from a branch. Another group of boulders forty yards downwind, with some strategically placed leafy branches, made a convenient blind. Three clients took their cats there in one six-week spell.

Once, late in the evening, one of the ladies in camp walked over to the shower room, the usual grass-walled affair with suspended bucket, and as she approached, a leopard loped off in the light of her gas lamp, looking a bit embarrassed, she said, at being caught in the shower without having hung the 'Occupied' notice across the entrance. Brita reckoned it was a Peeping Tom with voyeuristic tendencies.

My nephew Iain Waller, son of Rob who had taught me so much and introduced me to big game in Luangwa Valley, had joined us in Chete as a learner, or 'gopher' in safari circles (go for this, go for that) and provided all and sundry with much amusement, having an irrepressible sense of fun and an outrageously infectious giggle. A hefty two-hundred pounder, Iain had grown up on a tobacco farm and served in a specialised unit in the recently disbanded Rhodesian Army, and one could be forgiven for thinking that he was incapable of anything in the line of culinary arts. One would be correct.

Brita's mother had an uproarious time teaching him to make pancakes at home, so for safari lunches, as a change from cold meats and sandwiches, Iain could quickly pour dollops of batter onto a hot steel flat-iron sitting on a wood fire, and serve clients fresh flapjacks with sweet or savoury toppings according to taste. Simple, but a nice touch for a hot, tired and hungry

hunter needing something to accompany his iced water, coffee or cold beer.

The trial run went something like this: Brita prepared the mix and filled a large Consol glass jar with screw top and gave it to Iain with last minute instructions. The client, Herr Doktor Carl-Otto Industrial Magnate, Iain and I all piled into a boat with rifles, cooler boxes and stools for the leopard blind. A few miles along the shore we beached the boat, checked our bait and set up the blind comfortably for two huge guys and one small fellow, me, then went walking on the off-chance of finding a good kudu, impala or bushbuck.

Later in the afternoon, before taking up vigil at the leopard bait, we stopped by the boat for a snack and drinks. With a good deal of banter we had a fire going, the steel plate balanced over it on stones and a dash of cooking oil heating nicely. Iain gave the big glass container a quick shake with both hands and, with a flourish, whisked off the top. The batter of course contained baking soda which, with the hot weather and shaking had built up a really fine head of pressure, now released with formidable force. The volcanic mass of yellowish, sticky mixture burst out, hit the lid and Iain's hand, causing it to spray out in all directions for several yards, covering the client's face, designer safari suit, Gucci shoes, me, our rifles, the boat and a dozen tree trunks standing innocently around us. Too late, Iain tried desperately to slap the lid back on the container which simply directed the remnants of the explosion onto his shorts and shoes.

Cleaning up the debacle was hampered by the hysterics, but we eventually settled back into our camp chairs to watch Iain scrape the last of the batter out of the jar and cook just one medium-sized pancake, slightly burnt but edible, which we shared. Herr Doktor missed the leopard with his first shot, but an hour later it, or another one, came along and was trophied. We cruised slowly back to camp in the dark, happy but hungry.

Keeping the camp supplied with food, fuel and other essentials was a major task facing Brita and myself, particularly as communications were by written notes handed to pilots bringing and collecting clients, or by a sort of tug boat that Rupert van der Riet sent to us once a month with sacks of salt, maize meal and drums of fuel. We caught fish in the lake and occasionally, as a change from buffalo tail, tongue, steaks, stews and so on, we would have lion fillets or elephant trunk. Depending on the clients' preferences there was usually liver, kidney, fillets of various antelope, buffalo or warthog and guineafowl for variation when a client was staying for longer periods.

Life in Chete was full of surprises and amusing episodes like the rampant pancakes, like the lady creeping into Alan's bed in dead of night after her

husband had collapsed from an overindulgence of Scotch, like the elephant bull shot on an island jointly claimed by Zambia and Zimbabwe, and like the hyena shot by a client but for which I had no permit. It was an unusual hyena.

The Rhodesians had built a strange variety of armoured and mine-protected personnel carriers during the years of the bush war, using anything from 7-ton trucks to Land Rovers as the basic unit, with a V-shaped body of bullet-proof steel and seats inside. The shape would deflect a land-mine's blast, and AK 47 standard rounds could not pierce the bodywork. The groups of vehicle sizes were given animal names, so we had Rhinos, Leopards, Pookies, Hyenas and others.

One day a young policeman from Binga, the small administrative centre up the lake, called in at camp driving a Hyena. Alan, our two German hunters and I were present at the time and the vehicle intrigued the foreigners no end, but one of them, Eberhard by name, did not think much of the bullet-stopping ability of the steel plating. Bets were placed, Eberhard fetched his souped-up rifle, an 8mm calibre I recall, while our poor little policeman was white-faced, sweating and imploring us to stop this madness. Giving him a brotherly pat on the shoulder I assured him that even if the round dented his vehicle, we would put a dab of paint on the wound and his Senior Officer would never notice it.

From ten yards Eberhard fired and a neat 8mm diameter hole appeared in the steel. The policeman's eyes were out on stalks, his power of speech totally lost, and his knees knocking. I thought he was going to faint. The best was still to come: we all walked around to the other side to find out what had happened to the bullet, to see one of the two-inch-thick bulletproof glass windows had been in the line of fire on the opposite side of the V-body. It was cracked and a big crater of glass had been blasted out where the bullet struck. We now had a wounded Hyena on our hands in addition to its terrified driver. He was certain he would be fired, fined and jailed the moment he hit base.

"Now look, Charlie, don't panic," I soothed him. "Go and sit down, have some coffee or a beer and you'll see, all will be well."

I plugged the bullet hole with a short bolt, added washers and a nut so that it looked just like all the other seat-belt fixings along the sides of the hull. It was a few inches higher than the rest, but there is always the chance of an extra tall guy in the platoon, isn't there? The window, only a foot long by six inches high, I removed, threw into the lake and bolted back the steel frame, explaining to the young man he could quite plausibly state that either there never was glass in the frame or that the workshop people must

have removed it without anyone noticing. Nobody actually noticed anything and he remained a diligent and dutiful fellow in the police force but wisely kept clear of the safari camp.

Herbert and Biggy from Hamburg were with us once again, this time with the intention of getting a really big crocodile in addition to the statutory buffalo or two, and bull elephants. We found a spot where the stream had built up a sand bar some twenty yards long extending out into the lake's shallows, on which we found some huge croc tracks and belly-skin markings. Up on the hillside we built a blind amongst some thick bushes, approachable by an elephant path.

On our first available day we went to check on the sand bar, sneaking into the hide on the hill silently and training our binoculars on the scene below. To my horror, there on the tiny beach was a very delectable, dark-haired lass wearing a cute little bikini, watching two small children playing *in the water*. Dashing out of the blind, loading the .505 as I ran down the path, I reached the water's edge and called out: "For god's sake, get those kids out of the water, NOW!"

She of the desirable physique turned to me, shook her head and asked, "If I ignore you, will you go away?" I'll always remember those words as I stared at her across the ten yards of water, thinking of a huge crocodile sinking its teeth into her soft … Well, I could not let that happen.

"Lady, I'm sorry to disturb you. Those marks in the sand where you are standing are footprints of huge crocodiles that lie there every day. Right now, one could be approaching your kids under the water."

That galvanised her into action, and she quickly dragged the two little ones out of the water, along the sand bar and stopped near me on the shore. She apologised for sounding unfriendly but I assured her I quite understood that feeling of resentment when she must have thought there were no other humans within fifty miles. I explained what I was doing and pointed out the blind up the rise. A small boat appeared among dead trees in the lake some way off and the girl told me it was her husband out fishing, and that they lived at Triangle Sugar Estates in the lowveld. I could hardly believe that people living in this country would be so utterly foolish and ignorant about crocodiles!

Dande Safari Area in the Zambezi Valley bounded by the river to the north, Mozambique on the east, Chewore Safari Area on the west and the great Escarpment along the southern edge, had also been abandoned for many years due to the bush war. Land mines were again a definite possibility in the few tracks that existed in spite of efforts by the Department of Parks and Wildlife to get the army to clear every road. We did not dare use

those stretches which had not been cleared, and negotiated with Mike Drury and Arthur Wood of the department, who were responsible for such matters, to reduce our rent slightly in recognition that some of our concession was still 'out of bounds'.

It took many weeks of work before the hunting started just opening up some of the tracks, with sections having disappeared altogether, stream crossings washed away and tree after tree across the barely visible, overgrown roadways. The main access from the Angwa river bridge in the south to Kanyemba on the Zambezi was the only track which was passable. Kanyemba, a deserted spot on the water's edge, consisted of the ruins of a couple of huts, a roofless brick structure and overgrown clearings in the bush where the army used to pitch the tents. We built our grass-shelters-and-tents safari camp at a permanent stream, an hour and a half's drive over an atrocious track we had cut through from the Kanyemba road westwards towards Chewore.

Tsuro and I reminisced madly about our boyhood hunts in this part of the country fifteen to twenty years previously. We recognised the valley in which we had seen the two bull elephants fighting, after which I shot the wounded one with massive ivory. Over the years we had walked uncounted thousands of miles on the tracks of uncounted thousands of elephants, lived through myriads of adventures, dangers, laughs and unique experiences. I had long since surpassed my outlandish childhood fantasies of living in the wilds. Under the circumstances of the era in which I lived it was incredible that destiny had allowed my hunting imperative such fulfilment. For the first time it occurred to me that I had seen and done things that maybe would never be experienced by anyone else; everything had changed so much and would continue to do so. I had never been one to talk much about my personal hunting life, even to safari clients, but I suppose listening to them and other professional hunters brought out the slow realisation that I had been unbelievably fortunate with my experiences. The commercial safari game had much to commend it, and gave me the opportunity to be in the remaining undeveloped parts of Zimbabwe with big game, but the early years with Tsuro and later with Willie too, are the specially treasured memories.

Dande area was disappointing generally as far as populations of both big game and plains game were concerned, surely as a result of poaching by the Rhodesian military, the insurgent forces, the Mozambican military, the Frelimo rebels, Zambians from over the river and anyone else brave enough to move around there. I have no problem with working hard to hunt wary animals if they are present in one's concession, but in Dande it was hard

Hunting elephant and buffalo was 'my cup of tea'

Dande safari camp

Leopard damage

Tsuro, 40 years after our first elephant hunt

Marcel's leopard

work just finding spoor or other signs of game. The Wildlife Department had produced a quota of animals 'out of the hat', which Wood and Drury were quite honest about, as nobody had been there, let alone done a survey of the game. They were good enough to make a further reduction in the fees, taking our word on the lack of antelope species in particular.

Fritz Meyer had joined Alan Lowe and I as a partner in the company at this time. Twenty-plus years older than I was but lean and tough as buffalo bull biltong, Fritz was one of the country's characters and possessor of many talents and boundless energy, and he had already assisted me greatly in my cattle business. He was a member of the National Parks Advisory Board, had founded and managed the Mlezu Agricultural School, was at the same time managing director of a large cattle and game ranching concern, and served on various local and national conservation bodies, receiving several awards in recognition of his unselfish work. A true 'bush man', Fritz had an encyclopedic knowledge of trees, birds, game, fish and of course, hunting; all of which he would gladly share with those around him. Along with Rob Waller and Paul Grobler, I thank my old friend Fritz for the beneficial influence he had on my life.

Some years after I had left the safari company in pursuit of my other business interests, Fritz was still operating hunts in the Doma Safari Area. One day, while quickly following a buffalo just shot by the client, the trackers and client reached the animal as it dropped dead. Fritz had lagged a bit behind, battling a little to keep up with the younger men, and as he drew near he called to his tracker, "Michael, is the buffalo dead?" With those words, Fritz collapsed and died of heart failure.

Safaris in Dande with Fritz hold one especially vivid memory for me. Three French-speaking Swiss gents were in camp, two hunting and one along for the ride, with my client, Marcel, requiring a buffalo and leopard. Knowing this beforehand, I had hung half a zebra as bait a couple of days before the party arrived, as their stay in our camp was too short to risk delaying shooting a bait animal with Marcel, then setting about finding a leopard. The quick fly-in/fly-out hunt is rather unsatisfactory to my mind, but such is the way of today's world. The client is often on edge to shoot his allotted animals, the guide feels equally pressured but probably hides it well enough, and failures sometimes create icy atmospheres.

Marcel was a great guy, definitely relaxed and enjoying the safari, so no problems there. We were driving along the main track towards Kanyemba early in the morning when Tsuro, standing with Marcel behind me, called "Nyati." I stopped the open Land Rover, picked up my binoculars intending to look for said animals when Marcel's .375 exploded just above my head

without warning. No accidental discharge this, he had shot at one of a small group of bulls amongst the bushes at least eighty to a hundred yards away. I could not believe it. So out of character; French-speaking okay, but surely not *that* impetuous! Bloody hell.

"Tsuro, did he hit it?" I asked.

"Yes."

Marcel excitedly gabbled in French, meaning to say he thought it was a good shot. I smiled enthusiastically at him and replied "*Bon*, Marcel, *bon*," but thinking other, four-lettered things about my client as I climbed out of the vehicle and loaded my .458.

There was blood, good blood. Fifty yards on there was the bull plodding along between the green shrubs closely scattered over the otherwise grassy, undulating countryside. Both of us fired and the animal broke into a run, with us now running behind but not getting closer than sixty to seventy yards. When an opportunity arose where the buffalo was in the open briefly we shot again, a couple of times. Several hundred yards on he stopped in a grassy depression. Marcel fired, the buffalo turned to face us, Marcel fired again and the bull lay down on his brisket, then rolled over on his side. We approached cautiously and from ten paces I told Marcel to give it one more shot in the heart.

Having done that, and the buffalo lying dead at last, Marcel told me he had now used all seven rounds he had carried with him, handed his rifle to Tsuro who gave him the bag containing his camera, and advanced on the dead bull while looking down at his camera's controls. I stepped quickly in front of him, rifle at the ready, saying "*Attencion! Arretez*, Marcel. Watch out! Stop there." With my words the buffalo scrambled to its feet, beginning a lumbering attack from less than five paces away. A lightning thought crossed my mind, don't smash the horns, and I fired into its neck with no effect at all. Could just as well have missed it completely! The next bullet pierced the boss neatly, only a tiny hole, and went through the brain as I shot slightly downwards from the elevated edge of the little hollow. It was my fourth shot, making a total of eleven bullets in that animal. No wonder Marcel's face was white; it had become obvious this was not like picking off chamois in the Alps.

We checked our leopard bait on the trip back to camp, finding a good meal had been taken off the reeking five-day-old zebra, and saw good male leopard spoor in the sand of the dry stream bed below the bait. We sneaked back late in the afternoon and made ourselves comfortable in the blind: Marcel, Tsuro and I. As darkness closed in the leopard appeared on the rock below the hanging bait. Watching him through my binoculars I knew Marcel

would have a sufficiently illuminated view through his rifle scope to shoot. The leopard stood on its hind legs, front paws gripping the carcass, and began to feed. I whispered to Marcel, he fired and the leopard flipped around, disappearing into the blackness of the bushes along the stream bank.

We sat silently, listening, feeling the tension. Marcel whispered that he thought the shot was a good one, but I was unhappy with the way the cat had moved – it looked anything but seriously wounded. Telling Marcel to stay in the hide, Tsuro and I took a torch and my shotgun for a closer look and found blood, not much, some yards along the flight path of the leopard. We then drove back to camp, left Marcel to have dinner with everyone, grabbed a spotlight and car battery and returned. Tsuro, with the light in his hand and the battery on his shoulder, and me next to him carrying my Jeffrey side by side 12-bore, sneaked, slunk and eased our way through the undergrowth, following the odd spots of blood as well as checking around ourselves as we had no idea where the cat would be or how far it had travelled. After half an hour of this, we reached an expanse of solid-looking thicket, creepers and scrub which we could not penetrate other than on hands and knees. Strangely, I felt no intuition that the leopard was close, and decided that we were not going to find it and must leave things till morning.

Just after sunrise we arrived at the bait. The three clients stayed with coffee and biscuits at the vehicles while Fritz and his two trackers, myself, Tsuro and my other tracker, Damson set off on the search for the wounded leopard. Fritz had his .30-06 while I once again carried the double 12-bore with SSG loads. Not far from the streamside undergrowth the leopard's tracks had entered during the night, we found it had headed out across some quite open mopane forest with a ground cover of fairly sparse, knee-high yellow grass. The twelve-hour-old spoor was very difficult to follow; the dried blood was still only sporadic and the six of us fanned out, several yards between each individual, all searching for the faintest signs. I had been looking ahead and about, not seeing any cover that could hide a rabbit, let alone a leopard. A length of old mopane tree trunk drew my attention and next to it I found flattened grass. I bent down and felt the patch. It was warm. I stood up and clicked my fingers to draw the attention of the others, then signalled that the animal had left the spot only minutes earlier.

I glanced about, still seeing nothing that could hide a leopard within a radius of twenty to thirty yards, and began searching the ground for the cat's tracks as I walked forward. Bad mistake! Barely ten paces later the leopard

launched itself, with a deep grunt, out of the ground like a magician, straight at my face as I looked up. The first barrel, fired from the hip, took a chunk out of its right shoulder; the second barrel went off, probably into the treetops, because by then I was already going over backwards with the impact of the leopard and my left hand was pushed into his face to keep a mouthful of big teeth away from my face and throat. Before hitting the ground I had drawn my knees up to my stomach, with the leopard's weight on my legs and chest. He had bitten hard through my hand as well as digging the claws of his right paw deep into my left forearm. Lying on my back, I flung him off but felt utterly helpless and at his mercy as, for a split second, we eyed each other a yard apart. Suddenly the leopard turned its head away, a rifle shot boomed and he fell dead, the figure of Fritz with his weapon at the ready appearing from behind me. Tsuro was also only a few feet away, about to grab the leopard, he later told me, to pull it off me.

My major error was not leaving the tracking to the trackers and keeping a sharper eye out ahead. I should also have armed the four trackers with at least a basic weapon, if only an axe or spear. And I should have had a sidearm in a holster. And finally, why had my sixth sense failed to activate, the intuition of imminent danger that had been my guardian so often? The only explanation I felt answered the question, and partly accounted for the other oversights, was that the presence of another highly capable hunter and four other stalwarts had subconsciously produced a feeling of overconfidence and thus reduced my concentration and alertness. The team effort, as it were, was maybe overpowering and distracting. Possibly, with just two trackers, I would have never walked into that situation.

Those thoughts did not help the fact that I now had a well-crunched left hand, rips down both arms and a three-inch slice down to my ribs below the left collar bone. I felt sorry for the leopard though, who had spent the night with a smashed right forearm from Marcel's shot which was a few inches too low. Back at the camp we had coffee and Brita dressed the wounds which, apart from the hand aching a bit, gave no pain at all. It is a recognised fact that many injuries, including bullet wounds, produce a numbing or auto-anaesthetic effect for a period of time. In my case it was exactly two hours, after which severe pain, a burning sensation around the wounds, made it obvious I had to get to a doctor. Kariba Hospital was voted the sensible choice but still at least four hours drive on dirt tracks through the Zambezi Valley to the tar road, and nearly two hours more on to Kariba town. Brita drove while I writhed and sweated in agony next to her, once distracting her so much that she almost flipped the Land Rover going fast around a corner, but luckily bouncing the wheels against the edge of the roadside drain

which kept the vehicle upright. We stopped briefly for Brita to regain her shaken confidence before heading on.

Back at the hunting camp by noon the following day I thought I was feeling more comfortable but it was not to be. The claw wounds were not the problem, but the deep tooth holes in my hand and wrist were oozing badly, with my hand and fingers swelling and reddening in fine fashion. The zillions of organisms from the rotten zebra carcass, neatly implanted by the leopard's canines, were obviously loving the symbiotic situation. This time it was decided to head for Harare, more than six hours from camp.

A well-known surgeon, Mr. Rosin, was kind enough to attend to me on the Saturday Brita and I arrived in town. An elderly gentleman and friend of John Dryden of National Safaris, he mumbled away about how frequently he had amputated fingers, hands, arms and even a foot or two when his patient's leopard wounds turned bad beyond repair. Mostly Africans hunting killers of livestock. I really loved this topic as I watched him work on my own cuts and bites, which were actually relatively minor in themselves, but still could turn 'bad beyond repair'.

Just to really make my day, my briefcase was stolen from behind my back as I was paying the pharmacist for all the drugs Mr. Rosin had prescribed. I soon found the briefcase in an alleyway, minus thousands of dollars for staff wages and a fair bundle of foreign cash and cheques. It was actually a great relief to get back to the peace and tranquillity of the Dande camp. The bad hand festered on for a couple of weeks, with the infection plus heavy doses of antibiotics making me feel rotten in more ways than one. Everything cleared up eventually, with the only lasting effect being some loss of flexibility in my wrist.

Compared to Dande area, the Charara Safari Area, east of Kariba town along the lake shore, was a dream. Half an hour from a major airport and not much more to town for supply trips, game concentrated along the shorelines and a beautiful, cool camp site on the edge of a bay fringed with big trees were all much appreciated after the harsh operating conditions we had in other areas. During Herbert and Biggy's stay, the statutory couple of buffalo bulls, two elephant bulls and warthog, kudu and impala for the camp, were each dispatched before mid-morning, allowing plenty of champagne consumption before lunch. Brita actually got quite mad with us, having packed picnic lunches each day, only to find us back in camp not having opened the cooler boxes at all.

It was fortunate that we had no apprentice professional hunter with us in Charara. If he had harboured dreams of a rough, tough, scary, glamorous life of guiding clients, he could have suffered serious disillusionment. It was

more like a gentlemens' snooker club – pop one in the bag and reach for the G & T.

But changes were coming ever more rapidly. Competition for government hunting concessions hotted up, 'informal' agreements were nodded through, alliances formed, some good operators flourished as did some fly-by-nights. Others fell by the wayside. The Department of National Parks and Wildlife steadily deteriorated and eventually became yet another government department wrecked by greed, jealousies, corruption and stupid political bungling.

I moved on, but Fritz Meyer and Alan Lowe stayed with the safari business, mainly operating in the Doma area, augmented by quality plains game hunting on their own ranches in the Kwekwe district. Then disaster struck. Alan was killed by an elephant. One evening, at sundown, he told his trackers to walk the client back to the vehicle while he quickly checked out sounds of an elephant herd nearby. He never returned. His body was found pierced by tusks and no shots had been fired by his rifle. Fritz carried on the company for a few years until he died on the buffalo hunt. Although I had cut my ties with the hunting scene to pursue my own business interests, it was a great loss to Brita and I when these two old pals, partners and fine gentlemen were taken, while walking the big game trail, to a great new wilderness somewhere.

Epilogue

Brita and I acquired the ranch business from her father at Kwekwe, this time steadily building it into a small success. I then took over my family's farming enterprise at Rusape and set about revamping the cropping and cattle operations. Tsuro and his family settled on a plot near Rusape, where we helped build him a little house. We still see him regularly.

After some years of great pressure and many worries running the two diverse ventures, with a drive of two hundred and fifty miles between them, we had had enough. Approaching fifty, I made a decision to get our lives in order, according to the First Law of Survival: 'Whose life is it anyway?'

We cut ourselves out of eighty percent of our business activities within a year. Brita had more time for her art, being a very accomplished wildlife painter, and I found a fine channel for the hunting energies to flow down, being fly-fishing. And together we have pursued our joint passion for opera. This passion regularly leads us to the wonderful theatres of Vienna, New York, London and others where we have the exciting privilege of hearing the world's finest operatic singers performing some of the most glorious music. The travels are naturally designed to include trout fishing somewhere between here and there, or a diversion to fly-rod for tarpon, bonefish, kingfish, barracuda or whatever, in a quiet, warm corner of one of the great oceans.

Which brings to mind that wonderful guy, Ernest Hemingway. He said, "Before you write it you must have lived it, and when you write it you must live it again." And so I have. It was good both times.